AGAINST MARGINALIZATION

AGAINST MARGINALIZATION

CONVERGENCES IN BLACK AND LATINX LITERATURES

Jose O. Fernandez

THE OHIO STATE UNIVERSITY PRESS

COLUMBUS

Library of Congress Cataloging-in-Publication Data

Names: Fernandez, Jose O., 1976– author.

Title: Against marginalization : convergences in Black and Latinx literatures / Jose O. Fernandez.

Description: Columbus : The Ohio State University Press, [2022] | Includes bibliographical references and index. | Summary: "Analyzes the convergences of Black and Latinx literature—including works by Amiri Baraka, Luis Valdez, James Baldwin, Rudolfo Anaya, Ralph Ellison, Richard Rodriguez, Alice Walker, Helena María Viramontes, Edward P. Jones, and Junot Díaz—and how writers from both traditions fought against social, cultural, and literary marginalization"—Provided by publisher.

Identifiers: LCCN 2022021768 | ISBN 9780814215265 (cloth) | ISBN 0814215262 (cloth) | ISBN 9780814282427 (ebook) | ISBN 0814282423 (ebook)

Subjects: LCSH: American literature—African American authors—History and criticism. | American literature—Hispanic American authors—History and criticism. | Literature publishing—Social aspects—United States—History. | Marginality, Social, in literature.

Classification: LCC PS153.B53 F47 2022 | DDC 810.9/896073—dc23/eng/20220705

LC record available at https://lccn.loc.gov/2022021768

Other identifiers: ISBN 9780814258491 (paper) | ISBN 0814258492 (paper)

Cover design by adam bohannon
Text composition by Stuart Rodriguez
Type set in Minion Pro

For Joy

CONTENTS

ACKNOWLEDGMENTS

Numerous professors, mentors, and role models guided me through my academic journey, particularly Gary Brodsky, Melvin Terrell, Lemuel Watson, Mark Van Wienen, Tim Ryan, and Keith Gandal. I have received invaluable assistance from the University of Iowa, the College of Liberal Arts and Sciences, the Division of Interdisciplinary Programs, and the Latina/o/x Studies Program. I would like to thank an exceptional group of scholars and colleagues for their support, especially Kristy Nabhan-Warren, Rene Rocha, Claire Fox, Jorge Guerra, Eric Vásquez, Elizabeth Rodriguez Fielder, Lina Murillo, Karmen Berger, Lindsay Vella, Loren Glass, Roland Racevskis, Joshua Weiner, and Sara Sanders. A book subvention from the University of Iowa Division of Interdisciplinary Programs, the College of Liberal Arts & Sciences, and the Office of the Vice President for Research supported this project.

The English Department at Western Illinois University offered me an intellectual home and gave me the opportunity to teach courses in American, Black, and Latinx literatures. A sabbatical from the Office of the Provost allowed me to concentrate on my scholarship. Several colleagues, friends, and students made my time at Western Illinois University an extremely enjoyable experience; some of them include Tim and Magdelyn Helwig, Mark and Amy Mossman, Kathleen and Sean O'Donnell Brown, Chris and Becky Morrow, Alisha White, Sharon Thompson, Roberta Di Carmine, Marjorie Allison, Ron Williams, Alphonso Simpson, and Sue Martinelli-Fernandez. I would also like to acknowledge the several amazing graduate and undergraduate students who shared with me their enthusiasm for literature and writing.

I would like to thank the people at The Ohio State University Press. I am particularly fortunate to have met and worked with Ana Maria Jimenez-Moreno; this book greatly benefited from her diligent assistance and insights. I am also indebted to the two readers for providing extremely valuable feedback and suggestions for improving the manuscript. Many thanks also to Rebecca Bostock, Juliet Williams, Caitlin Sacks, Olivia Sergent, and Tara Cyphers.

An earlier version of chapter 2 appeared in the *Journal of American Drama and Theatre,* vol. 29, no. 1 (2016): 1–18. Reprinted with permission of the Graduate Center, CUNY. Chapter 3 is a revised and extended version of an article published in the *MELUS Journal,* vol. 45, no. 2 (2020): 173–93. Reprinted with permission of Oxford University Press.

Lastly, I would like to thank my family, especially my parents, José and Martha Fernández, as well as other members of the Fernández family—Gabriela Fernández, Salvador Guerrero Fernández, Aurora Martínez, and Rolando Cruz—who followed the development of this project from Mexico City. A special thanks to Francisco Perez, Ignacio Perez, Israel Mendoza, and their families for their friendship. I am also grateful to the Lockhart family, especially to the group of strong and smart women who welcomed me into their family and shared parts of their life stories with me: Ernestine Griffin, Eunice Jean Lockhart-Moss, Evelyn Williams, and Joyce Goins. Finally, this book is dedicated to my wife, Joy Goins-Fernandez, my most relentless and enthusiastic supporter.

Contextualizing Black and Latinx Literatures

Now more than during any other period in American letters, contemporary authors from diverse racial and ethnic backgrounds have gained visibility and recognition in university curricula, at major publishing houses, and among the literary establishment. Colson Whitehead recently became one of the few American authors to have won both the National Book Award and the Pulitzer Prize for fiction for *The Underground Railroad*; equally remarkable, Whitehead became the only Black author to win multiple Pulitzer Prizes for fiction for *The Underground Railroad* and *The Nickel Boys* despite the prize's centuries-old longevity. Other recent recipients of the Pulitzer Prize for fiction include Edward P. Jones's *The Known World*, Junot Díaz's *The Brief Wondrous Life of Oscar Wao*, Viet Thanh Nguyen's *The Sympathizer*, and Louise Erdrich's *The Night Watchman*. In poetry, Natasha Trethewey, Juan Felipe Herrera, Tracy K. Smith, and Joy Harjo became United States Poet Laureates. In drama, Nilo Cruz, Lin-Manuel Miranda, Lynn Nottage, Jackie Sibblies Drury, Michael R. Jackson, and Katori Hall have won the Pulitzer Prize in recent years. The inclusion of authors of color by literary and cultural institutions in these lists of prizes and recognitions represents a significant change from only a few decades earlier. It is common today that in any given year authors of color are largely represented in the finalists' list for the National Book Award for fiction.[1] The status of writers of color among award-granting institutions is that today it would be hard to imagine if they were not represented as finalists or possible winners of these awards.

The recognition of authors of color by literary institutions such as the Pulitzer Prize Board or the National Book Foundation exemplifies the gains made by these authors given that only a few decades earlier the literary landscape was male-dominated and predominantly white. A watershed moment in American literature occurred when Toni Morrison received the Nobel Prize for literature in 1993. Morrison's place in American letters only increased in the following years, and *Beloved* was recognized in 2006 by writers and critics as the single most important novel of the past twenty-five years, ahead of other literary luminaries including Don DeLillo, Cormac McCarthy, John Updike, and Philip Roth.[2] It is worth noting that while Morrison came ahead of a group of predominantly white male authors, Edward P. Jones was the only other writer of color in the list. Writers of color in the 1980s and 1990s, for the most part, lacked the mainstream visibility and recognition from literary and cultural institutions of their white male counterparts; Morrison was perhaps the most visible of a relatively small group of women writers of color that includes Alice Walker, Maya Angelou, Gloria Naylor, Sandra Cisneros, and Lorna Dee Cervantes who were signed by mainstream publishers in the 1980s and 1990s.[3] While at first glance these authors' mainstream publishing successes would indicate an increasing literary plurality in the cultural landscape, there was another equally important group of women writers of color, which included Barbara Smith, Audre Lorde, Ana Castillo, Gloria Anzaldúa, and Cherríe Moraga, among others, who were published by small independent publishers such as Third Woman Press and Aunt Lute due in part to the lack of publishing opportunities by mainstream publishers.[4]

Trends by mainstream publishers in the publication of works by authors of color and authors' recognition by cultural institutions relate to changes in US readers' demographics. For most of the twentieth century, readers tended

---

1. For example, out of the five finalists for the National Book Award for fiction in 2019, four (Susan Choi, Kali Fajardo-Anstine, Marlon James, and Laila Lalami) were writers of color ("National Book Awards").

2. A. O. Scott discusses in detail the methodology for classification and acknowledges the subjective nature of evaluating and ranking works of fiction and the competing views and interpretations in establishing the criteria for such rankings ("In Search of the Best").

3. For discussions on the emergence of Black and Latinx writers during the 1980s and 1990s, see Griffin, "Thirty Years," and Bruce-Novoa, *RetroSpace*.

4. For a discussion on the publication of women writers of color by independent publishers such as Kitchen Table: Women of Color Press, Third Woman Press, and Aunt Lute Books, see M. González, "Beyond Mainstream Presses"; and Blackwell, *Chicana Power!* 156–59.

to be affluent and educated, which has not been the prevalent experience of people of color. Publishing houses became an extension of these elites that still in contemporary times function within "particular protocols and gate-keeping procedures" (Kaestle and Radway 20). While general readership remains predominantly white, current statistics show that among reading populations, women are more likely to have read a book in the past twelve months, and these numbers increase among women with higher incomes and college degrees (Zickuhr and Rainie); however, a significant trend is that among this population, Black women are at the top of this demographic (Zickuhr and Rainie). In other words, and as reported by one news outlet, Black women with higher incomes and levels of education are statistically the single highest demographic group of readers.[5] Part of the continuing increase in the recognition and visibility of contemporary women authors of color such as Jesmyn Ward, Ayana Mathis, Tayari Jones, Carmen Maria Machado, and Susan Choi, among others, reflect publishers' attempts to respond to these demographic changes. Despite these apparent signs of progress, writers of color today remain on the margins of the publishing industry.[6]

Colleges and universities play a significant role in the creation of a readership base for authors of color that reaches beyond numbers and statistics through the institutionalization of academic programs and fields of study such as Black literature and Latinx literature that have been developed over the past decades. College students are becoming increasingly racially and ethnically diverse; in relation to changing student demographics, the number of students of color enrolled at colleges and universities in the US has steadily increased and in 2016 constituted almost half of the entire undergraduate enrollment across the nation.[7] A number of scholars have discussed the emergence at colleges and universities of social protest movements led by activists, faculty, and students in the 1960s and 1970s and their calls for the inclusion of ethnic

---

5. Philip Bump cautions that readers' preferences from all demographics, including college-educated Black women, varies significantly and encompasses several literary and non-literary genres ("Most Likely Person").

6. For example, Chris Jackson, editor in chief of One World imprint at Penguin Random House, who published Ta-Nehisi Coates's *Between the World and Me*, explains that he is "often asked to speak about a thing that doesn't actually exist: diversity in publishing" (223).

7. A report from the American Council on Education on race and ethnicity in higher education shows that nearly half of the undergraduates (45.2 percent) were students of color in 2016 (Espinosa et al.). Through humanities general education courses, literature courses, and ethnic and gender studies programs, college students have increasingly been exposed and have read authors of color. While not all students who attend college may become lifelong readers, the likelihood is that students of color who attend or graduate from college would be more likely to read fiction, and part of their reading preferences would be influenced by their academic experiences.

studies and the reading of authors of color.[8] The increasing study and recovery of Black and Latinx texts by a growing number of scholars after the 1960s was instrumental in the fight for inclusion into the American literary tradition; formerly neglected authors such as James Weldon Johnson, Zora Neale Hurston, María Amparo Ruiz de Burton, José Antonio Villarreal, and several others were introduced, read, and studied on college campuses. Contemporary university-trained educators and scholars who received a broader instruction in American literature and encountered the works of authors of color would often teach some of these texts, which in turn would increase the visibility of a larger number of authors of color through the publication of essays, articles, reviews, and monographs. Universities and scholars have also published the works of authors of color through initiatives such as the Recovering the US Hispanic Literary Heritage Project led by Nicolás Kanellos, which has played a fundamental role in the publication and dissemination of past Latinx texts that otherwise would not have come to light through mainstream publishers.

The reading and visibility of authors of color in the past decades closely relate to the means of literary production—including the printing, publication, dissemination, promotion, and reading of texts—and the way mainstream publishers have attempted to respond to changes in readership demographics and trends in academia.[9] The current American literary landscape—or market—is partly the result of a process primarily sustained by major publishing companies, which embody the traditions and legacies of centuries of book production in the US that has led to business consolidations and the formation of the American literary canon.[10] The current publishing industry is dominated by a small group, often referred as the "Big Five," that includes Penguin Random House, HarperCollins, Simon & Schuster, Hachette, and Macmillan—along with their several subsidiaries. For most of its history, the American publishing industry has played a major role in aesthetic and artistic creation through its ecosystem of signed writers, agents, editors, marketers, and publishing executives. The publishing industry is also associated with the literary establishment in the form of foundations, literary boards, and so forth,

---

8. See Smethurst, *Black Arts Movement*; Acuña, *Making of Chicano/a Studies*; Bona and Maini, *Multiethnic Literature and Canon Debates*; Rojas, *From Black Power to Black Studies*; and Cutler, *Ends of Assimilation*.

9. Carl Kaestle and Janice Radway explain that literature and publishing have been tied to educational trends since the emergence of the modern publishing industry; for instance, Kaestle and Radway discuss the developing of the modern publishing industry in relation to high school attendance, which "increased from less than 5 percent in 1880 to more than 50 percent in 1940" (7).

10. For in-depth discussions on literature as cultural capital, the cultural and economic value of literary prizes, and the rise of the conglomerate US publishing industry, see Guillory, *Cultural Capital*; English, *Economy of Prestige*; and Thompson, *Merchants of Culture*.

that grant literary awards, which in turn generate more readers and book sales.[11] As part of their disseminating power, major publishing companies advertise and promote authors who at times achieve national recognition;[12] however, it is only in the last few decades that major publishing companies have increasingly promoted and celebrated authors of color. One only needs to peruse through some of these publishers' book catalogs marketed to educators to find the work of authors of color prominently displayed, particularly authors who have previously been recognized through literary awards such as Whitehead, Díaz, and Morrison, to name a few. In the case of Díaz, the allegations of sexual misconduct toward women show the drawbacks of highlighting and promoting the work of only a handful of authors of color; due in part by the dearth of writers of color in mainstream publishing and cultural institutions, the legitimate concerns regarding Díaz's writing and its depiction of women of color are discussed at times as representing the entire body of Latinx literature.[13]

While some writers of color have attained literary recognition that has created a sense of inclusion, the reality is that contemporary authors of color continue to face major obstacles. When it comes to mainstream publishers, the books of authors of color constitute a small fraction of their catalogs. Authors of color continue to be excluded, and their number is disproportionately lower than that of white authors; Richard Jean So and Gus Wezerek, in their 2020 *New York Times* piece, "Just How White Is the Book Industry?" write that while a small number of authors of color occupy the bestsellers' lists in any given year, almost 90 percent of fiction books published are by white writers, and when it comes to publishing opportunities, they unequivocally state, "It helps to be white." Despite recent attempts at inclusion, power structures at major publishing companies continue to be predominantly white.[14] For finan-

---

11. A glance at the winners of the Pulitzer Prize for Fiction in the last couple of decades shows that these awards are dominated by authors published by the "Big Five" publishing houses such as HarperCollins and Random House, or some of their own subsidiary imprints such as Viking and Alfred A. Knopf.

12. Most of the recent authors of color who have been awarded the Pulitzer Prize for Fiction, including Jones, Díaz, and Whitehead, have been published by one of the "Big Five" publishing companies or subsidiaries. Nguyen's novel, however, was published by Grove Press, an independent publisher. Similarly, all of the four authors of color who were finalists for the 2019 National Book Award for fiction, including the winner Susan Choi, were published by one of the "Big Five" publishers ("National Book Awards").

13. For a thorough analysis of Díaz's writings in light of the allegations of abuse of power, verbal abuse toward women, sexual harassment, and the role of the publishing industry and mainstream magazines such as the *New Yorker*, see Gil'Adí, "'I Think about You, X—'"

14. While there have been major changes in US demographics, a 2015 survey in *Publishers Weekly* shows that within the publishing industry, 79 percent of people identify as white (Deahl). These numbers only increase when it comes to decision making in the publishing industry as "85 percent of the people who acquire and edit books" are white (So and Wezerek).

cial and market-driven reasons, major publishers often operate in a winner-takes-all dynamic in the publishing industry as only a small number of writers are recognized, which in turn results in publishers' investment and advertisement of the same few authors. While these statistics are telling, they primarily reflect larger historical forces regarding centuries of historical exclusion of authors of color in the publishing industry; the story I tell in this book is not only about the historical and literary exclusion of Black and Latinx authors in mainstream publications and the publishing industry, it is also the story of how countless Black and Latinx authors fought against centuries of literary, artistic, and cultural marginalization through their sustained efforts to write, publish, and reach a sustaining readership while aesthetically depicting the struggles of their respective groups.

Before moving to my argument, I describe some of the terminology employed in this study. I use the term "Black" to invoke broader articulations of African American, diasporic, and Afro-Atlantic identities and literatures theorized by scholars such as Paul Gilroy, Brent Hayes Edwards, and Yomaira Figueroa-Vásquez, among others.[15] While my study engages with the experiences of a group of Black writers within the context of the US, I explore these writers under the larger and more encompassing field of Black literature. In addition, I employ the term "writers of color" throughout this study primarily as a form of racial and ethnic self-identification as opposed to the term "minority" writers. In contrast, I resist the term "brown." Due to processes of racialization and otherness in the context of US identity formation, Linda Martín Alcoff observes that the use of the term "brown" has been used by Latinx people in a "positive rather than derogatory way" (*Visible* 237). Nonetheless, the term "brown" in the context of *Latinidad* is worth questioning in relation to the indigenous and African-descent groups encompassed under the panethnic identification of "Latinx." I follow the lead of Latinx scholars including Ed Morales, Claudia Milian, and Arlene Dávila by using the term "Latinx" in the spirit of new possibilities for a more encompassing ethnic identification—and racial and ethnic solidarity—among distinct racial and ethnic groups of Latin American backgrounds that have traditionally been discussed under the term "Latino/a,"[16] thus, resulting in terms such as Latinx writers, Latinx literature, and the Latinx literary tradition.

Against Marginalization argues that a way to comparatively examine instances of convergence in post-1960s Black and Latinx texts is through

---

15. See Gilroy, *Black Atlantic*; Edwards, *Practice of Diaspora*; and Figueroa-Vásquez, *Decolonizing Diasporas*.

16. For discussions on the promising possibilities of the term "Latinx," see Morales, *Latinx*; Milian, *LatinX*; and Dávila, *Latinx Art*.

the study of the ways some representative Black and Latinx writers moved from a position of literary marginalization vis-à-vis the mainstream publishing industry and the American literary tradition that characterized past literary periods. I examine comparatively the efforts to map and theorize about the origins and development of the Black and Latinx literary traditions and investigate how racial and ethnic identities in the US have shaped the study of literary production and have opened avenues for competing or contested views of racial and ethnic identities within the framework of literary studies; moreover, I argue that the shared fight by Black and Latinx writers against historical, social, and literary marginalization—which is reflected in the development of their respective literary traditions—represents a key characteristic that unites not only Latinx writers from different racial, ethnic, and cultural groups but also other writers of color in the US context. *Against Marginalization* studies comparatively the development of the Black and Latinx literary traditions showing how the marginalization of Black and Latinx authors from mainstream publishing and their limited opportunities to publish their books and gain an audience has played a key role in the formation of both literary traditions. I employ the publication histories of representative Black and Latinx texts to explore how Black and Latinx authors began from a position of marginality, neglect, and isolation and how Black and Latinx authors fought against what Jacqueline Goldsby aptly calls "cultural segregation" when it came to publishing opportunities in the literary world for Black writers (lvi), which is similarly applicable to Latinx writers.

My comparative study tracing representative instances in the development of the Black and Latinx literary traditions is informed by the work of numerous scholars who have focused on different aspects of the means of literary production (the publication, dissemination, and reading of texts) in the creation of Black and Latinx texts. In my discussion of the "long" nineteenth century, I rely on a number of scholars who have focused on aspects of Black and Spanish-language print culture and the writing printed in local newspapers and periodicals in some major cities such as New York City, Boston, Philadelphia, San Francisco, and New Orleans during the antebellum and postbellum periods.[17] The Black and Spanish-language print cultures speak of authors' shared literary exclusion from mainstream presses, newspapers, and magazines, while at the same time reflect their remarkable attempts to build resilience, commu-

---

17. Representative examples include Ernest, *Liberation Historiography*; Gardner, *Unexpected Places*; Cohen and Stein, *Early African American Print Culture*; McHenry, *Forgotten Readers*; Foreman, *Activist Sentiments*; Spires, *Practice of Citizenship*; Gruesz, *Ambassadors of Culture*; Meléndez, *So All Is Not Lost*; Lazo and Alemán, *Latino Nineteenth Century*; Coronado, *World Not to Come*; and Lazo, *Letters from Filadelfia*.

nity, and a local readership. While scholars have focused on different aspects of either Black and Spanish-language print culture, fewer studies have explored them comparatively or by analyzing their similarities in relation to the position of Black and Latinx authors within the larger publishing trends in the US.[18] My discussion of representative twentieth-century Black and Latinx texts and authors builds on the works and insights of several scholars who have focused on some aspects of the creation, production, dissemination, reception, and reading of texts.[19] The nineteenth-century fight for literary inclusion and the development of local newspapers and weeklies continued into the decades of the twentieth century; representative publishing histories of Black and Latinx texts show the obstacles and challenges faced by Black and Latinx authors, editors, and small publishers during their quests for representation in mainstream publications, which continued into the 1960s and 1970s, and how this history has continued to influence the writing of subsequent decades.

Against Marginalization's main argument is twofold; first, I argue that a group of Black and Latinx texts in different literary genres—novels, drama, essays, and short story collections—written from the 1960s to the last decade of the twentieth century shared compelling instances of convergence related to the ideological and thematic elements incorporated in these texts to challenge the historical, social, and economic marginalization of their respective communities vis-à-vis an Eurocentric and English-speaking mainstream society. The major authors and works explored in this study include Amiri Baraka's *The Slave*, Luis Valdez's *Bandido!*, James Baldwin's *Tell Me How Long the Train's Been Gone*, Rudolfo Anaya's *Bless Me, Ultima*, Ralph Ellison's *Shadow and Act* and *Going to the Territory*, Richard Rodriguez's *Days of Obligation* and *Brown*, Alice Walker's *The Third Life of Grange Copeland*, Helena María Viramontes's *Under the Feet of Jesus*, Edward P. Jones's *Lost in the City*, and Junot Díaz's *Drown*.[20] Baraka's *The Slave* and Valdez's *Bandido!*, for instance, share thematic and narrative strategies in the way they present the marginalized position of

18. One notable exception is Cécile Cottenet's edited collection *Race, Ethnicity and Publishing in America,* which focuses on writers of color in relation to publishing trends at different periods in literary history; Cottenet notes that her collection seeks to highlight "how print culture has contributed, time and time again, to the construction, consolidation and preservation of an ethnic identity" (14).

19. Some of these scholars include Farah Jasmine Griffin, George Hutchinson, John K. Young, James Smethurst, Valerie Babb, Jacqueline Goldsby, Gene A. Jarrett, Autumn Womack, Jean-Christophe Cloutier, Nicolás Kanellos, Juan Bruce-Novoa, Juan Flores, Manuel Martín-Rodríguez, John Morán González, Kirsten Silva-Gruesz, Rodrigo Lazo, and John Alba Cutler.

20. My study's overall organization, and structure of each chapter, follows a chronological order that presents a Black author followed by a Latinx author. Moreover, the inclusion of a representative Black writer at the start of most sections, and chapters, situates the historical, social, and cultural context of both Black and Latinx texts.

Blacks in the antebellum South and Mexican Americans after the Mexican–American War in the Southwest, respectively; both playwrights challenge prevalent historical narratives by rewriting history and staging revolutionary uprisings led by archetypal figures of resistance inscribed in the historical memory of each group. In another comparative case study, I analyze the essays by Ellison and Rodriguez and their shared similarities in their response to challenges to mainstream American culture and literature brought by Black and Mexican American social protest movements during the late 1960s and early 1970s. While Ellison and Rodriguez interpret the racial, ethnic, and cultural composition of the US through a broader and pluralistic view of the historical, cultural, and artistic connections among different racial and ethnic groups, their essays similarly avoid confronting the way in which different racial and ethnic groups have experienced a process of racialization and otherness that had permeated, as Toni Morrison cogently argues, the American literary tradition and the society that created it.

A second argument developed in *Against Marginalization* is that case studies of post-1960s Black and Latinx authors show that one of their shared strategies in the way they fought against literary exclusion from the American literary tradition was by engaging, appropriating, and subverting the literary tradition. At different periods and in different genres, a number of aesthetic works of post-1960s Black and Latinx writers share formalistic, aesthetic, and stylistic strategies that reflect the influence of literary movements such as naturalism, modernism, and postmodernism. These authors engage in some of their writings with some of the American tradition's most enduring preoccupations such as the tension between art and social protest and the place of writers of color in the literary tradition; some Black and Latinx writers were influenced in a similar manner by authors from the tradition including Harriet Beecher Stowe, Mark Twain, Theodore Dreiser, Tennessee Williams, and William Faulkner, among others. My comparative analysis suggests that rather than rejecting the influence of a Eurocentric and English-speaking literary tradition advocated by prominent social activists, writers, and artists during the emergence of Black and Chicanx nationalist movements of the 1960s and 1970s, representative authors from each tradition developed as writers and artists under the influence of the American literary tradition that is similarly presented in some of their formalistic, thematic, and aesthetic strategies. Post-1960s Black and Latinx authors fought against literary invisibility in part by engaging with the literary tradition's literary movements; in turn, as the tradition became more encompassed by the publication, reading, and literary study of Black and Latinx texts, such literary and publishing dynamics contributed to increasing changes and publishing opportunities for authors of color.

Against Marginalization contributes to the body of scholarship that has focused on critical comparative studies of Black and Latinx writers and artists during or after the civil rights struggles of the 1960s and 1970s. There is an increasing number of scholars who have studied comparatively the work of Black and Latinx authors from different cross-cultural, intercultural, and interacial perspectives ranging from communal theater performances; intercultural commonalities among Black, Puerto Rican, and Chicanx authors; mix-raced and hybrid identity narratives by women of color; or intercultural exchanges by Black authors through their Latin American experiences.[21] My study is particularly indebted to Harry J. Elam's *Taking It to the Streets: The Social Protest Theater of Luis Valdez and Amiri Baraka*, a groundbreaking comparative analysis that studies the theater performances of Amiri Baraka and Luis Valdez during their early years in their fight for social justice and cultural representation from 1965 through 1971. The trajectories of the Black and Latinx literary traditions—not only after their post-1960s period but throughout most of their histories—show that both traditions share several commonalities and points of convergence that are yet to be studied thoroughly. Marta Sánchez, for instance, cogently observes that "histories and literatures of diverse cultural groups are, I believe, more often than not presented in college and university curricula in disconnected ways, taught and researched as separate areas of study, quarantined into separate camps, . . . or only in relation to a presumably homogeneous dominant white population" (10).

While it is important and necessary to study, recover, and historicize the richness and uniqueness of distinct literary traditions and of writers from different racial and ethnic groups, cross-ethnic literary studies are also needed to show instances of shared historical, cultural, and literary struggles that unite writers and people of color in the US. Scholars such as Charles Mills, Linda Martín Alcoff, David Theo Goldberg, and Paul C. Taylor have studied the distinct experiences of different racial and ethnic groups within the larger historical, social, and economic context of US race relations and the constructions of racial and ethnic identities; likewise, they have also shown the parallels in the processes of racialization, othering, and marginalization inflicted not only upon Blacks but other people of color.[22] Mills reminds readers that "we live in a world which has been *fundamentally shaped for the past five hundred years by the realities of European domination and the gradual consolidation of global*

21. See Elam, *Taking It to the Streets*; M. Sánchez, *"Shakin' Up" Race and Gender*; Bost, *Mulattas and Mestizas*; Acampora and Cotten, *Unmaking Race, Remaking Soul*; Cotera, *Native Speakers*; Romero, *Activism and the American Novel*; Milian, *Latining America*; A. López, *Unbecoming Blackness*; and Figueroa-Vásquez, *Decolonizing Diasporas*.

22. See Mills, *Racial Contract*; Alcoff, *Visible Identities*; Goldberg, *Racial Subjects*; and P. Taylor, *Race*.

white supremacy" (20). *Against Marginalization* emphasizes shared instances of convergence in the development of the Black and Latinx literary traditions by emphasizing shared histories and experiences while acknowledging the different experiences of particular groups. Similar to the way racial and ethnic identities have evolved at different historical moments due to the racialization and otherness of nonwhite groups at different moments in US history, the present historical moment with its shifting demographics and increasing acknowledgement of how race and identity are formed—and the disparities and inequalities they create—represents an opportunity for racial and ethnic solidarity among writers, scholars, and communities of color.[23]

Although authors of color have gained increasing literary recognition in the twenty-first century, and there have been major changes in the ways their works are published, disseminated, and read by an increasingly multiethnic population, the struggles are far from over. In a sense, my study tells a story of shared literary exclusion of Black and Latinx writers, but one that is equally characterized by perseverance, resistance, and communal work in their struggle to write, get their work published, and gain a readership. The increasing recognition of authors of color in the literary realm points toward an increasingly multiethnic and more encompassing American literary tradition, away from a once-monolithic, Western-influenced, and monolingual literary heritage. As the Black and Latinx literary traditions continue to evolve and flourish—and increase their visibility and recognition—authors of color will increasingly influence readers and writers from a multiplicity of racial and ethnic backgrounds, who in turn will lead to a single more encompassing American literary tradition in the twenty-first century.

CONFLUENCES AND DEBATES IN THE FORMATION OF THE BLACK AND LATINX LITERARY TRADITIONS

Since the early decades of the twentieth century, scholars began to delineate the origin and trajectories of Black and Latinx literary histories either in book-length studies, compendiums, or single or multivolume anthologies that focus on one or more aspects of the cultural histories within each tradition. The writings and scholarship of W. E. B. Du Bois, Alain Locke, James Weldon Johnson, Sterling Brown, Arthur P. Davis, J. Saunders Redding, Jovita González, and Américo Paredes, among others, are representative of early attempts at compiling and studying the literary or cultural heritage of their

---

23. For a detailed analysis on the unprecedented opportunities and challenges due to the major shift in US demographics from a white to a multiracial society, see Alcoff, *Future of Whiteness*.

respective group. Before the 1970s, there had been attempts to anthologize the work of Black writers and poets; however, the systematic study of each literary tradition was a direct result of the struggle for civil rights and student protests in the 1960s and 1970s, which expanded the curriculum to include ethnic studies and the study of authors of color at colleges and universities. A similar gain was the increasing number of scholars of Black and Latinx literature who began to study and recover representative texts from each tradition. In-depth or encompassing anthologies of Black literature that began to emerge in the 1990s built upon the scholarship and expertise of post-1960s literary critics including Frances Smith Foster, William Andrews, Bernard Bell, Barbara Christian, Hortense Spillers, and Hazel Carby, among others. Similarly, the scholarship of post-1960s critics such as Francisco Lomelí, Francisco Jiménez, Juan Bruce-Novoa, and Nicolás Kanellos, among others, informed and contributed to the creation of anthologies of Latinx literature in the 1990s. These critics offered the first answers to the question of how Black and Latinx authors who found themselves on the literary margins—either through social and economic disenfranchisement during the era of slavery or the aftermath of the Mexican–American War—set the foundations of either the Black or Latinx literary tradition.

A function of the increasing number of literary anthologies is to reconstruct a complex history of well-known, lesser-known, and continuously reevaluated and emerging texts with the goal of tracing and contextualizing the histories, achievements, and unique characteristics by writers of a particular group. Among the various comprehensive anthologies, *The Norton Anthology of African American Literature* edited by Henry Louis Gates Jr. and Nellie Y. McKay is representative of the efforts by leading scholars to map the tradition.[24] A similar systematic effort to anthologize Latinx literature is Ilan Stavans's *The Norton Anthology of Latino Literature*.[25] Gates, McKay, and Stavans are representative among several scholars who have contributed to the development and increasing visibility of each tradition and the efforts to compile, evaluate, and study texts that despite each tradition's unique origins and developments, share a common attempt to "celebrate" writings and authors

---

24. Notable contributions to canon formation in the Black literary tradition include Andrews, Foster, and Harris, *Oxford Companion to African American Literature*; Graham and Ward, *Cambridge History of African American Literature*; King and Moody-Turner, *Contemporary African American Literature*; and Miller, *Routledge Introduction to African American Literature*.

25. Other representative works that map the Latinx literary tradition include Augenbraum and Fernández Olmos, *Latino Reader*; Kanellos, *Herencia*; Bost and Aparicio, *Routledge Companion to Latino/a Literature*; and González and Lomas, *Cambridge History of Latina/o American Literature*.

who form part of the nation's cultural and literary heritage.[26] While these two anthologies, and certainly similar projects, set to highlight and contextualize the contributions of authors in their respective traditions, their process of selection, interpretation, and methodology—and attempts to contain an ever-increasing body of texts—render the process of literary periodization, classification, and canon formation open to scrutiny and debate.

The ever-evolving project of mapping the Black and Latinx literary histories has been marked by debates related to periodization, geographical or linguistic delimitations, and the categorization of authors and texts from different groups. Gates and McKay, for instance, address the criteria for selecting the works in their anthology by focusing on the works that are more significant or representative for their resonance, historical significance, or aesthetic value (xl); however, these criteria are subjective and not exhaustive. Depending on their general editors and contributors, different anthologies would include or exclude certain authors represented in one anthology but not in others. More specifically, debates on periodization in Black literary history, although not unique, are representative of the competing views in canon formation. Kenneth Warren, for instance, questions the function of periodization in the history of Black literature as he maintains that the body of works that forms this literary tradition lacks cohesion since Black writers before the Harlem Renaissance were authors who did not consider themselves primarily as artists (*What Was* 7). Warren's views on periodization efforts specifically, and in relation to prevalent notions of Black literature more generally, exemplify those challenges in the study of Black texts.

An additional critique regarding the project of comprehensively mapping the Black and Latinx literary traditions is based on the larger number of texts, fiction, essays, and poetry published throughout most of the nineteenth century in small or regional presses that remain unexplored and require detailed archival work.[27] In the context of Latinx literary history, some scholars have questioned anthologies' methods of classification, issues of representation, and claims of unity in light of the still-ongoing projects related to the recovery of Latinx texts, particularly from the nineteenth century.[28] To further confound efforts of mapping the Latinx literary tradition, *The Norton Anthology of Latino Literature*, for example, presents two different forms of classifica-

26. For an example of the shared goals in anthologizing Black and Latinx texts, see Gates and McKay xxxvi, and Stavans, *Norton* liii.

27. Ernest has argued in *Chaotic Justice* for a rethinking of Black literary history since early Black texts that constitute part of the tradition have been only partially recovered and are yet to be thoroughly studied and incorporated into the tradition.

28. For discussions focusing on the need for further archival research and recovery of Latinx literary texts, see Martín-Rodríguez, *Life in Search of Readers* 139–56; Gruesz, "Once and Future Latino" 116–17; and Lazo, "Trajectories of ExChange" 190–99.

tion of authors: one places Latinx authors from different national and ethnic backgrounds in a chronological order; the second presents authors as clusters or groups based on the countries from which authors trace their heritage;[29] moreover, shifting geographical and historical circumstances due to the influence of colonial legacies in US regions such as the Southwest further complicate classification in literary recovery efforts.[30]

Anthologies and literary studies that have traditionally mapped Black literary history have taken into consideration a strict notion of national boundaries and geographical spaces; however, a growing number of scholars of Black literary studies have questioned prevalent nationalistic and monolinguistic perspectives. A number of critics and theorists have argued for transnational, transcontinental, or diasporic perspectives in the study of Black texts beyond the confines of the African American tradition that situate texts and authors beyond national or linguistic borders.[31] In his often-cited study, Paul Gilroy questions the emphasis on "nationalistic perspectives" in the study of African American cultural and literary texts; in contrast to national, racial, and cultural absolutes, he proposes a Black diasporic emphasis in which "cultural historians could take the Atlantic as one single, complex unit of analysis in their discussions of the modern world and use it to produce an explicitly transnational and intercultural perspective" (15).[32] Such scholarly inquiries have demonstrated that Black literary history is culturally and linguistically porous since it contains instances of cross-cultural exchanges that have not been sufficiently acknowledged in the mapping of the tradition.

Similar to scholars who have argued for a broader geographical interpretation of the Black literary tradition, some scholars of Latinx literature have made similar arguments regarding the need to expand the national and geographical boundaries of Latinx literature by proposing a hemispheric, transnational, or global South perspective to map the Latinx literary tradition that

---

29. For a discussion on the classification and periodization of the *Norton Anthology of Latino Literature*, see Gruesz, "What Was Latino Literature?"

30. Marissa López and Vanessa Fonseca-Chávez, among others, have argued for the need to study more closely the colonial legacies of Spain, Mexico, and the US in studies of Mexican American or Chicanx literature from the Southwest.

31. Representative works of transnational, transcontinental, or diasporic approaches to Black literature include Gilroy, *Black Atlantic*; Edwards, *Practice of Diaspora*; Carretta and Gould, *Genius in Bondage*; Gruesser, *Confluences*; Goyal, *Romance, Diaspora, and Black Atlantic Literature*; and Spires, "Genealogies of Black Modernities."

32. Edwards, however, acknowledges the challenges of a transatlantic perspective in the study of Black authors; he notes that studying authors from the Harlem Renaissance from a Black internationalist theoretical lens "is to move against the grain of much of the scholarship on African American culture of the 1920s, which has tended to emphasize US-bound themes of cultural nationalism, civil rights protests, and uplift in the literary culture" (2–3).

goes beyond US borders.[33] José David Saldívar has led these lines of inquiry by taking into consideration the broader geographies, texts, and cultures from the American continent and arguing for "a new, transgeographical conception of American culture—one more responsive to the hemisphere's geographical ties and political crosscurrents than to narrow national ideologies" (xi). The task of reconceptualizing a Latinx literary history that acknowledges the influences of the American continent is significant—particularly when taking into consideration the history of territories such as the Southwest—and the geographical, historical, and cultural trajectories of Latinx writers. Efforts by scholars who have interrogated the boundaries and scope of the Black and Latinx literary traditions based on historical interdependences and shared linguistic and cultural elements are necessary to thoroughly recognize the complex origins and developments of both traditions. However, there is equal value in cross-cultural studies that point toward instances of shared commonalities among distinct literary traditions, particularly when several Black and Latinx texts have been similarly influenced by the cultural and literary marginalization prevalent within the US. The historical, social, and cultural marginalization in which Black and Latinx texts originated and evolved in the US presents points of reference and possibilities for cross-cultural investigations that add an additional layer of interpretation to the study of both traditions.

THE MEANING OF BLACKNESS AND *LATINIDAD* IN THE CONTEXT OF BLACK AND LATINX LITERARY HISTORIES

Scholars who have focused on the historical, social, and economic trajectories of race and ethnicity in the US context and the workings of racism, otherness, and racialization, suggest their large, complex, and evolving process.[34] As Charles Mills and Paul C. Taylor explain, the development of racial and ethnic categories has a long history on the American continent that dates back to the legacy of the European colonial project that began in the sixteenth century.[35] In her analysis of the formation of racial and ethnic identities in the US context, Linda Martín Alcoff analyzes how racial and ethnic identities in the

---

33. For critical studies that have reinterpreted the Latinx literary tradition by emphasizing a broader hemispheric perspective, see J. Saldívar, *Dialectics of Our America*; Gruesz, *Ambassadors of Culture*; Levander and Levine, *Hemispheric American Studies*; M. López, *Chicano Nations*; and Lazo, *Letters from Filadelfia*.

34. See, for example, Goldberg, *Racial Subjects*; P. Taylor, *Race*; and Alcoff, *Visible Identities*.

35. For discussions on the origin of racial classification, racism, and European colonialism in the American continent, see Mills 19–31, and P. Taylor 73–74.

US are dynamic and have been in constant flux (*Visible* 232); Alcoff correctly posits that discussions of racial and ethnic identify formation "need to be contextualized and processes of identity formation need to be historicized" (*Visible* 85). I follow Alcoff's lead by discussing Black and Latinx identity in the context of the development of the Black and Latinx literary traditions; both traditions show the evolving meaning and agency in the way race and ethnicity are articulated in the context of the creation of Black and Latinx texts. At the start of the Black literary tradition, early texts and anthologies were those of "Negro" literature that reflected the Jim Crow era and attitudes; the civil rights movements of the 1960s and 1970s gave way to modes of racial identification that emphasized an African heritage that also served as a form of self-identification and Black empowerment that manifested in the term "Afro-American," which was reflected in Black literary studies.[36] The 1990s shows a shift to the term "African American" in literary studies that has continued until recently; there is an increasing number of literary scholars of Black literature who favor a more encompassing interpretation of Blackness that emphasizes its cultural and diasporic elements and invokes a broader interpretation of the writing produced by Black authors in the US that goes beyond traditional meanings of race.[37]

In the context of Latinx literary history, the focus on geographies, language, and past histories closely relates the multiplicity of ethnic, racial, cultural, and national groups encompassing under terms such as "Chicana/o/x," "Hispanic," or "Latina/o/x"—and other positionings that fall under *Latinidad*—which problematize notions of Latinx people, and their literatures, as part of one group. A first point of contention regarding a panethnic identification acknowledged by scholars of Latinx literature is that the term risks erasing geographical, historical, and cultural differences among members of diverse racial and ethnic groups.[38] A number of scholars of Latinx literature have focused on the distinct characteristics of groups of writers in part as a result of the emergence of ethnic studies at colleges and universities after the 1960s; literary scholars began to theorize about the distinctiveness of their identities and the literary and aesthetic contributions from each group that began to be classified as Mexican American, Chicano/a, Puerto Rican, Cuban American, Dominican Ameri-

36. The titles of some post-1960s studies of Black literature reflect an emphasis on an "Afro-American" racial identity; see, for example, Baraka and Neal, *Black Fire*; Stepto, *From Behind the Veil*; and Baker, *Blues, Ideology, and Afro-American Literature*.

37. See, for instance, Gilroy, *Black Atlantic*; Ernest, *Liberation Historiography*; Jarrett, *Representing the Race*; and Warren, *What Was African American Literature?*

38. While discussing the contemporary trajectory of Latinx literature, María Saldaña-Portillo, for instance, questions "false unities and tidy histories" of different groups and their histories in the US that are often invoked in the formation of the Latinx literary tradition (475).

can, Latina/o, and Afro-Latina/o literatures.[39] Marta Caminero-Santangelo and Arlene Dávila have correctly demonstrated that terms such as "Hispanic" or "Latino," if used uncritically, ultimately erase or efface the distinct histories, geographies, social, and cultural characteristics among different groups since those terms have often been used by government entities and business conglomerates for homogenizing and economic reasons.[40] While scholars rightly contest uncritical uses of panethnic labels and engage with the various historical, social, and cultural characteristics that distinguish different groups, it is equally valuable to explore characteristics or experiences that unite different groups in solidarity and in resisting forms of oppression, disenfranchisement, and segregation within the larger context of race and social dynamics within the US.

Against Marginalization acknowledges the need to interrogate panethnic rubrics such as "Latino/a/x" that are at times invoked on social discourses seeking to efface distinct racial, ethnic, national, or cultural identities; however, it appears equally important to emphasize the histories and experiences that unite Latinx people—and people of color more broadly—within the US context. Scholars of Latinx literature are right to emphasize the markedly distinct experiences of different Latinx groups that go beyond racial, ethnic, or national origins such as the role and impact of government policies, legal status, language fluency, educational attainment, and economic resources;[41] however, most of these experiences are influenced by the legacy of historical marginalization and the experience of becoming "other" socially and culturally vis-à-vis the dominant white mainstream society. As Alcoff observes, just as with Black identity, "the category Latino generally operates as a racialized category in the United States" (*Visible* 241). Even a second-generation, middle-class Cuban American of European descent may not escape a degree of racialization or otherness if she speaks Spanish in a white-dominated or historically white-dominated social space. Similarly, an upper-class Black physician living in a Virginia suburb may not escape these processes of racialization and

---

39. Literary critics who have theorized about racial and ethnic identity in relation to the literary or artistic output of a particular Latinx group of writers starting in the 1990s include R. Saldívar, *Chicano Narrative*; Luis, *Dance between Two Cultures*; Flores, *From Bomba to Hip-Hop*; Pérez-Torres, *Mestizaje*; Caminero-Santangelo, *On Latinidad*; and Irizarry, *Chicana/o and Latina/o Fiction*.

40. For in-depth analyses of *Latinidad* in the context of Latinx literature and culture, see Caminero-Santangelo, *On Latinidad*, and Arlene Dávila, *Latinos, Inc.*

41. Caminero-Santangelo does not reject the term "Latino"; instead, she concedes that such a panethnic term is at times necessary as when studying a body of literature that shares elements in common but "without assuming any more fundamental connections between the various groups but in acknowledgement of the fact that a sense of a larger group identity has tentatively been constructed—often by popular culture—in the United States" (*Latinidad* 31).

otherness when he enters a department store. While Black and Latinx people possess distinct and unique historical memories and experiences, my examination of post-1960s Black and Latinx writers focuses on shared historical, literary, and cultural legacies and their similar strategies to fight against social, cultural, and literary marginalization.

The emerging panethnic rubric "Latinx" represents the latest attempt to reformulate from within, rather than imposed from outside, a panethnic identity that remains necessary while exploring the historical, cultural, aesthetic, and linguistic characteristics of a literature that, although rich and multifaceted, has struggled for recognition and had been traditionally excluded—just as its Black counterpart—from the larger literary tradition until the 1970s. Similar to the way Black literature began as "Negro literature" and then moved from "Afro-American" to "African American," the development of Latinx literary studies shows the evolution in representative efforts to anthologize it from "Hispanic," "Latina/o," to "Latinx."[42] Suzanne Bost and Frances Aparicio, for instance, point out the need to study the Latinx literary tradition through an encompassing panethnic Latinx perspective since those texts constitute "a corpus that has struggled against the invisibility of its authors within the larger context of mainstream American literature, [and] the role of anthologies becomes ever more significant as a strategy and site for inclusion and for claiming public legitimacy" (8). Due in part to the complex history of race relations in the US, racial and ethnic terms, particularly those used to describe historical disenfranchised groups, have remained in constant flux through different historical periods; the terms "Black" and "Latinx" represent the latest permutations of ongoing social and cultural processes.

My study builds on the works of critics and scholars who have interpreted a broad array of literary periods, texts, and groups of either Black or Latinx writers engaging or thematizing the disenfranchised position of their communities and some of their writings and texts vis-à-vis the larger white dominant group.[43] Among these scholars, the development of my argument or comparative analysis and the exploration of these texts as reflecting a shared fight against marginalization particularly draws from formulations in studies such as Ramón Saldívar's *Chicano Narrative,* which focuses on Mexican American literature after the 1960s as a form of "resistance literature" (10), Rafael Pérez-

---

42. See, for example, Kanellos, *Herencia*; Stavans, *Norton Anthology of Latino Literature*; and Bost and Aparicio, *Routledge Companion to Latino/a Literature.*

43. In formulating a comparative interpretation of the Black and Latinx literary traditions as a fight against marginalization, I have drawn particularly from the insights by Ramón Saldívar, William Luis, Rafael Pérez-Torres, John Alba Cutler, Harry J. Elam, Kenneth Warren, Lawrence Jackson, and Phillip Brian Harper.

Torres's *Mestizaje* on Chicanx literature as Chicanx subjects writing with an "awareness of exclusion" (12), and particularly William Luis's *Dance Between Two Cultures* that analyzes the writing of post-1960s Latinx Caribbean writers through a "culture of resistance" based on their shared position of marginality vis-à-vis mainstream society (x).[44] While this element of marginalization affecting writers and communities from different groups has been identified, my study contributes to these ongoing scholarly inquiries by focusing on the shared literary experiences of Black and Latinx authors.

Against Marginalization argues that the fight for social, literary, and aesthetic recognition constitutes a shared trait contained in the drama of Baraka and Valdez; novels by Baldwin, Walker, Anaya, and Viramontes; the essays by Ellison and Rodriguez; and in the short story collections of Jones and Díaz. Their shared struggles and literary strategies have not been studied comparatively as a distinct characteristic that permeates and informs the work of several representative post-1960s Black and Latinx writers. My study acknowledges that race, ethnicity, national origin, and cultural heritage play a key role in the experiences of distinct Black and Latinx authors; however, the works of some Black and Latinx writers also show a shared emphasis in their fight for the social recognition of their respective communities.[45] Most times, historical interpretations of different racial and ethnic groups in the US are studied separately from the perspective of each group; however, cross-cultural and comparative racial and ethnic histories of Black and Latinx people are emerging. Paul Ortiz, for instance, studies the struggles of Black and Latinx people against the legacies of slavery and imperialism as two forms of oppression that people of color have endured and fought against through their histories on the American continent.[46] It is equally important to note that this fight

44. William Luis's study emphasizes, at different times, that the struggle against a hegemonic, white-dominated society is shared not only among Latinx people but also by other people of color more broadly; for example, Luis explains that "many Latinos in the United States continue to live, as Puerto Ricans do, a colonial existence within the colonizing country. Whereas Anglo-Americans profit from the American dream, Latinos and African Americans, as a group, have been kept at a distance" (278).

45. Historians and scholars including John Hope Franklin, William Julius Wilson, Cornel West, Charles Mills, Paul C. Taylor, Linda Martín Alcoff, Rodolfo Acuña, Juan González, and Paul Ortiz, among others, have documented, studied, and contextualized the history of marginalization and disenfranchisement of Black and Spanish-speaking communities going back to the establishment of the country, which continued uninterrupted in other forms, and improved to a certain degree after civil rights gains of the 1960s and 1970s.

46. Ortiz's *An African American and Latinx History of the United States* takes a comparative approach to historicize the ways in which slavery, imperialism, and social systems of oppression—particularly white supremacy in different forms—have shaped and influenced US history and how Black and Latinx communities have fought for social recognition, particularly through community organizing and social activism.

against marginalization that is present in Black and Latinx texts is also present in the fiction of other writers of color, including Native American and Asian American writers.[47] This fight against marginalization serves to articulate not only a pan-Asian, pan-Native-American, or pan-Latinx form of unity, but a solidarity among people of color based on their shared past histories and current social and economic conditions since racism, discrimination, and disenfranchisement continued to be the reality for many communities of color in the twentieth-first century.[48]

POST-1960s BLACK AND LATINX WRITERS AND THE AMERICAN LITERARY TRADITION

The civil rights era of the 1960s and 1970s marked a critical moment in the fight for social justice by people of color, including the creation of the first ethnic studies programs at colleges and universities; scholars have focused and interpreted the work of post-1960s Black and Latinx writers in relation to these social and cultural changes, identifying how their thematic, aesthetic, and social concerns relate to the fight for social justice and the civil rights struggles of the 1960s and 1970s.[49] John Alba Cutler's analysis, for instance, pays particular attention to the role that universities played before the civil rights era in "reproducing national culture" (*Assimilation* 19), which, in the case of literature, was represented by the American literary tradition and its canon, and how changes brought by the fight for civil rights and cultural representation altered those dynamics in relation to the production, dissemination, and reading of Chicanx texts. These studies of either post-1960s Black or Latinx literature inform my study, particularly through their insights on

---

47. Arnold Krupat and Viet Thanh Nguyen, for instance, have identified tendencies in Native American and Asian American literary traditions, respectively, in relation to the writers' emphasis on the history of oppression of their respective groups.

48. Michelle Alexander, for instance, has incisively written in *The New Jim Crow* about the continued legacy of discrimination against Black communities and the criminalization of the Black body through mass incarceration that had its origins in slavery times and has continued in different forms to the present; likewise, Alexander has drawn parallels between the mass incarceration of Black bodies and the mass deportation of mostly Latinx immigrants ("Injustice"). Ortiz correctly observes that the shared struggles against oppression of Black and Latinx people in the US continues to be as important as in previous decades in light of the resurgence of federal and state policies and legislation that target communities of color (179).

49. For interpretations of either post-1960s Black or Latinx literature, see Smethurst, *Black Arts Movement*; Levy-Hussen, *How to Read African American Literature*; Dalleo and Machado Sáez, *Latino/a Canon*; and Cutler, *Ends of Assimilation*.

how student-led social protests and the emergence of university-sponsored independent publishers influenced the trajectory of both literary traditions.

While post-1960s Black and Latinx authors began to move away from the legacy of the civil rights struggles of the 1960s and 1970s, a premise of *Against Marginalization* is that several post-1960s Black and Latinx writers continued to grapple with the history of social and cultural marginalization as their narratives thematize the legacy of their past position of marginality. Current developments in Black and Latinx writing—particularly in the twenty-first century—indicate an increasing multiplicity of cultural, thematic, and stylistic concerns and incursions into different genres. Lovalerie King and Shirley Moody-Turner correctly contend that contemporary Black writers have made innovations in their thematic and aesthetic approaches in part by moving away from the historical and social legacies of race relations in the US.[50] In the case of Latinx fiction, critics have made a similar case arguing that contemporary Latinx authors engage with themes beyond the confines of their histories, social justice, and cultural heritage;[51] instead, more Latinx writers emphasize stylistic and formal experimentation, or as Ramón Saldívar notes, write fiction that "requires the invention of new forms to represent [them]" ("Historical Fantasy" 574). Nonetheless, it would be difficult to analyze the post-1960s essays of Ellison and Richard Rodriguez, for example, without taking into consideration competing interpretations of the meaning of race and ethnicity among communities of color developed during the 1960s and 1970s civil rights era. My study places the fight against historical and literary invisibility at the center of my analysis of post-1960s Black and Latinx authors; however, I cover the period from the 1960s to the end of the twentieth century, since I agree that the trajectories of contemporary Black and Latinx fiction have increasingly expanded beyond the realms of racial, ethnic identity, social justice, and historical memory.

In making a case for studying Black and Latinx writers as engaged in a shared struggle against literary exclusion, my comparative analysis of selective case studies of post-1960s Black and Latinx authors explores the degree to which some of these writers engaged with the American literary tradition, its authors, and literary movements; however, my study does not engage with

---

50. King and Moody-Turner make a strong case by arguing that "within the realm of so-called literary fiction, we are witnessing a new generation of writers who locate themselves firmly within the African American tradition, while refusing to be bound by monolithic and imaginary notions of authentic blackness or respectability" (4).

51. For interpretations of contemporary Latinx fiction as moving away from previous concerns regarding the social struggles of the 1960s, see Dalleo and Machado Sáez, *Latino/a Canon*; R. Saldívar, "Historical Fantasy"; and Ralph Rodriguez, *Latinx Literature Unbound*.

debates among literary critics regarding the intrinsic value or cultural valid-ity of Black or Latinx texts within the American literary canon. The field of American literature has moved from rigid interpretations of the literary can-on's intrinsic quality and aesthetic value exemplified by critics such as Harold Bloom that were restrictive, biased, or blatantly discriminatory.[52] What was seen as radical and politicized by some predominantly white literary schol-ars starting in the late 1960s was viewed by writers and artists of color such as Baraka as a legitimate critique on a literary tradition that had rejected or marginalized Black writers. Baraka exemplifies other authors who identified the American literary canon as a form of cultural and artistic oppression and sought to undermine it rather than advocating for the inclusion of Black writ-ers; he interprets the literary canon, not simply based on intrinsic or aesthetic value, but as a representation of the legacy of racism and colonialism masked under the premise of apolitical artistic merit.[53] Black and Latinx literary schol-ars who attended English graduate programs during the 1980s and 1990s have written about the efforts to integrate Black and Latinx literatures as part of the larger American literary tradition.[54] It is important for my argument to note that while Baraka explicitly ties his critique of the literary canon to the fight for social justice of the 1960s by people of color, the influence of the Ameri-can literary tradition in authors of color, including Baraka, speaks of a more complex relation.[55]

---

52. Bloom's interpretation of canon formation exemplifies the excesses while theorizing about the worth of literature measured by its intrinsic "aesthetic value" without regard to its social and cultural implications (*Western* 22). While attempting to defend the aesthetic value of literary works against writers and critics with an alleged left-wing agenda, Bloom, in his role as literary gatekeeper, reverts to an ideologically and politically charged, rather than aesthetic, defense of the canon.

53. Baraka situates his critique within the emergence of the Black Nationalist movement of the late 1960s that advocated for the "continued struggle for equality and self-determination," along with its Black aesthetic component represented by the Black Arts Movement, which sought "to challenge the 'whiteness' of art as posited by a white supremacist society" ("Cultural" 152–53).

54. Gates's *Loose Canons* discusses in detail how critics of Black literature in the 1980s and 1990s had to grapple with the scholars' perceptions regarding the integrity and intrinsic aes-thetic value of canonical texts and the secondary place of Black writers within the larger literary tradition. R. Saldívar similarly discusses how emerging scholars of Chicanx literature in these decades fought to integrate the "works by Mexican-American authors [that were] absent from the American literary histories, the anthologies of American literature, and from the syllabi of courses on American literature" (*Chicano* 11).

55. Although Baraka excoriates the Western and American literary canons while partici-pating in the Black Arts Movement in the 1960s and 1970s, some of his drama and fiction, such as his novel *The System of Dante's Hell*, was influenced by his knowledge and engagement with the Western and American literary traditions.

Against Marginalization consists of comparative case studies that show how some Black and Latinx writers after the 1960s fought against the exclusion of Black or Latinx texts by engaging, appropriating, and subverting elements from the American literary tradition. Critics of Black and Latinx literature have called attention to ways in which Black and Latinx writers at different periods have been influenced by, and how they engaged with, the American literary tradition and the ways a number of Black writers shared formalistic, stylistic, and aesthetic techniques associated with literary movements during the early decades of the twentieth century.[56] Gates, for example, explains that "the most formally complex and compelling black writers . . . have always blended forms of Western literature with African American vernacular and written traditions," offering as examples writers such as Jean Toomer, Sterling Brown, Langston Hughes, James Baldwin, and Toni Morrison, among others (*Loose Canons* xvii). Similarly, scholars of Latinx literature have studied how some Latinx writers since the turn of the twentieth century have engaged in their writings with literary legacies and movements such as realism and modernism.[57] After the 1960s, not only Black writers—but Latinx writers as well—have been influenced by the American literary tradition, its literary movements, aesthetic concerns, and canonical authors to different degrees. For instance, while the influence of the literary tradition has been discussed in the writings of Ellison and Rodriguez, less attention has been given to the use of literary naturalism themes, tropes, and stylistic elements in the fiction of Edward P. Jones and Junot Díaz. *Against Marginalization* studies the shared formalistic and aesthetic strategies in the work of post-1960s Black and Latinx writers in part as a conscious attempt to inscribe their work in the literary tradition in a predominantly white literary and publishing world that has historically struggled to either acknowledge their presence or meaningfully include them.

Chapter 1 builds on the work of several scholars who have studied either the Black or Latinx literary traditions to present a comparative analysis that focuses on the publication and reading of representative authors and texts at key junctures in literary history. The consensus among scholars of Black and Latinx literature is that the late 1960s and early 1970s represented perhaps the most important transformation in the writing, publishing, and reading of Black and Latinx texts due, to a great extent, to the gains of social justice

---

56. For discussions on the American literary tradition and Black writers, see Gates, *Loose Canons*; Spillers, *Black, White, and in Color*; Baker, *Modernism and the Harlem Renaissance*; Jackson, *Indignant Generation*; Hill, *Ethics of Swagger*; and Nowlin, *Literary Ambition*.

57. See R. Saldívar, *Chicano Narrative*; Moya, *Learning from Experience*; Aranda, *When We Arrive*; Cutler, "At the Crossroads"; and Contreras, "'I'll Publish Your Cowardice.'"

movements in political and academic realms. Based on the work of scholars who have focused on either Black or Spanish-language print culture, this chapter explores how the increase in the publication and reading of Black and Latinx authors was not only the result of the period of social protest of the 1960s and 1970s, but it was also a direct result of the changes and struggles to be published and read in the white-dominated mainstream publishing industry dating back to the start of both literary traditions.

Chapter 2 traces the historical, thematic, and aesthetic convergences in Black and Mexican American theater and the influence of the Black and Mexican American civil rights movements of the 1960s. I focus on how Amiri Baraka's *The Slave* and Luis Valdez's *Bandido!* challenge the marginalized position of Blacks in the antebellum South and Mexican Americans in California after the Mexican–American War of 1848, respectively, by transforming a field slave and a Mexican American outlaw into revolutionary leaders who led armed confrontations against white oppression. I trace how these plays equally resist dominant historical narratives by subverting the figures of the disenfranchised slave and Mexican American outlaw into characters who gain agency in part by the playwrights' use of postmodernist aesthetics including the contestation of hegemonic histories, the use of irony and parody, and self-reflexivity. Despite both plays' emphasis on open confrontation, they similarly present their protagonists' divided allegiances toward the US as their revolutionary efforts collapse, which reflect the tensions between racial and ethnic self-determination and the protagonists' sense of national belonging.

Chapter 3 examines how Black and Latinx authors after the 1960s contested the prevailing history of World War II, which often overlooks the role, sacrifice, and courage of soldiers of color by depicting in fiction the experiences of Black and Latinx soldiers who were deployed overseas and fought for their country despite widespread discrimination in the army. James Baldwin's *Tell Me How Long the Train's Been Gone* and Rudolfo Anaya's *Bless Me, Ultima* situate the war and its influence during the 1940s and 1950s within the "long civil rights movement" as soldiers of color fought for liberty abroad only to return to a segregated society at home. Baldwin and Anaya similarly struggled to reconcile the tension between art and social protest that has been present from the start of the literary tradition. Both writers similarly grappled and struggled to navigate their dual roles as artists and spokespersons for their respective groups at the height of the fight for social justice in the 1960s and 1970s among communities of color, which sheds light on the authors' shared thematic, structural, and narrative strategies in relation to the depiction and the role of soldiers of color in their novels.

Chapter 4 focuses on the emergence of Black and Chicanx nationalist movements in the 1960s and 1970s, along with their emphasis on racial and ethnic difference, and how some writers of color challenged those ideological premises. I examine Ralph Ellison's two collections of essays, *Shadow and Act* and *Going to the Territory*, and Richard Rodriguez's *Days of Obligation* and *Brown*; in their roles as essayists and intellectuals, Ellison and Rodriguez similarly explore elements in American culture, history, and literature to argue that since the country's inception, American mainstream culture has been influenced, in various degrees, by cross-cultural exchanges and the contributions of diverse racial, ethnic, religious, and immigrant groups that were once considered outsiders. A characteristic shared by the nonfiction of Ellison and Rodriguez is the way in which both authors fail to acknowledge the racialized and marginalized position of Black and Latinx people both in the literary tradition and society at large. The essays of Ellison and Rodriguez share a similar belief in American ideals based primarily on their personal experiences that, while insightful and necessary, ultimately place into question their claims of a dual or pluralistic cultural identity.

Chapter 5 analyzes fictional representations of systems of segregation, discrimination, and economic exploitation affecting Black rural communities in the South and Mexican American communities in agricultural fields in California during the 1950s and 1960s. Alice Walker's *The Third Life of Grange Copeland* exposes the dehumanizing effects of the system of sharecropping in Black rural communities in the South while Helena María Viramontes's *Under the Feet of Jesus* similarly presents the economic and social marginalization experienced by Mexican American farmworker families created by large-scale agricultural practices in the Southwest. These narratives render agency to women of color in these communities while employing aesthetic, linguistic, and formalistic techniques associated with literary modernism, including complex imagery and symbolism, narrative fragmentation, and multiple points of view, thus creating instances of intertextuality with previous literary works.

Chapter 6 concentrates on the social and economic inequalities in communities of color in urban areas denounced by Black and Latinx civil rights activists at the height of the struggles for social justice in the 1960s and 1970s. I focus on two short story collections, Edward P. Jones's *Lost in the City* and Junot Díaz's *Drown* that present similar critiques of the legacy of systematic employment discrimination and disenfranchisement in urban communities of color. Short stories in both collections explore the interconnections between racial discrimination and economic stagnation and reflect the influence of literary naturalism—particularly the fiction of Richard Wright—through their shared thematic and stylistic elements such as the influence of social and economic forces on individuals including unemployment, violence, and addiction. The fiction of Jones and Díaz presents another instance in which writers of color continued to appropriate and subvert aesthetic and stylistic techniques to inscribe their work in the American literary tradition.

The final section reflects on the possibilities for further comparative or cross-cultural analyses of Black and Latinx authors in different genres, including the poetry of Sonia Sanchez and Lorna Dee Cervantes, the political writings of Huey Newton and Rodolfo "Corky" Gonzales, the fiction and poetry of Gwendolyn Brooks and Sandra Cisneros, and the novels of Toni Morrison and Ana Castillo. I conclude with a discussion on the seemingly paradoxical position that contemporary authors of color confront; while a few are nationally and critically recognized, the large majority—particularly women of color—continue to fight for access and opportunities in a still predominantly white publishing industry and academia, even when college students and readers in general in the US are increasingly more racially and ethnically diverse.

CHAPTER 1

Convergences in Black and Latinx Literary Histories through Publishing

Beginnings to 1970s

This chapter presents a comparative study of instances of convergences in the development of the Black and Latinx literary traditions by focusing comparatively on the creation, publication, and reading of representative texts at key junctures from both traditions' beginnings to the 1970s.[1] The development of both literary traditions reflects the historical fight against marginalization that relates to the efforts of Black and Latinx writers to publish their work in local and mainstream venues; both literary traditions show their gradual transition from the literary margins—when Black and Spanish-language texts were excluded from social, cultural, and institutional discourses—to a position of inclusion as Black and Latinx writers began to be published and read by mainstream audiences in a sustained manner. My analysis draws particularly from the works and insights of numerous scholars who have studied the publication histories of Black and Spanish-language texts during the colonial period, the publishing dynamics in Black and Spanish-language print culture in the "long" nineteenth century, and the printing, publishing, and reading of Black

---

1. As noted in the introduction, I use the terms "Latinx literary history" and "Latinx literary tradition" as opposed to "Latina/o literary history" and "Latina/o literary tradition" throughout this chapter to emphasize a project of Latinx identity formation and Latinx literature in the US that encompasses authors and peoples from different racial and ethnic backgrounds, including African and indigenous. Similarly, I refer to the "Black literary tradition" and "Black literary history" while historicizing Black authors within the US context in this and subsequent chapters.

and Latinx texts in the twentieth century up to the 1970s.[2] These critics have studied aspects of how pamphlets, newspapers, magazines, weeklies, serialized novels, poetry, and print books, among others, were printed and read, or in some cases how they were not printed or only marginally read by mainstream audiences. My study contributes to efforts to map aspects of those traditions comparatively and to call attention to some of the shared commonalities in the trajectories of Black and Latinx literatures, which despite the considerable instances of convergence have traditionally been studied, mapped, and anthologized separately for the most part.[3]

While it is necessary to study the distinct historical, social, and cultural differences that have made possible the formation and development of the Black and Latinx literary traditions, it is also important to investigate instances of convergences in the development of each tradition to call attention to the shared commonalities and struggles that allowed early Black and Spanish-language texts to emerge from their position of marginality vis-à-vis a white-dominated and English-speaking literary tradition. Representative instances of convergence during the late nineteenth century and early twentieth century in each tradition, such as Black and Latinx authors' attempts to gain a wider audience with different cultural expectations, and the choices made by writers to appeal to those readers, show that Black and Latinx writers often contended against similar obstacles. While both literary traditions share a position of marginality, authors' struggles attest to the shared history of resistance and attempts to gain access to printing presses, publishing houses, and a sustaining readership. While the social, political, and literary experiences of marginalized groups and writers of color differ in marked degrees—as no other group has experienced the legacy of slavery, racism, and discrimination in the United States as Blacks—the fight against literary marginalization sheds light on the commonalities that unite Black and Latinx writers at most instances in the development of both literary traditions.

---

2. Some of these scholars include Barbara Christian, Henry L. Gates, Robert Levine, Eric Gardner, John Ernest, Valerie Babb, Elizabeth McHenry, P. Gabrielle Foreman, Ivy Wilson, Derrick Spires, James Smethurst, George Hutchinson, John K. Young, and Jean-Christophe Cloutier. In the case of the Latinx literary tradition, they include Nicolás Kanellos, María Herrera-Sobek, Juan Bruce-Novoa, Ramón Saldívar, Genaro M. Padilla, A. Gabriel Meléndez, Francisco Lomelí, Manuel Martín-Rodríguez, John Morán González, Kirsten Silva Gruesz, Rodrigo Lazo, Jesse Alemán, John Alba Cutler, and Vanessa Fonseca-Chávez.

3. A notable exception is the collection *Race, Ethnicity and Publishing in America*, edited by Cécile Cottenet, which presents a cross-cultural and diasporic analysis related to the creation, publication, and dissemination of representative American texts by writers of color.

This chapter studies chronologically representative authors and texts from both traditions by exploring aspects of the authors' publication histories and their targeted audiences. Some instances in the publication histories of Phillis Wheatley and Gaspar Pérez de Villagrá, by far the most asymmetrical comparison in terms of the authors' historical and social positions—the latter a Spanish expeditioner and soldier in a territory that would form part of the Southwest, the former an emancipated slave in the US colonies; nonetheless, the publication histories of their books of poetry illustrate these authors' position of literary exclusion vis-à-vis the larger American literary tradition. The emergence of Black and Spanish-language print culture in the early nineteenth century and the proliferation of texts during much of the nineteenth century share parallels in the way both Black and Spanish-language newspapers and weeklies began to disseminate writings in different types of genres that were excluded from mainstream print culture and publications. The shared similarities of both Black and Spanish-language print culture in the latter part of the nineteenth century are exemplified by Frederick Douglass and José Martí and their efforts at gaining access to the means of literary production by producing and editing their own newspapers.

The late nineteenth century and the turn of the twentieth century illustrate how previously marginalized authors struggled to publish their work with mainstream publishers, and in the cases of Charles Chesnutt and María Amparo Ruiz de Burton, their challenges in appealing to white and nonwhite readers. The early decades of the twentieth century shed light on the influence of Black and Spanish-language newspapers and magazines in New York City as shown by the aspects of the publication histories of James Weldon Johnson and Jesús Colón. The middle part of the twentieth century shows that despite decades of writers' struggles to be published by mainstream houses and gain a white readership, those struggles continued as reflected in the literary careers of Ann Petry and Josefina Niggli. The fight to create, publish, and gain an audience continued into the twentieth century and intensified with the institutionalization of both literary traditions at college campuses and universities in the late 1960s and early 1970s when, for the first time, authors of color were published by independent and mainstream presses in significant numbers and were able to gain a sustaining readership composed primarily of college students. While the Black and Latinx literary traditions emerged as independent from one another, their shared traits and characteristics came into full view with the institutionalization of both literary traditions at colleges and universities starting in the 1960s. The consensus among scholars is that the late 1960s and early 1970s represent the most important transformation in the development of both literary traditions due to the gains of protest and social justice movements in social and academic realms.[4] This chapter makes the case that the changes that took place in the publication, teaching, and reading of Black and Latinx authors starting in the 1960s represent the culmination of decades, or even centuries, of Black and Latinx writers struggling to break into a white-dominated publishing industry and gain a mainstream audience dating back to the formation of the United States.

As I explored in the introduction, terms to describe people of African descent and from Latin American backgrounds in the US have evolved and continue to evolve in response to historical, social, and cultural changes that are often complex, and when related to literary history and past authors, require additional considerations. In discussing the publication histories of Black and Latinx texts, I follow the lead of literary scholars to position and describe authors within their geographical and historical moments; however, I similarly attempt to describe authors who have been studied and anthologized in "Latina/o literature" as "Latinx" writers. In the context of Black literature, I use the term "Black" rather than "African American," thus acknowledging the evolving meaning of the term "Black" in the context of Black studies and Black literary history. In the development of the Latinx literary tradition, most writers that presently are considered Latinx writers were studied in relation to their historical and geographical context, giving way to Chicana/o/x, Caribbean-American, Puerto Rican, Latino/a, Afro-Latino/a literatures. Prior to the 1960s, most Latinx authors did not consider themselves as part of a larger panethnic group or a panethnic Latinx literary tradition. For instance, in the late nineteenth century, María Amparo Ruiz de Burton did not identify herself as a member of a racial or ethnic group; other writers such as Eusebio Chacón identified as *Nuevomexicano,* rather than Latinx, and others such as José Martí writing in New York City has been considered primarily a Cuban writer in exile. Rodrigo Lazo, for instance, brings attention to "the challenges of historical scholarship and literary history, which are always in dialogue and tension with the conceptual frames of the present" (*Letters* 15). One goal of my study is an attempt at cohesion by describing these authors as "Latinx," while at the same time considering their historical and geographical contexts.

Most studies that attempt to analyze and map the Black and Latinx literary traditions would encounter intrinsic limitations, and *Against Marginalization* is no exception; both literary traditions cover vast historical, geographical, and social trajectories that mark their uniqueness or distinctiveness. Equally

4. See, for example, Smethurst, *Black Arts Movement*; Warren, *What Was African American Literature?*; Martín-Rodríguez, *Life in Search of Readers*; Lima, *Latino Body*; and Cutler, *Ends of Assimilation*, among others.

important, literary scholars have called attention to the large number of texts from different past periods in both traditions that are still to be studied, published, and archived thoroughly and critically.[5] Moreover, my comparative analysis of representative Black and Latinx texts does not attempt to oversimplify significant moments and circumstances unique to each literary tradition such as the place of early chronicles of the New Spain in Latinx literature, the emergence and development of the slave narrative genre in the first half of the nineteenth century, and the access to mainstream publishers by a number of the authors of the Harlem Renaissance. While each literary tradition possesses distinct histories, developments, and characteristics, some of these histories share commonalities due to the dynamics of a society and mainstream publishing industry that at almost each step excluded Black and Latinx writers. Likewise, instances in both traditions demonstrate how Black and Latinx writers have fought to be published and gain a readership in both local and mainstream venues.

COLONIAL PERIOD AND NINETEENTH-CENTURY BLACK AND SPANISH-LANGUAGE PRINT CULTURE

Phillis Wheatley and Gaspar Pérez de Villagrá represent what it meant to be on the literary margins in relation to the publishing and reading of their texts within the social and geographical circumstances during the colonial period. The publication of the poetry of Wheatley and Villagrá reflects the initial social, political, and historical circumstances in which both literary traditions emerged: Wheatley, a former slave and a writer in colonial Boston during the years preceding the formation of the country, and Villagrá, a European expeditioner and soldier writing about the Spanish territory of New Mexico. The reception, limited circulation, and place in the American literary tradition, until a few decades ago, reflect the position of marginality in which the Black and Latinx literary traditions began. The authenticity of Wheatley's poetry was questioned by Bostonian readers, and Villagrá's poetry, while written in Spanish and intended for a select continental Spain audience, was peripheral to literary and critical discourses in the US for centuries despite its historical, literary, and cultural significance as one of the earliest texts written about a territory that would become part of this country.

---

5. See, for example, Ernest, *Chaotic Justice*; Cloutier, *Shadow Archives*; Martín-Rodríguez, *Life in Search of Readers*; and Kanellos, "Exiles, Immigrants, and Natives."

Instances in the publication history of Wheatley's poetry show how early Black writers lacked access to the means of literary production and how they actively struggled to be published; while Wheatley succeeded, her literary legacy was primarily kept in Black periodicals and weeklies during the nineteenth century and only available to a wider readership after the 1970s.[6] Wheatley wrote before the Revolutionary War when Boston was still a colony, and the extraordinary craft of her poetry allowed her to publish and reprint it in various periodicals such as the *Newport Mercury*, the *Boston Evening-Post*, and the *Massachusetts Gazette* (Rezek 25). The publication of her book of poetry, *Poems on Various Subjects, Religious and Moral*, published in London in 1773, is considered one of the earliest Black books.[7] *Poems on Various Subjects* is distinct also for the obstacles its author encountered within the learned society of the emerging colonies. Wheatley was supported by her master, John Wheatley, as they tried to get the book published in Boston in 1770 without success; however, she remained a literary outsider with no access to an American publisher (Carretta xvi). Even the London publication of *Poems on Various Subjects* was conditional until some of the most prominent men in Boston attested at a public gathering that Wheatley was in fact the person who wrote those poems, an attestation that was printed in the first pages of *Poems on Various Subjects* (Gates, *Loose Canons* 51–53). Readers' reactions to her poetry were mixed; a few British readers became her earliest admirers and realized the potential of her poetry to assist with the abolitionist cause in England, while others such as Thomas Jefferson, in the oft-quoted passages from his *Notes on the State of Virginia*, were less enthusiastic of Wheatley's poetry and remained skeptical about equality among Blacks and whites (Rezek 29–30). Although Wheatley was legally recognized as the author of her poetry and was able to gain freedom from her master, her subsequent poetry did not garnish as much interest from readers as *Poems on Various Subjects* had, resulting in the end of her career as a poet. In the early nineteenth century, Wheatley's poetry was republished in book format by Black and white abolitionists such as Isaac Knapp and William G. Allen (Cavitch 220); thus, it was within a dedicated group of Black writers, editors, and readers that Wheatley found her readership in posterity.

---

6. For a detailed discussion on the republishing of Wheatley's poetry, see Cavitch, "Poetry of Phillis Wheatley."

7. Vincent Carretta notes that Wheatley has become one of the best-known early Black writers; however, other Black poets such as Lucy Terry and Jupiter Hammon were also able to publish their poetry in periodicals at the time (xv). Joseph Rezek, however, notes the distinctiveness of Wheatley's *Poems on Various Subjects* is due to its length and publication dynamics, which differ from "shorter, occasional, and more ephemeral texts" by other Black writers (24).

The place of Villagrá in Latinx literary history illustrates the complex ways in which Spanish-language texts remained outside the margins of American literary history when they did not conform to an English-speaking tradition despite Villagrá's inexorable link to the history of the Southwest.[8] Villagrá was a Spanish-born soldier who participated in Juan de Oñate's expedition of New Mexico in 1598. Villagrá's *Historia de la Nueva México* (A History of New Mexico) was printed and published in Alcalá de Henares, Spain, in 1610 (Fonseca-Chávez 34). The poem's publication dynamics relate in part to the patronage tradition and printing trends that developed in Europe after the Gutenberg press; one of Villagrá's goals in the publication of his epic poem was to entice a recompense from Spanish King Felipe III in the form of a government post in one of the Spanish provinces (Leal 114). *Historia de la Nueva México*, however, remains a work linked in geography, cultural relevance, and subject matter to the history of New Mexico. Villagrá's poetry documents the presence of Spanish-language writing about a territory that would become part of the US; however, it is also a text valuable for its aesthetic and artistic elements, which had remained overlooked in American literary studies until recently (Padilla, *Daring Flight* 3). Villagrá's poem, similar to Wheatley's *Poems on Various Subjects,* reflects the influence of classical Greek and Roman sources;[9] these classical allusions, however, were often interrogated due in part to the "otherness" of their authors rather than studied within the context of Renaissance and Enlightenment influences, as with other colonial writers.[10] Likewise, their poetry shows the difficulty of accepting and incorporating the work of writers who fell outside Western and English-speaking conventions in the new colonies, which has also contributed to the lack of critical engagement with their work in American literary studies.[11]

Similar to Wheatley's poetry, Villagrá's poem was kept alive in Spanish-language print culture in New Mexico in the late nineteenth century as a form

---

8. The editors of the 1992 annotated Spanish-English edition of Villagrá's poem, for instance, state that the "salient themes and facts regarding the founding of New Mexico in 1598, an event tantamount to the founding of Jamestown, Virginia, in 1607, is as much part of the United States' national story as it is that of Mexico's" (Encinias et al. xxv).

9. Genaro Padilla's book-length study of *Historia de la Nueva México* explores the numerous Greek and Roman classical allusions in Villagrá's poem (*Daring Flight* 11–37). For a discussion on the influence of classical sources in Wheatley's poetry, see Carretta xiii–xiv.

10. Wheatley's poetry has been scrutinized for an overreliance on classical sources (Gates, *Loose Canons* 78); similarly, Villagrá's poem was criticized by early readers who thought the poem indistinctly mixed classical references and Amerindian cultural sources (Martín-Rodríguez, "Epic Return(s)" 668).

11. For discussions on the challenges that Spanish-language texts pose to literary scholars working primarily with English sources, see Lazo, "Trajectories of ExChange," and Gruesz and Lazo, "Spanish Americas."

of cultural memory, despite the poem's depiction and fictionalized version of Oñate's expedition and the military conquest of the Pueblo people of New Mexico. It was *Nuevomexicanos* in the 1890s who printed parts of Villagrá's poem in local Spanish-language newspapers (Fonseca-Chávez 36). Subsequent republications of *Historia de la Nueva México* in the twentieth century became tied to historical moments that coincided with moments in US territorial expansions such as the Spanish-American War.[12] Villagrá's literary legacy was kept alive by Latinx people in the Southwest and increased its significance; some of the poem's cultural references, including the concept of Aztlán, were embraced by activists, artists, and students during the Chicanx Movement of the 1960s and 1970s (Martín-Rodríguez, "Epic Return(s)" 666). However, efforts to reconceptualize the writings of Spanish explorers in the Southwest remain a complex endeavor since several of these early texts engage with the conquest of indigenous people in the North American continent, and in the case of *Historia de la Nueva México*, the conquest of the Pueblo people.[13]

The ongoing debate regarding whether early texts from *conquistadores*, Spanish explorers, and early Spanish-speaking settlers of the Southwest and Florida can be considered Latinx literature, or part of the larger American literary tradition, is representative of the extensive periods of neglect, obscurity, and subsequent recovery that characterize early Spanish-language texts from the New World. Early Spanish-language texts consisted mainly of chronicles of expeditions and diaries that were written after Columbus's first exploration to the American continent; those chronicles continued for centuries and were printed for audiences primarily in Spain and Europe. Perhaps the most discussed *relación* (chronicle) among Latinx scholars is the *Chronicle of the Narváez Expedition* by Álvar Núñez Cabeza de Vaca as a member of a Spanish expedition to Florida in 1528. Some of these chronicles have been studied by scholars of Latinx literature while acknowledging the texts' shortcomings in relation to the social, economic, and political motives that created those texts.[14] Due in part to the complex legacy of these texts, some literary schol-

---

12. Fonseca-Chávez explores in detail the publication history of *Historia de la Nueva México* and how these publications relate to social and demographic dynamics in New Mexico between *Nuevomexicanos* and Anglos (35–41).

13. Lima, for instance, reads Villagrá's depiction of Amerindians, in this case the Acoma people who originally inhabited parts of New Mexico, as the product of conquest and colonization in the name of the Spanish empire (121).

14. These scholars trace the beginning of the Latinx literary tradition to the discovery of the American continent when chroniclers from Spain and Mexico traveled or settled in the New Spain territories that will become part of the United States; see, for example, Herrera-Sobek, Introduction to *Reconstructing a Chicano/a Literary Heritage*; Bruce-Novoa, "Shipwrecked in the Seas of Significance"; and Padilla, "Discontinuous Continuities."

ars considered them outside of the Latinx literary tradition.[15] Critics on both sides, however, agree on the need to contextualize these texts.[16] Constant reexamination of the legacy of Spanish settlers in the Americas—including the Southwest—and their devastating consequences for indigenous populations, reflects the complicated histories and legacies in Latinx literature.

Nineteenth-century Black and Spanish-language print culture reflect the ways in which Black and Spanish-speaking authors emerged and made inroads by writing and publishing in newspapers and weeklies that were read and sustained by their respective Black and Spanish-speaking audiences, and in some cases by acquiring printing presses. Nineteenth-century print culture shows parallels between the Black and Latinx literary traditions; both print cultures developed and were sustained throughout most of the nineteenth century in larger cities such as Philadelphia as sites of social and political activism and as a form of counterpublics.[17] As the decades progressed, Black and Spanish-Language print culture spread to other geographical regions, concentrated in small and larger cities with Black or Spanish-speaking populations, whom in most cases either migrated or immigrated to those cities.

Antebellum Black local newspapers and weeklies in several cities represent the ways in which Black residents began to build a literary infrastructure in Northern cities with readers and communities that actively kept alive the literary legacies of former writers by reprinting or promoting their works.[18] Black newspapers in the 1840s and 1850s expanded beyond Boston, New York, and Philadelphia to other cities such as St. Louis, New Orleans, and San Francisco. Writings in these newspapers and weeklies such as the *Anglo-African Magazine,* the *Colored American Magazine,* and the *Christian Reader* consisted of essays, editorials, columns, fiction, poetry, and travel narratives, among oth-

15. Héctor Calderón and José Saldívar propose that texts written in Spanish about the Southwest before 1848 should be considered Mexican or Spanish literature, not Latinx literature (2). They point to the Mexican–American War of 1848, and the annexation of the Southwest by the US, as the start of Mexican American literature since most of its inhabitants before the war were either of Mexican or Spanish descent and lacked a Mexican American or Chicanx consciousness. In a similar way, Lima questions Cabeza de Vaca's position as a foundational author in Latinx literature (102).

16. As Martín-Rodríguez notes, the retroactive recovery of some of these texts represents a recent post-1960s phenomenon that may require a different classification methodology (*Life in Search* 139–41). Gruesz and Lazo have made a case for the incorporation of chronicles of the New Spain not only into Latinx literature but also into the larger American literary tradition, while also acknowledging the challenges of traditional national and linguistic classifications prevalent in American literary studies ("Spanish Americas" 642–43).

17. See, for instance, Ernest, *Chaotic Justice*; Spires, *Practice of Citizenship*; and Lazo, *Letters from Filadelfia.*

18. See Gardner, *Unexpected Places*; Ernest, *Liberation Historiography*; Cohen and Stein, *Early African American Print Culture*; and McHenry, *Forgotten Readers.*

ers.[19] Through the *Anglo-African Magazine,* for instance, its editor Thomas Hamilton offered a publishing space for Black writers and activists who saw print culture as means for creating community, social activism, and Black literary aesthetics (Spires, *Practice* 176). Equally important was the role of Black communities and literary societies during the antebellum period in the dissemination of Black writing and social and political ideas (McHenry 19–20). Notably, the start and development of Black fiction is closely connected to antebellum print culture as some of the earliest Black novels and short stories were first fictionalized in Black newspapers and weeklies.[20] The close relationship between Black print culture and the development of Black fiction relates to the emerging opportunities at the time for some Black writers to publish their work, which contrasts to Wheatley's difficulties finding a publisher and an audience for her book of poetry some decades earlier. As Black newspapers and weeklies shaped textual, social, and political attitudes, this independent publishing infrastructure allowed some Black writers to be published for the first time in meaningful numbers and reach a local audience.

The early attempts to gain access to the means of literary production through printing presses is exemplified by Frederick Douglass's work as a newspaper writer and editor in New York and Washington, DC. Douglass began to write for newspapers under the oversight of white editors, most famously for William Lloyd Garrison's *The Liberator,* an antebellum publication targeted toward a white readership. The unbalanced literary relationship between Douglass and Garrison—a white editor and a Black writer—and its power dynamics has permeated the Black literary tradition ever since.[21] Douglass's appropriation of the means of literary production through the printing of his own newspaper is representative of the various acts of literary independence sought by Black publishers and writers. Douglass writes in *My Bondage and My Freedom* about raising funds to acquire a printing press and "to start a paper, devoted to the interests of my enslaved and oppressed people" since at the time "there was not, in the United States, a single newspaper regularly published by the colored people; that many attempts had been made to estab-

---

19. For analyses of nineteenth-century Black print culture, see Gardner, *Unexpected Places;* Babb 9–19; I. Wilson, "Brief Wondrous Life of the *Anglo-African Magazine*"; Fagan 121–25; and Spires, *Practice of Citizenship* 161–79.

20. For example, Hamilton's *Anglo-African Magazine* serialized Martin Delany's *Blake; or the Huts of America* (Spires, *Practice* 178); Delany's novel was not published in a book format until the 1970s. Frances E. W. Harper's short story "The Two Offers" also appeared in the *Anglo-African Magazine* in 1859 (Ernest, *Liberation* 305–6).

21. For an account of the schism between Garrison and Douglass, see Fanuzzi, "Frederick Douglass's 'Colored Newspaper.'"

lish such papers[,]" but "up to that time, they had all failed" (286, 287). Douglass's work as founding editor of *The North Star* based in Rochester, New York, from 1847 to 1863, reflects the struggles against literary exclusion as Black writers began to create outlets to publish their work and find a readership. In 1851, *The North Star* merged with the *Liberty Party Paper* and was renamed *Frederick Douglass' Paper*, which contributed to the dissemination of Black writers including Frances E. W. Harper and Henry Bibb (McHenry 117–18). Douglass himself participated in these early attempts to create a body of Black fiction with his novella, *The Heroic Slave*, published in his own newspaper in 1853;[22] however, similar to other early works of fiction by Black writers, *The Heroic Slave* remained a forgotten text in scholarly conversations with only a few references until 1975 (Levine et al. xxxiii). After the Civil War, Douglass continued his involvement as editor with the *New National Era* printed in Washington, DC, up to 1874 when the paper failed. Douglass remained active as a speaker and as a writer in newspapers up to his last years in the 1880s, focusing on the social and political struggles of Blacks, a work dating back to his early 1840s writings.

In the decades leading to the Civil War, slave narratives constitute a singular moment in the development of the Black literary tradition. The publication of slave narratives reflects the historical and social circumstances that allowed slavery and former slaves' attempts to abolish it with the assistance of the printed word. Most of these narratives were published in abolitionist bastions such as Boston, Philadelphia, and New York City (Foster 18). In their efforts to depict the cruelties and inhumanity of slavery, slave narratives found an audience in abolitionists and a wider white audience in the North, who increasingly opposed slavery. The slave narrative genre marks one of the early episodes when Black writers were able to take part in US national and political debates and publish texts with large circulation among white readers. For example, Douglass's *Narrative of the Life of Frederick Douglass, an American Slave, Written by Himself*, printed in 1845 by an abolitionist society in Boston, with a preface by Garrison, sold well and went through several reprints.[23] The circulation of slave narratives as a genre, however, was short-lived; their publication rested in the hands of white publishers and with the end of the Civil War and Reconstruction, the interest in these narratives almost came to a complete stop (Foster ix). A renewed interest returned only

---

22. Scholars had pointed out that *The Heroic Slave* was first published a few months earlier in *Autographs for Freedom* in 1853, and then serialized in Douglass's newspaper (Levine et al. xii).

23. Douglass's narrative had seven editions in four years and sold more copies than works by Thoreau, Melville, or Hawthorne at the time (Foster 18–23).

after the 1970s when scholars and publishers began to study and reissue some of these narratives.

Similar to the emergence of Black newspapers, Spanish-language newspapers and weeklies in the early nineteenth century circulated in some cities such as Philadelphia. Early exiles from Latin American and Caribbean countries gave rise to a Spanish-language print culture by publishing texts including Manuel Lorenzo de Vidaurre's *Cartas americanas, políticas y morales* (American Letters on Politics and Morals) published in Philadelphia in 1823 (Lazo, *Letters* 7).[24] In subsequent decades, a substantial Spanish-language print culture emerged with the support of Spanish-speaking communities in the Southwest, particularly in Texas and New Mexico, around the time of the Mexican–American War of 1848.[25] Independence movements across Latin American countries in the early nineteenth century and the subsequent political and territorial reconfigurations, such as the Texas independence and the incorporation of the Southwest by the US after the war, influenced the emergence of Spanish-language print culture.[26] Spanish-language newspapers in New Mexico and Colorado show the development of local centers of writing that spanned the nineteenth century and contributed to the development of the Latinx literary tradition (Meléndez and Lomelí 3).[27] Similar to the way early Black newspapers allowed for the serialization of some of the first Black novels, Spanish-language newspapers serialized some of the earliest Latinx fiction such as Eusebio Chacón's "El hijo de la tempestad" (The Son of the Storm), which was serialized in 1892 in *El Boletín Popular* (The Popular Bulletin), a Spanish-language newspaper published in New Mexico that was sustained by a Spanish-speaking local readership (Meléndez and Lomelí 9). The Southwest was not the only region where Spanish-language print culture emerged; economic conditions and migration movements due to social and political upheaval in previously held Spanish territories allowed Spanish-language print culture to emerge in the antebellum period in cities such as

24. According to Lazo, Spanish-language print culture in Philadelphia was "the product of a conjunction between the collective political aspirations of individual actors such as [Vicente] Rocafuerte, discourses of revolution and independence, and the robust commerce of print in Philadelphia" (*Letters* 21).

25. For analyses of Spanish-language print culture, see Meléndez, *So All Is Not Lost*; Coronado, *World Not to Come*; and Lazo and Alemán, *Latino Nineteenth Century*.

26. As Coronado argues, "Though nineteenth-century communities in Texas, New Mexico, and California had very little communication with one another, they were embedded in larger discursive worlds" ("Historicizing" 55).

27. Examples of Spanish-language periodicals in New Mexico and Colorado in the late nineteenth and early twentieth century include *La Bandera Americana* (The American Flag), *La Revista Ilustrada* (The Illustrated Magazine), and *Las Dos Repúblicas* (The Two Republics), among others (Meléndez and Lomelí 2–6).

New York City and New Orleans.[28] Similar to Black newspapers, Spanish-language newspapers allowed authors to participate in the country's social and political life; for instance, Spanish-language newspapers such as *El Independiente* (The Independent), *La Verdad* (Truth), and *La Patria* (Homeland) were sustained by political exiles, new immigrants, and emerging Spanish-speaking communities in New Orleans (Gruesz, *Ambassadors* 112).[29]

The significance of the means of literary production in the form of Spanish-language print culture in Latinx literature is reflected in José Martí's writing in New York City newspapers and weeklies in the latter part of the nineteenth century. While Douglass had been active writing for newspapers since the 1840s and Martí started decades later, Douglass and Martí were writing and publishing in the 1880s in newspapers, voicing their social and political views. Martí had a long publishing career writing for newspapers and as a political activist and exile in various Latin American countries and Spain dating back to the 1870s; when Martí first arrived in New York in 1880, he began to write for the English-language newspaper *New York Sun* and for the weekly magazine *The Hour*. Some of Martí's newspaper writings engage with the ideological struggle for Cuba's independence from Spain, but others cover topics pertaining to racial and ethnic groups in the US, including his often-discussed postulations on Pan-Americanism, a shared identification of people and cultures from Latin American countries (Lomas, "El negro" 302). In the 1880s, at a time when Douglass was still writing and lecturing on the political rights of Blacks, Martí also wrote for Spanish-language newspapers advocating for communities of Latin American backgrounds in the US and writing at times against American racism and imperialism.[30] Just as Douglass's fiction was serialized in his newspapers decades earlier, Martí's only novel, *Amistad funesta* (Fatal Friendship) was serialized in the New York magazine *El Latino-Americano* (The Latin American) in 1885 (Echevarría xxx). In other parallels to Douglass, Martí launched his own newspaper *Patria* (Homeland) in 1892 based in New York City,[31] and both Douglass and Martí offered other Black and Afro-Latinx writers, respectively, editorial opportunities in their

---

28. See Gruesz, *Ambassadors of Culture* and "Transamerican New Orleans"; and Lazo and Alemán, *Latino Nineteenth Century*.

29. For a discussion on the origins and significance of the newspaper *La Patria* (Homeland) in nineteenth-century Spanish-language print culture in New Orleans, see Gruesz, *Ambassadors* 112–20.

30. Laura Lomas explores Martí's writings in relation to his critique of American racism and expansionism in *Translating Empire*.

31. Martí was active in creating, editing, and writing for *Patria*, which served as part of his Cuban revolutionary goals and had an audience of Cuban exiles in the US (Echevarría xxxi).

newspapers.[32] While Martí's writings and political goals extend beyond the US, his newspaper writings and publishing enterprises in New York make him an early precursor, along with other writers such as Sotero Figueroa, in the fight of Spanish-speaking communities in the US to gain access to a means of literary production in the form of a printing press.[33]

Black and Spanish-language print culture allowed for the emergence of an intellectual tradition and publishing infrastructure for their respective Black and Spanish-speaking communities throughout most of the nineteenth century. Just as in the case of Black print culture, a multiplicity of Spanish-language newspapers in different geographical regions illustrates the presence of editors, writers, and local readerships that fought against the literary exclusion from mainstream newspapers, magazines, and publishers.[34] The late nineteenth century marks a transitional period when writers such as Frances E. W. Harper, Charles Chesnutt, and María Amparo Ruiz de Burton fought to be published in mainstream periodicals and publishing houses with the goal of reaching a predominantly white readership. While the publication histories of these authors and their involvement with either local or mainstream newspapers and magazines differ in important respects, what unites their literary struggles are their attempts to break into mainstream publishing and reach a broader white readership that had a set of preconceived ideas and expectations about fiction.[35] The tensions and conflicting views confronting Black and Latinx writers represent a "dilemma" that James Weldon Johnson would famously identify decades later as "the problem of the double audience," or rather a "divided audience," one Black and one white with divergent reading tastes and expectations (Johnson, "Dilemma" 202). These conflicting readers' expectations have influenced the direction of the Black and Latinx literary traditions in significant ways and have remained with writers of color to the present moment.

---

32. Douglass coedited the *North Star* with Martin R. Delany (Foreman 100), and Sotero Figueroa assisted with the editing of Martí's *Patria* (Kanellos, "Sotero" 330).

33. For a detailed discussion of Figueroa's newspaper writings, his work as editor of the *Revista Ilustrada de Nueva York* (Illustrated Magazine of New York), and his collaboration with Martí's *Patria* in the 1890s, see Kanellos, "Sotero" 323–34.

34. Critics have discussed the preponderance of print culture during the Reconstruction Era, or more broadly during the "post-bellum, pre-Harlem" era; see, Gardner, "African American Literary Reconstructions"; and the *MELUS* special issue on "African American Print Cultures," edited by Joycelyn Moody and Howard Rambsy II.

35. Kaestle and Radway point out that mainstream publishers at the turn of the twentieth century catered to the "social and cultural elites" and that "book reading in the United States tends to correlate with education and wealth" (19). For discussions on the influence of white readerships in representative Black writers, see Hutchinson and Young, *Publishing Blackness*; and Young, *Black Writers, White Publishers*.

Instances in Frances E. W. Harper's writing career show the transition of some late nineteenth-century Black writers from writing to local audiences to appealing to a white readership. While active in the antislavery movement in Philadelphia in the 1850s, Harper published her poetry in the Black-owned *Weekly Anglo-African* and abolitionists newspapers such as Garrison's *Liberator* (McGill 64). While a prolific poet, Harper also wrote fiction; her first novel, *Minnie's Sacrifice*, published in 1869, was serialized in the *Christian Recorder,* a Black newspaper (Gardner, "Reconstructions" 436).[36] Garrigues Brothers, a publisher with ties to the temperance movement, published Harper's best-known novel, *Iola Leroy,* in 1892. Harper's extensive social activism and public lecturing put her in contact with social organizations and white publishers that allowed her to reach a white audience; Harper's envisioned readership for *Iola Leory* speaks of the dynamics faced by Black writers as the novel develops a set of competing themes and concerns for two different audiences. Harper attempted to balance themes and messages of resistance for Black audiences while at the same time *Iola Leroy* tries to dismantle for a white readership the prevailing racist stereotypes about Blacks depicted in Reconstruction Era novels written by white authors such as Thomas Nelson Page (Christian 11). It was only after the 1970s that an emerging number of scholars of Black literature began to study the literary and social nuances in Harper's fiction.[37]

Chesnutt's writing career offers a notable case study of a Black writer in the late nineteenth century fighting to enter mainstream publishing and ultimately struggling to manage the competing expectations of Black and white readers. Early in his career, Chesnutt was able to publish a short story, "The Goophered Grapevine," in the influential *Atlantic Monthly* in 1887, due in part to the interest by white editors and readers in plantation stories (Andrews, *Literary* 11); however, similar to Harper, Chesnutt fought to challenge stereotypes about Blacks among white readers with mixed results. While some of Chesnutt's stories were collected in *The Conjure Woman* and published in 1899 by Houghton Mifflin, a Boston publisher and owner of the *Atlantic Monthly,* several other stories with more marked social critiques were not included; equally telling, Houghton Mifflin in its advertisement of *The Conjure Woman* withheld the fact that Chesnutt was a Black author (Andrews, *Conjure* xiii). *The Conjure Woman* received positive reviews that led to the publication of

---

36. Gardner notes that Harper's published works, such as *Minnie's Sacrifice,* are still yet to be studied in light of Harper's extensive publishing history in the Black periodicals during the Reconstruction Era ("Reconstructions" 436).

37. On Harper's social activism and its relation to the major themes in *Iola Leroy,* see Christian 19–32; Carby 62–94; K. Mitchell, *Iola Leroy* 13–50; Foreman 73–96; and Spires, *Practice of Citizenship* 211–26.

Chesnutt's first novel, *The House behind the Cedars,* also published by Houghton Mifflin in 1900. *The House behind the Cedars* is significant in literary history as it was one of the early instances in which a mainstream publisher sought to appeal to Black and white audiences. Chesnutt's second novel, *The Marrow of Tradition* published by Houghton Mifflin the following year, did not sell well despite its command of realist tenets popular at the time; one reason was the novel's open treatment of race relations in the South. Just a few years after Chesnutt's initial success breaking into a white-dominated publishing industry, his career as a writer began to decline as his subsequent novel, *The Colonel's Dream,* was rejected by Walter Hines Page, his editor at Houghton Mifflin.[38] Although *The Colonel's Dream* was later published in 1905 by Doubleday Page & Company, this would become Chesnutt's last novel due to the lack of white readership interest reflected by its poor sales, which brought Chesnutt's collaboration with mainstream editors and publishers to a halt.[39] Similar to the way Douglass and Hamilton promoted the legacy of previous Black writers in the Black press, it was the *Chicago Defender,* the Black newspaper led by Robert S. Abbott, that kept Chesnutt's work in circulation for Black readers by serializing *The House Behind the Cedars* decades after its initial publication (Browner and Price 171).

The publication of Ruiz de Burton's two novels resonates with the struggles experienced by Chesnutt as Ruiz de Burton sought to publish her fiction in mainstream publishing houses and reach a white audience. Ruiz de Burton was part of the *criollo* elite families in California around the Mexican–American War, which partly accounts for her ability to start a writing career since her family had the economic resources that allowed her to write (Lazo, "Trajectories" 211). Ruiz de Burton's first novel, *Who Would Have Thought It?* published by J. B. Lippincott in Philadelphia in 1872, has gained a place in literary history as one of the earlier Latinx novels written in English despite Ruiz de Burton's conflicted allegiances to her ethnic background (Sánchez and Pita 12). Similar to Chesnutt, Ruiz de Burton actively tried to promote her novel among white readers, sending letters asking Lippincott, her publisher, to send copies to book reviewers in mainstream publications; however, reviews in newspapers were scarce and mostly negative (Montes xx). Ruiz de Burton's

---

38. Page wrote to Chesnutt explaining that Houghton Mifflin could not overlook "the fact that the public has failed to respond adequately to your other admirable work . . . , and that we have netted a large aggregate loss on the several volumes of which we had such hopes" (qtd. in Andrews, *Literary* 133).

39. Notably Chesnutt actively sought to promote *The Marrow of Tradition* among Black readers by seeking the endorsement of W. E. B. Du Bois and Booker T. Washington, but his effort to court Black readers failed (Babb 59).

racial and ethnic identification has been the subject of study since she used the ambiguity of her ethnicity in part to appeal to a white readership albeit unsuccessfully.[40] She published *Who Would Have Thought It?* anonymously in part because she feared that white readers would doubt that a Mexican American was "capable of writing such a book" (Montes xxi). Ruiz de Burton's second novel, *The Squatter and the Don*, uses a pseudonym, "C. Loyal," and was originally printed in San Francisco in 1885 by Ruiz de Burton with borrowed money in part to gain a larger profit from sales;[41] otherwise, she feared "all the profits will go to the pocket of the publisher and book-sellers" (qtd. in Sánchez and Pita 13). By including Ruiz de Burton as an early Latinx writer who fought to gain the recognition of mainstream publishers and readers, it is necessary to acknowledge her complicated ethnic identification and cultural allegiances, which in turn reflect the troubled legacy of racial and ethnic hierarchies that marginalized early Black and Latinx authors.

PUBLISHING AND READING OF BLACK AND LATINX TEXTS: EARLY TWENTIETH CENTURY TO 1950

The emerging epicenter of the writing and publishing of Black and Latinx texts in the early decades of the twentieth century, particularly in the 1920s and 1930s, was New York City. The influence of New York City as a hub for Black writing at the time was related to the city's position as one of the two most important centers of the mainstream publishing industry.[42] While New York City was the major center of Black and Spanish-language writing, there were other significant hubs of creativity and literary production sustained by a robust presence of Black residents in Chicago, Pittsburgh, and in Spanish-speaking communities in San Antonio, Corpus Christie, and New Orleans.[43] New York City in the early twentieth century reflects the continued influence of Black and Spanish-language newspapers, weeklies, and magazines that sup-

---

40. Lazo points out that Ruiz de Burton, as a member of a California family of European descent, "engages [in her fiction] with racial hierarchies, privileging white skin and portraying indigenous and black characters as inferior" ("Trajectories" 211).

41. *The Squatter and the Don* was later copyrighted by Samuel Carson & Co. in San Francisco in 1885 (Sánchez and Pita 13).

42. Hutchinson describes the Harlem Renaissance as depending "upon unique processes of production, distribution, and reception" of texts that centered around the prominence of mainstream white magazines such as *The Nation* and the *New Republic* (*Harlem* 126–27).

43. For discussions of creative hubs in the early twentieth century beyond New York City, see Hine and McCluskey, *Black Chicago Renaissance*; Whitaker, *Smoketown*; John González, *Border Renaissance*; and Gruesz, "Transamerican New Orleans."

ported Black and Latinx writers, who in turn were sustained by growing local communities composed of migrating Blacks from the South and Spanish-speaking immigrants from Latin America and the Caribbean.[44] New York City boasts arguably the single most important literary movement by writers of color of any period in the Harlem Renaissance due in part to the publishing dynamics in the city and the cultural and ideological exchanges among individuals from different racial and ethnic backgrounds.[45] While much has been written regarding some of the brightest stars of the movement, including Claude McKay, Langston Hughes, Nella Larsen, Zora Neale Hurston, and Jean Toomer, my comparative analysis focuses on instances in the publication histories of James Weldon Johnson and Jesús Colón, the role of Black and Spanish-language newspapers, magazines, and the increasing number of readers of color in the early decades of the twentieth century.

While a number of authors of the Harlem Renaissance were able to publish some of their work in mainstream publishing houses, these writers, almost without exception, began their careers writing in Black newspapers and magazines; some of the most influential publications supported by Black organizations include W. E. B. Du Bois and Jessie Fauset's *The Crisis,* Charles Johnson's *Opportunity,* and A. Philip Randolph and Chandler Owen's *The Messenger. The Crisis* was instrumental in publishing the work of emerging Black writers as part of a social and cultural project to raise the profile of Blacks that was sustained by the National Association for the Advancement of Colored People (NAACP).[46] Similarly influential were the efforts of Charles Johnson in gathering and providing an outlet for publication to most Harlem Renaissance authors.[47] Writers such as Hughes and Larsen published their writing in Black publications such as *The Crisis* and *The Brownies' Book,* respectively, prior to being supported by fellow white writers or published by Alfred A.

---

44. David Levering Lewis explains that the large increase of Blacks in Harlem started at the turn of the twentieth century and increased with the first great migration during World War I (25–45). Acosta-Belén and Korrol place the number of Latinx people in New York during the 1920s and 1930s at over 100,000 (14).

45. As Hutchinson notes, the publishing industry in the 1920s for the first time "expanded and diversified, nourished by a rapidly growing market, the recent, massive waves of immigration, and a stimulating clash of ideologies" (*Harlem* 8).

46. For example, Countee Cullen's early poetry first appeared in *The Crisis* and *Opportunity* before it was published by national magazines such as *The Bookman, Harper's,* and *The American Mercury* (Lewis 75). Hutchinson, however, argues that highbrow white magazines, along with Black publications, influenced the trajectory of the Harlem Renaissance (*Harlem* 125–29).

47. For a discussion of Charles Johnson's support of Black writers before some of them were able to sign book contracts with mainstream publishers, see Lewis 89–93; and Hutchinson, *Harlem Renaissance* 166–69, 173–79.

Knopf.[48] In these cases, mainstream publishing did not equate to white publishers; Jewish immigration to New York City gave rise to an emerging type of publishing houses that were more willing to experiment and bet on novelty and were themselves on the periphery from more established Boston and New York publishers.[49] While the goals of emerging publishing houses were both economic and literary, the publication of first marketed Black novels by Jewish publishers in the early 1920s and 1930s represents an early instance of racial and ethnic solidarity.[50] Just a few years into the 1930s, due in part to the major economic upheaval brought by the Great Depression, interest in Black writers by emerging and mainstream publishers and white readers faded.[51] While the literary and cultural influence of the Harlem Renaissance increased as the decades progressed, most of its writers were unable to escape the fate of Chesnutt's writing career decades earlier as they failed to gain a readership that could sustain their careers, as attested by the writing careers of Fauset, Larsen, and Hurston, just to name a few.[52]

Instances in James Weldon Johnson's publication history are representative of the fight against literary exclusion in the early decades of the twentieth century. The first edition of Johnson's first novel, *The Autobiography of an Ex-Colored Man*, was published in 1912 anonymously by a small Boston publisher, Sherman, French, and Company; the novel, however, was not advertised and did not sell well.[53] Similar to Chesnutt's first book publication, a telling aspect of the publication of *The Autobiography of an Ex-Colored Man* is that Johnson did not meet with his publisher in person before the novel was published;

---

48. For instance, Alfred A. Knopf published Hughes's *The Weary Blues* in 1925 and Larsen's *Quicksand* in 1928, both with the support of Carl Van Vechten (Lewis 85; and Hutchinson, *Harlem* 169). For a discussion on Larsen's publication in *The Brownies' Book*, see Hutchinson, *In Search of Nella Larsen* 128–29.

49. Young describes both Jewish publishers and Harlem Renaissance authors as groups "marginalized by the mainstream Protestant New York firms" (*Black Writers* 8).

50. Hutchinson counters the critique of the role of publishers in the Harlem Renaissance since some white writers and publishers such as Van Vechten and Alfred A. Knopf proved to be some of the "chief white allies" of Black writers (*Harlem* 134). James Weldon Johnson, for instance, writes fondly of Van Vechten and "his many personal efforts [on] behalf of individual Negro writers and artists" (*Along This Way* 382).

51. For the impact of the Great Depression years on Harlem Renaissance authors and mainstream publishing houses, see Lewis 264–68.

52. Years later, Hurston took a critical view of white publishers during the Harlem Renaissance when she wrote that "publishing houses . . . are in business to make money. They will sponsor anything they believe will sell"; however, they frowned upon the social and emotional complexity of Black characters since "they are not in the business to educate, but to make money. Sympathetic as they might be, they cannot afford to be crusaders" (118).

53. Andrews, Introduction to *Autobiography of an Ex-Colored Man* xii.

thus, obscuring his identification as a Black writer (Goldsby xlvi). In the 1920s, Johnson became involved in political activism as the leader of the NAACP, and along with Du Bois, Fauset, and Alain Locke, worked in promoting Black writing and showcasing the work of Black authors and their contributions to American arts and culture.[54] Johnson, for example, edited *The Book of American Negro Poetry,* published by Harcourt Brace in 1922, an anthology of Black writers that echoes early efforts by Douglass and Hamilton to publicize the work of past Black poets in their newspapers. In his preface to his anthology, Johnson makes the explicit argument that white readers have been unaware of Black writers not because of the lack of Black writers but rather white editors have not published and disseminated their works.[55] When Harcourt Brace and Boni & Liveright began to publish Black writers at the height of the Harlem Renaissance, Alfred A. Knopf also reissued *Autobiography of an Ex-Colored Man* in 1927, this time with favorable reviews (Andrews, *Autobiography* xiv).[56] The reissuing of Johnson's novel also shows the literary influence of publishers such as Alfred A. Knopf whom by personal inclination and publishing decision-making was able to associate Johnson's writing with other modernist texts (Goldsby xlvi). Similarly, the practice of reissuing neglected works by Black writers is telling of publishers' influence and motives as this would be replicated on a larger scale in the late 1960s and 1970s as interest for Black texts resurged.[57] Johnson, just as Chesnutt before him, pondered about the challenges of reconciling in his writing the distinct interests and concerns of white and Black readers.[58] This dilemma was resolved in part when in 1930 Johnson gained a position as literature professor at Fisk University in Nashville, Tennessee; this institutional support allowed him to remain one of the few Harlem Renaissance writers who continued to publish his work after the 1930s.

Writers and intellectuals such as Bernardo Vega and Jesús Colón writing in Spanish-language newspapers in New York City illustrate how the Latinx

---

54. See Hutchinson, *Harlem Renaissance* 142–49; and Lewis 143, 147–48.

55. Johnson remarks, "The public, generally speaking, does not know that there are American Negro poets—to supply this lack of information is, alone, a work worthy of somebody's efforts" (*Negro Poetry* vii).

56. Goldsby shows how book deals between Black writers and white publishers were made through her discussion of the letter exchanges between Johnson and Blanche W. Knopf (xlviii). These exchanges also reflect the asymmetrical power dynamics between white publishers and Black writers as editors had the ability to launch the careers of Black writers with the stroke of a pen, but most times decided against it.

57. Autumn Womack has studied the history of Arno Press, an independent publisher acquired in part by the *New York Times,* and the publishing house's role in launching in 1968 *The American Negro: His History and Literature,* a series of reprints of Black texts in response to the renewed interest in Black literature in the late 1960s.

58. Andrews discusses the dilemma that Johnson faced trying to please different Black and white audiences (*Autobiography* xvi).

literary tradition in the early decades of the twentieth century continued to be sustained by newspapers and weeklies and by an increasing Spanish-speaking readership not only on the East Coast but also in the Southwest.[59] Bernardo Vega founded the weekly newspaper *El Gráfico* (The Graphic) in 1927, which was sustained by the increasing migration of people from Puerto Rico and Cuba to New York City (Acosta-Belén and Korrol 21). Similar to the role of Black newspapers and magazines, Spanish-language print culture served as a space to promote social and cultural causes, including the dissemination of Latinx writings through local publishing venues.[60] Colón arrived in New York City in 1918 and began to write in Spanish-language newspapers such as *Justicia* (Justice) and *Unión Obrera* (Workers' Solidarity). In the 1920s and 1930s, Colón wrote for Vega's *El Gráfico* and other Spanish-language newspapers published in New York City.[61] Although Colón started his newspaper career in the 1920s, Colón's book of essays or "sketches,"[62] *A Puerto Rican in New York and Other Sketches* was published until 1961 by Masses and Mainstream, a small publisher with ties to *New Masses* since Colón was a supporter of the Communist Party in New York City, particularly during the decade between the Great Depression and World War II (Flores, Foreword xii). Colón's attraction to communism echoes a similar ideological alliance between communists and Black writers, including Hughes and Richard Wright, that was significant for creating publishing opportunities for them.[63] Colón's choice of writing in English in *A Puerto Rican in New York* reflects his attempt to reach

---

59. The early 1930s also represents the emergence of Mexican American civil rights organizations in the Southwest—similar in principles and goals as the NAACP—in the form of the League of United Latin American Citizens (LULAC), which had its own publication, *LULAC News,* showcasing the work of Mexican American writers. For a detailed analysis of *LULAC News* and some of its writers, see González, *Border Renaissance* 95–126.

60. In his memoir, Vega directly connects his desire to acquire a newspaper in New York City and use it as a venue to highlight and "addres[s] problems of housing, crime, inadequate services, civil rights, culture, and the arts" serving not only Puerto Ricans but "all Hispanic people" (149). For an analysis of Vega's writings and his attempt to document the experiences of the Puerto Rican community in New York City in the early decades of the twentieth century, see Luis 99–127.

61. Colón's writings in newspapers extended for five decades, including contributions to *Pueblos Hispanos* (Hispanic People), *Liberación* (Liberation), and the *Daily Worker,* among others (Acosta-Belén and Korrol 20–21).

62. Writing in the 1950s for the newspaper the *Daily Worker,* Colón uses the form of "sketches" (or *crónica* or chronicle), a literary genre present in Spanish-language newspapers since the time of José Martí in the late nineteenth century (Holton 10–11).

63. Likewise, the publication histories of Colón and Hughes in local newspapers share parallels. Colón wrote newspaper columns for the *Daily Worker* and Hughes for the *Chicago Defender* during the 1950s; both wrote about discrimination and racial segregation in their respective communities in simple or colloquial language intended for an audience composed of working-class Black and Latinx readers, respectively.

an audience beyond his Puerto Rican community.[64] Although decades apart, Colón's objective in *A Puerto Rican in New York* resembles that of Johnson's anthology of Black poets, as Colón attempts to introduce white readers to the cultural vitality of Puerto Ricans and to serve as a counternarrative to the stigmatization of his community in mainstream newspapers.[65] The time between the writing of Colón's sketches and their publication in a book format decades later reflects the continuing challenges for Latinx writers to publish well into the first half of the twentieth century.

While some authors of the 1940s and 1950s, such as Richard Wright, Margaret Walker, and José Antonio Villarreal, struggled to sustain a mainstream readership after the publication of their early work, other writers such as Mario Suárez were unable to interest mainstream publishers despite their efforts. Wright became one of the most successful Black writers when *Native Son* was published in 1940 by Harper and Brothers and was selected as the Book-of-the-Month Club reading the same year;[66] he became one of the few Black writers to enter the national literary conversation since Frederick Douglass. Wright, along with an increasing number of Black writers, began to benefit from the sustained support of social, cultural, and literary organizations;[67] however, despite his literary output in subsequent years, white readers increasingly stopped reading his work, particularly after his exile in France. In a similar publishing dynamic, Margaret Walker's poetry collection, *For My People,* was published by Yale University Press in 1942, but despite this coveted recognition, she did not publish another book for twenty-four years until the publication of her novel, *Jubilee,* by Houghton Mifflin in 1966 (Graham, "Introduction" ix). During these in-between decades, Walker taught at Jackson State University and wrote without the challenges of appealing to a

---

64. Flores discusses the singularity of Colón's use of English among other Puerto Rican writers in New York City at the time (Foreword xv–xvi).

65. In his preface to *A Puerto Rican in New York,* Colón sheds light on the lives of Puerto Ricans since the writings about them in mainstream newspapers, such as the *New York Times,* describe them as a "problem" or as "The Puerto Rican Problem" (9). According to Colón, Puerto Ricans in New York "remain unsung, unheralded and practically unknown to their fellow New Yorkers, except through the filters of an assiduously cultivated hostility, distrust, and ignorance" (*Puerto Rican* 10).

66. Wright's publication with Harper and Brothers and the novel's promotion represent a key moment in the publication history of Black authors. Founded in 1817, Harper and Brothers was one of the earliest publishing houses in the US, and the Book-of-the-Month Club, created by Harry Sherman in 1926, was one of the most influential forces in mainstream publishing at the time (Shatzkin and Riger 49–50). For an incisive discussion on the influence of white editors on Wright's *Native Son* and *Black Boy,* see Young, "Quite as Human as It Is Negro."

67. Wright, for example, benefited from sponsorships by government and nonprofit organizations such as the American Communist Party, the Federal Writers' Project, and the Julius Rosenwald Fund, among others (Jackson, *Indignant* 12).

white readership as in the case of Wright.[68] As Black novelists struggled to be published and read in sustaining numbers, Latinx writers encountered similar publishing dynamics. José Antonio Villarreal's *Pocho,* published by Doubleday in 1959, was one of the earliest Mexican American novels to be published by a major publishing house, but the novel did not sell well, was negatively reviewed, and soon went out of print (Cutler, *Assimilation* 51). Villarreal continued to write and publish but none of his subsequent novels gained a mainstream readership. The case of Suárez, who was writing at the same time as Villarreal and attempted to publish his fiction with New York publishers, appears more vexing since Suárez was unable to find a publisher for his fiction, which led to his transition from fiction writing to investigative journalism for the newspaper *Prensa Mexicana* (Mexican Press) based in Tucson, Arizona (Lomelí 3).

Ann Petry's publication history reflects the opportunities and challenges still faced by writers in the 1940s and 1950s who began writing in Black publications and were subsequently able to break into mainstream publishing but were unable to maintain sustained interest by white readers. Petry's career began by writing for Harlem newspapers, including the *Amsterdam News* and the *People's Voice* (Christian 63). She then published fiction in Black magazines and benefited from the support of mainstream publishers;[69] Petry's short fiction brought her notoriety, and she received a Houghton Mifflin Literary Fellowship that allowed her to complete her first novel, *The Street,* published in 1946 by the same publisher (Holladay 11–12). *The Street* was a commercial success, and Petry became the first Black woman writer "to sell over one million copies" of her novel since it was marketed to both Black and white audiences (Babb 99).[70] However, just as in the case of Wright, Petry's breakthrough novel represented the height of her career as a novelist, as her two subsequent novels, *Country Place* and *The Narrows,* both published also by Houghton Mifflin in 1947 and 1953, respectively, received considerably less attention from white readers. Petry's subject matter for her two novels after *The Street* are significant in relation to Petry's targeted readership—and a number of other now canonical Black writers—as she began to write novels with white protagonists and deemphasized social conditions created by racism as presented in

68. In an interview, Walker discusses the role that academia and teaching had on her writing career and her perception of herself as a writer (Rowell 24).

69. Petry's emergence as a writer came in 1943 when *Crisis* published her story "On Saturday the Siren Sounds at Noon," which prompted a Houghton Mifflin editor to inquire about her fiction (Holladay 10).

70. As Holladay notes, Petry "became a representative figure, a black woman whose achievement was recognized by a white publishing company and white readers" (14).

her early work;[71] these publishing dynamics further accentuate the major role of white editors and publishers even in the aesthetic work of now-canonical Black writers. Petry's writings are representative of the influence of a white-dominated publishing industry of the 1940s and 1950s as Petry, and other Black writers, including Claude McKay and Wright, left significant unpublished works that until recently had been stacked at archival collections at major research universities.[72]

Latinx authors in the 1940s and 1950s such as Mexican American playwright and novelist Josefina Niggli attempted to gain a mainstream readership by thematizing in her novels her experiences growing up in Mexico.[73] Niggli worked in radio and theater in the 1930s and subsequently would complete a master's degree in theater in 1937 at the University of North Carolina (UNC)–Chapel Hill. Similar to Petry and other Black writers at the time, Niggli's writing was supported by mainstream cultural organizations; Niggli's plays, produced and staged at the Carolina Playmakers' program at UNC, engaged with Mexican history, Aztec culture, and folklore. In subsequent years, she began to write fiction. Her first novel, *Mexican Village*, published by University of North Carolina Press in 1945 was well received by mainstream reviewers; her second novel, *Step Down, Elder Brother*, published by Rinehart & Company in 1947, became a Book-of-the-Month Club selection (Orchard and Padilla 25–27). In contrast to Petry, who attempted to gain a broader readership by deemphasizing race after *The Street*, Niggli engages in *Mexican Village* with her Mexican cultural background with mixed results.[74] Similar to the recognition of Wright's *Native Son* as a Book-of-the-Month Club selection, Niggli's novels represent a significant historical antecedent in Latinx writers'

71. Paula Rabinowitz discusses in detail Petry's attempt in *Country Place* to move away from the emphasis on racism by substituting Black characters with white characters in an attempt to appeal to a broader white audience. Other writers at the time such as Wright, Baldwin, Willard Motley, and Hurston also wrote novels that include white protagonists (56–59).

72. Jean-Christophe Cloutier in *Shadow Archives* documents the large number of unpublished Black novels and writings by some of the most representative Black authors that are only accessible through research university archives (20–21).

73. Niggli's position in the Latinx literary tradition has been debated by scholars due to her European background and privileged-class status; however, the consensus among scholars is that Niggli forms part of the Latinx literary tradition. Following María Herrera-Sobek's lead, for example, William Orchard and Yolanda Padilla describe Niggli as a "border writer" "who lies at the interstices of many figurative borders—between American and Mexican, between Mexican and Chican[a]" (4–5).

74. Stavans interprets Niggli's emphasis on Mexican culture as a way to take advantage of white readers' interest in novelty; Stavans argues that the initial interest in Niggli's novels by mainstream critics and readers was due to the popularity of novels that depicted Mexico from the perspective of the outsider similar to Malcolm Lowry's *Under the Volcano* (Foreword xiv).

struggles to gain a mainstream readership. In contrast to earlier Latinx works of fiction such as Chacón's "El hijo de la tempestad" (The Son of the Storm) that were written in Spanish, Niggli's novels were written in English and intended for mainstream audiences rather than a regional readership. Despite her recognition as a novelist, Niggli was not able to maintain her career as a writer; instead, similar to James Weldon Johnson, Margaret Walker, and a few others before her, Niggli found a permanent academic position at Western Carolina University that allowed her to continue her writing career (Orchard and Padilla 28).[75]

While some Black and Latinx authors found in academia a respite from an exclusionary publishing market, several others, such as Toomer, Larsen, and Hurston, fell into literary hard times after their initial publishing success; it wasn't until the 1960s and 1970s that their literary achievements and significance began to be recovered by scholars and disseminated among college readers. A few of them, including Hughes, Gwendolyn Brooks, Ralph Ellison, and James Baldwin, successfully transitioned from their pre-1960s writing careers to the post-1960s literary landscape. Some of the novels studied today from the Latinx canon, such as *Mexican Village* and *Pocho*, were reissued, or in the case of Américo Paredes's *George Washington Gomez* and Jovita González and Margaret Eimer's *Caballero*—novels that were written in the 1930s—were not published until the 1990s.[76] A characteristic of pre-1960s Black and Latinx authors was their marginalized position in mainstream publishing and literary and cultural organizations, a position that continued over decades and changed only after the increase of civil rights and student-led protests for changes in academia across the nation.

THE EMERGENCE OF THE ACADEMIC INFRASTRUCTURE FOR BLACK AND LATINX TEXTS: 1960s AND 1970s

The structural changes at colleges and universities in the late 1960s and early 1970s that began with student protests across the nation allowed for the first time an increase in Black and Latinx literature courses, scholars of color, and monographs that studied the emergence and development of each literary tra-

---

75. Other writers of the 1940s and 1950s who taught at the college level include Sterling Brown, Ralph Ellison, and Américo Paredes, among others.

76. In his analysis of González and Eimer's *Caballero*, John M. González discusses how their novel was "rejected by publishers despite numerous efforts" (183).

dition.[77] These transformative changes in the study of Black and Latinx literature from previous efforts made by writers, publishers, and scholars of color
contributed to the development and institutionalization of both literary traditions, which in turn allowed emerging writers to gain publishing opportunities and have a sustaining readership.[78] While the social protest movements
of the 1960s and 1970s marked a turning point, as they were instrumental for
Black and Latinx authors to be published and gain a wider multiethnic readership, it is also necessary to connect these gains to the historical fight by Black
and Latinx writers to gain access to the means of literary production and their
search to gain a sustained readership dating back to the beginning of both
literary traditions. The emergence of academic infrastructure of the 1960s and
1970s stands as the most important development in the study of Black and
Latinx literatures as it represented the first time that some authors were able
to gain—in meaningful numbers—access to publishers, readers, and scholarly
recognition that they had been denied in previous decades.

The changes in the academic infrastructure allowed an increasing number
of scholars of Black and Latinx literature to study and recover texts from their
respective literary traditions in a systematic manner since previous efforts had
lacked wider institutional support. While there have been efforts to study,
promote, and anthologize the work of Black writers in the early decades
of the twentieth century by scholars, including Du Bois, Alain Locke, and
James Weldon Johnson, these projects were supported primarily by social
and cultural organizations, Black periodicals, and a few mainstream publishers. Before the 1960s, Black scholars entered academia primarily teaching at
Historically Black Colleges and Universities (HBCUs) as they contributed to
the creation of scholarship that shaped the field of Black literature; however,
these scholars represented the exception within the field of American literary
studies.[79] Some of these scholars included Charles Eaton Burch, J. Saunders
Redding, Sterling Brown, Arthur P. Davis, Ulysses G. Lee, Dorothy B. Porter,
Darwin T. Turner, and Hugh Gloster, among others. Before the 1960s, there

---

77. For discussions on the importance of the university in the institutionalization of Black
and Latinx literatures during the 1960s and 1970s, see Gates, *Loose Canons*; Griffin, "Thirty
Years"; Smethurst, *Black Arts Movement*; Bona and Maini, *Multiethnic Literature and Canon
Debates*; Martín-Rodríguez, *Life in Search of Readers*; Acuña, *Making of Chicano/a Studies*;
Rojas, *From Black Power to Black Studies*; and Cutler, *Ends of Assimilation*.

78. For a competing view and critique of the way universities and colleges have attempted
to co-opt race, ethnic, and gender studies, see Ferguson, *Reorder of Things*.

79. David Shumway describes the pre-1960s field of American literary studies not only
as lacking inclusion of Black and other authors of color, but as openly exclusionary and elitist; writing about the emergence of American literature as a discipline in the first half of the
twentieth century, Shumway describes American literary studies as a field where "white male
hegemony" was the norm (9).

was a similar group of active scholars of Latinx literature, folklore, and culture that included Aurelio M. Espinosa, Arthur L. Campa, Jovita González,
George I. Sánchez, Américo Paredes, and Luis Leal who primarily taught at
PWIs in the Southwest and made contributions to the study and preservation of Mexican American narratives and Spanish-language texts.[80] Increasing
academic opportunities for scholars of Black and Latinx literature after the
1960s allowed for the sustained and systematic study of both literary traditions; scholars considered pioneers in their fields who emerged around the
1970s include Larry Neal, Sarah Webster Fabio, George E. Kent, Robert Stepto,
Frances Smith Foster, Barbara Christian, Arnold Rampersad, Houston Baker,
Nicolás Kanellos, Jorge Huerta, Rolando Hinojosa, Juan Bruce-Novoa, and
Francisco Lomelí, among others. It is important to highlight not only writers
but also scholars who were responsible in large part for the recovery, study,
and reading of several texts that today form an integral part of either the Black
or the Latinx literary tradition.

The emergence of the university infrastructure that started in the late
1960s not only allowed for a substantial increase in the number of scholars
but also gave a significant number of Black and Latinx authors a way to participate in the process of anthologizing and recovering Black and Latinx texts.
Amiri Baraka, Luis Valdez, Alice Walker, Toni Cade Bambara, Toni Morrison,
and others attended colleges and universities in the 1950s and 1960s when the
Western and American literary canons were represented by predominantly
white and male authors.[81] Emerging Black and Latinx writers experienced
firsthand the need to incorporate authors who had been previously marginalized from academia and the American literary tradition. Alice Walker, for
instance, read Ernest Hemingway and William Faulkner in college but sought
to raise the profile of former Black writers such as Jean Toomer by writing
articles and opinion pieces and famously contributing to the recovery of the
writings of Zora Neale Hurston.[82] Black and Latinx writers actively worked to
compile anthologies in part to meet the need for primary texts at university
courses (Bona and Maini 3); some of these anthologies include Baraka and
Larry Neal's *Black Fire: An Anthology of Afro-American Writing*, Arthur Davis's
Cavalcade: Negro American Writing from 1790 to the Present, Valdez and Stan
Steiner's *Aztlán: An Anthology of Mexican American Literature*, and Bambara's
edited collection of contemporary Black women writers, *The Black Woman:*

---

80. For a critique of Aurelio M. Espinosa's scholarship and his efforts to link Spanish culture
to the culture of New Mexico while diminishing the influence of Mexico, see Vélez-Ibáñez et al.

81. For a thorough analysis regarding the whiteness of the field of American Literature in
the academy before the 1960s, see Shumway, *Creating American Civilization*.

82. Walker, *In Search of Our Mothers' Gardens* 93–116, 132–33.

An Anthology, all published in the late 1960s and early 1970s. Other authors such as Morrison began to influence editorial decisions at mainstream publishing houses for the first time; while working as an editor at Random House, Morrison assisted in publishing the work of Gayl Jones, Henry Dumas, and Bambara (Babb 187). The need for primary texts created by Black and Mexican American literature courses at college campuses allowed authors previously on the margins to participate in the process of literary production and canon formation.

Along with the emergence of the academic infrastructure, smaller presses began to publish experienced and emerging authors of color in the 1960s and 1970s, which offered writers new degrees of creative liberty and the opportunity to sustain their writing careers. An element of the Black Arts Movement of the 1960s and 1970s was its deliberate attempt to reject the cultural and literary hegemony of mainstream publishers and find alternatives to create, publish, and focus on a Black readership that had been neglected by white publishers (Smethurst 179–80). This period saw the emergence of Black presses such as Broadside Press created by poet Dudley Randall in Detroit and Third World Press in Chicago founded by Haki Madhubuti, Carolyn Rodgers, and Johari Amini (Babb 126). These Black publishers offered new outlets for seasoned and emerging writers; some of the works published by Broadside Press during the 1960s included Margaret Walker's *The Ballad of the Free*, Baraka's *A Poem for Black Hearts*, and Gwendolyn Brooks's *The Wall* and *In the Mecca* (Young, *Black Writers* 98). These small publishers also served as an alternative for writers who worked with mainstream publishers; Brooks stopped working with Harper and Brothers, which had published her books up to 1963, and subsequently switched to Broadside Press and Third World Press.[83] A number of Black publishers that emerged at this time also gave Black writers for the first time ideological and artistic liberties to depict social and racial relations, thus overcoming the asymmetrical Black author–white publisher dynamics that had haunted pre-1960s authors such as Chesnutt, James Weldon Johnson, Petry, and Wright, among several others.[84]

The emerging academic infrastructure, which began in the 1960s contributed to the creation of small printing houses Quinto Sol, Bilingual Press, Third Woman Press, and Arte Público that as a group allowed publishing opportu-

---

83. For a discussion of the publication history of Gwendolyn Brooks with Third World Press, see Young, *Black Writers* 94–118.

84. Subsequent decades reflect the development of the relation between the university infrastructure and the publication of previously neglected Black texts; a notable example is *The Schomburg Library of Nineteenth-Century Black Women Writers*, a thirty-volume collection of works written by Black women from the start of the Black literary tradition to the 1920s edited by Henry L. Gates and published by Oxford University Press in 1988.

nities for Latinx writers who had previously been unable to publish in mainstream printing houses. Quinto Sol, an independent publishing press created by Octavio Romano-V., Nick C. Vaca, and Herminio Ríos from University of California–Berkeley, played a key role in the publication of Latinx writers such as Tomás Rivera, Rudolfo Anaya, and Rolando Hinojosa.[85] Romano sought to increase publication venues for Mexican American authors, and similar to Luis Valdez, Romano wanted to highlight and promote the work of Mexican American writers, particularly among university students. Quinto Sol's publication of Anaya's *Bless Me, Ultima* in 1972 is representative of the new publishing dynamics related to the publication and reading of Mexican American texts made possible by the university infrastructure. Before the 1960s, Anaya tried to publish *Bless Me, Ultima* in New York City and Boston without success, and it was almost by accident that he learned about Quinto Sol while reading a journal, *El Grito* (The Shout), one of the few Mexican American academic publications also affiliated with Quinto Sol (Fernández Olmos 7–8).[86] Anaya's novel won the Quinto Sol Award, a literary recognition created by Romano to encourage the dissemination of Mexican American fiction. Romano's vision followed the strategies of mainstream publishers who had used literary awards as recognitions but also as a means to increase interest among readers. Although short-lived, the Quinto Sol Award contributed to the canonization of its other two recipients, Rivera's *... y no se lo tragó la tierra* (And the Earth Did Not Devour Him, 1971) and Hinojosa's *Estampas del Valle* (The Valley, 1973). Bilingual Press, an independent publishing effort, started at the City College of New York in 1973 under the direction of Gary Francisco Keller;[87] similarly, the influential Third Woman Press was created by Norma Alarcón in 1979; Arte Público Press, a publishing house founded by Nicolás Kanellos in 1979 and supported by the University of Houston, has significantly contributed to the dissemination of Latinx texts.[88] Quinto Sol, Bilingual Press, Third Woman Press, and Arte Público exemplify the close

---

85. For extended analyses on the influence of Quinto Sol, see Martín-Rodríguez, *Life in Search of Readers*; Dennis López, "Good-Bye Revolution—Hello Cultural Mystique"; and Cutler, *Ends of Assimilation*.

86. Other notable examples are *Aztlán: A Journal of Chicano Studies*, started by Juan Gómez-Quiñones, Roberto Sifuentes, Jaime Sena, and Alfredo Cuéller at the University of California, Los Angeles, in 1970 (Villaseñor Black 88); and *Revista Chicano-Riqueña* (Chicano-Puerto Rican Review), a magazine focusing on Latinx literature started by Nicolás Kanellos and Luis Dávila in 1973.

87. Bilingual Review Press, now hosted at Arizona State University, in its early years published the work of now canonical Latinx writers such as Alurista, Estela Portillo-Trambley, and Ana Castillo (Brito 84).

88. Arte Público has continued to play a critical role in subsequent decades by recovering and reissuing neglected Latinx texts through the Recovering the US Hispanic Literary Heritage Project, an initiative led by Kanellos and other Latinx literary scholars.

connections in the university infrastructure that support writers, scholars, and a readership composed primarily of college students.

The university infrastructure similarly created an incentive for mainstream publishers to sign and reissue works by writers of color as a direct response to a demand for texts among college students, a key readership demographic absent in previous decades.[89] Mainstream publishing houses such as Alfred A. Knopf and Harcourt Brace began to reissue works of their previously published writers such as Larsen, Weldon Johnson, and McKay for a new generation of readers; for instance, Jean Toomer's *Cane*, first published in 1923, was reissued in 1975 by Boni & Liveright. Similarly, Villarreal's *Pocho*, originally published by Doubleday in 1959, was reissued by Anchor in 1970, which had the Doubleday copyrights.[90] Publishers also responded to changes in the university infrastructure by publishing an increasing number of Black and Latinx writers in the 1970s; representative examples include Morrison's *The Bluest Eye* (Holt McDougal, 1970) and *Song of Solomon* (Knopf, 1977), the latter novel won the National Book Critics Circle Award, perhaps the most significant literary recognition given to a Black author since Ellison's *Invisible Man* won the National Book Award in 1953, Walker's *The Third Life of Grange Copeland* (Harcourt, 1970), Ernest Gaines's *Autobiography of Miss Jane Pittman* (Dial, 1971), Ishmael Reed's *Mumbo Jumbo* (Doubleday, 1972), Oscar "Zeta" Acosta's *Autobiography of a Brown Buffalo* (Random House, 1972), Victor Hernández Cruz's *Mainland* (Random House, 1973), Charles Johnson's *Faith and the Good Thing* (Viking, 1974), Gayl Jones's *Corregidora* (Random House, 1975), and Nicholasa Mohr's *El Bronx Remembered* (Harper and Row, 1975). This renewed interest in Black and Latinx texts became a permanent aspect of the publishing and literary landscape for the very first time since the beginning of both literary traditions.

Small printing presses and mainstream publishing houses were able to publish Black and Latinx authors in larger numbers as a response to newly developed programs and curriculum changes at college campuses brought in part by the increasing enrollment of students of color after the 1950s, which allowed authors of color for the first time to gain a sustaining readership. The Black and Latinx literary traditions show that authors, particularly at the turn of the twentieth century, benefited from demographic changes such as

---

89. Independent publishers such as Arno Press also began to reissue the work of Black and Mexican American authors to meet the interest in these texts starting in the late 1960s; see Womack, "Reprinting the Past"; and Meléndez, "Growing Up" 137–38.

90. Cutler notes the direct link between the second publication of *Pocho* in relation to the renewed interest in Mexican American authors created by the Chicanx Movement (*Assimilation* 50–51).

the migration of Blacks toward the North, which increased after World War I, and the growth of Latinx populations in larger cities from the 1920s to the 1950s; these demographic changes allowed for the emergence of newspapers and magazines written for an either Black or Latinx readership. The increase of students of color after the 1950s contributed to the resurging militancy and social protest movements of the late 1960s and early 1970s that forced changes in academia.[91] These social and institutional changes resulted in the implicit partnership between the academic infrastructure and the publishing industry as publishers met the increasing demand for Black and Latinx texts. The teaching of authors of color contributed to the recognition of writers as their works were assigned and read in college classrooms, and scholars of Black and Latinx literature began to critically study them. Toni Morrison exemplifies this point when she discusses in an interview her eventual success as a novelist after she left her job as an editor to focus on her fiction, noting that "it was the academic community that gave *The Bluest Eye* its life. . . . People assigned it in class. Students bought the paperback" (Als, "Ghosts"). Morrison's statement captures the post-1960s publishing dynamics among authors, universities, publishers, and readers that contributed to the long-overdue literary recognition of authors of color.

The institutionalization of Black and Latinx literature that emerged in academia as a result of the social activism and increasing militancy of the 1960s and 1970s stands as a breakthrough in the struggles against literary exclusion by the Black and Latinx writers and scholars that came before them. Nonetheless, the fight was not over; it continued from the 1970s through subsequent decades into the twentieth century. The following chapters present comparative case studies that show how Black and Latinx authors, despite their increased literary recognition, have continued to shed light on the historical, cultural, and artistic struggles of previous writers and their respective groups.

---

91. Griffin discusses changes in academia that allowed for the expansion of Black literary production as the result of social protest movements (165). Acuña explains the relation between the growth of the Mexican American population, particularly in the Southwest, and the emergence of student activism on college campuses (*Making* 36–58).

CHAPTER 2

Imagining an Independent Nation

Archetypal Revolutionaries in the Theater of Amiri Baraka and Luis Valdez

The emergence of the Black and Mexican American theater traditions dates back to the second part of the nineteenth century; however, these traditions remained excluded from mainstream theater venues and critical discussions until the 1960s. The Black theater tradition developed alongside other types of performances such as minstrels and vaudevillians that resulted in hybrid productions created by Blacks exemplified by Bob Cole's *A Trip to Coontown*, staged in 1898 (Hay 32). At the turn of the twentieth century, Black theater evolved through the plays of Willis Richardson, Randolph Edmonds, W. E. B. Du Bois, Alice Dunbar Nelson, and Langston Hughes, among others, who either wrote or staged drama, or theorized about it.[1] While a number of Black plays were staged locally in subsequent decades, particularly at HBCUs, it wasn't until the production of Lorrain Hansberry's *A Raisin in the Sun* in 1959 that Black drama coalesced into a broader national movement and gained access to mainstream venues for the first time in the long history of the tradition.[2] Spanish-language

---

1. For studies on the development of the Black theater tradition, see Hay, *African American Theatre*; H. Miller, *Theorizing Black Theater*; K. Mitchell, *Living with Lynching*; and Prentiss, *Staging Faith*.

2. Smethurst observes that while there had been Black drama before the 1960s, the theater produced starting with Hansberry's *A Raisin in the Sun* was unique in its combination of social, political, and artistic objectives that would also characterize the Black Arts Movement (79–83). Hay similarly argues that an "analysis of plot synopses of the more than seven hundred musical comedies produced between Cole's *Coontown* in 1898 and Hughes's *Simply Heavenly* in 1957 shows almost no evidence of social consciousness" (32).

plays in the United States, with Spanish and Mexican influences, became a staple of the cultural production of the Southwest in the second half of the nineteenth century and turn of the twentieth century.[3] Similar to the Black theater tradition, there had been local theater productions exemplified by the plays of Josefina Niggli in the 1930s and 1940s;[4] however, the Mexican American theater that emerged in the 1960s represented a distinctive type of performance closely connected to the reinvigorated struggles for social justice by Mexican Americans in the Southwest. A shared trait of the Black and Chicanx theater traditions from their inceptions to the 1960s is their exclusion from mainstream theater venues and cultural organizations.[5]

Playwrights of the 1960s such as Amiri Baraka and Luis Valdez combined in their grassroots theater an emerging social and political militancy among their respective groups with the goal of creating performances beyond the influence of the Western and American theater traditions.[6] Baraka and Valdez began their artistic and social projects as independent and community-based, due in part to their theater and literary experiences as college students, which were dominated by the Western tradition. When Baraka attended Howard University, the Western literary tradition was predominant in humanities courses;[7] Baraka's early theater performances with the Black Arts Repertory in

---

3. Scholars have debated whether Spanish-language theater productions in the Southwest before the 1960s form part of the Mexican American theater tradition; Kanellos, for instance, explains that in "style, content, and genre, the Hispanic stage in the United States during the nineteenth and early twentieth centuries was almost completely dominated by the Spanish tradition" (*History* 199). Yolanda Broyles-González dates the origin of Mexican American theater to the "Mexican oral culture or the popular performance tradition" that had its roots in the "Mexican popular tradition of comedy associated in the past two hundred years with the *carpa,* or tent show" (7).

4. Orchard and Padilla have discussed in detail Niggli's "folk drama" and her position in the Mexican American theater tradition (3–21).

5. Scholars use the term "Chicano/a theater" in reference to the work of playwrights of Mexican American descent living in the Southwest during the 1960s and 1970s. I use the terms "Mexican American" and "Chicanx" synonymously. For a detailed description of the social and political connotations of the terms Chicano/a, Mexican American, and Mexican in the context of Chicanx theatre, see Huerta, "When Sleeping Giants Awaken" 23.

6. In later years, Baraka explains that Black artists in the 1960s "wanted to create a poetry, a literature, which directly reflected the civil rights and black liberation movements. We wanted an art that was recognizably African American . . . [and] was mass-oriented" ("Cultural" 152). Valdez similarly discussed the link between the politics and militancy of the Chicanx Movement and his theater aesthetics, "Chicano theatre must be revolutionary in technique as well as content. It must be popular . . . ; but it must also educate the pueblo toward an appreciation of *social change,* on and off the stage" ("Notes" 7–8).

7. In his *Autobiography,* Baraka discusses being introduced to the literary tradition through the works of Dante, Gertrude Stein, Ezra Pound, and Federico García Lorca, among others (75, 88). Years later, in his essay, "Cultural Revolution and the Literary Canon," Baraka would offer a scathing assessment of the literary tradition that before the 1960s excluded artists and writers of color.

Harlem, and his role as one of the leading exponents of the Black Arts Movement, reflected an attempt to create a new aesthetics for Black artists. Valdez experienced a similar artistic development; when Valdez studied theater at San Jose State University, his courses relied on either the American or Spanish theater traditions.[8] Jorge Huerta, for instance, situates Valdez's theater performances of the 1960s and his engagement with Chicanx themes as the proper start of the Mexican American theater tradition in contrast to the Spanish- or Mexican-inspired performances of the past.[9] The political militancy and social engagement of the 1960s marked either a development or a new start in the Black and Chicanx theater traditions.

While several scholars have focused on either the theater of Baraka and Valdez, Harry J. Elam has studied comparatively their early theater performances and their close connection to the social protest, militancy, and the Black and Chicanx nationalism of the 1960s.[10] The early works of Baraka and Valdez reflect some of their aesthetic, social, political, and ideological convergences that coincided with the tumultuous period of social protest during the 1960s and 1970s. Both playwrights defined their social and artistic work by engaging with issues of race, ethnicity, justice, and nationalist aspirations for their respective groups at a critical juncture in American history. The death of Malcolm X marked an ideological shift in Baraka's artistic work when he formed the Black Arts Repertory in Harlem in 1965; for Valdez, it was the Delano grape strike of 1965 in California that led to the creation of the strike's artistic unit, *El Teatro Campesino* (The Farmworker's Theater). Elam systematically explores their social protest theater by focusing on their points of convergences and similarities.[11] Elam argues that living in a multiethnic society "demand[s] not only that we acknowledge diverse cultural experiences but also that we investigate and

---

8. Valdez writes that while at college, "Chicanos in Spanish classes [were] frequently involved in productions of plays by Lope de Vega, Calderón de la Barca, Tirso de Molina and other classic playwrights" ("Notes" 7); Valdez also questioned whether the emerging Chicanx theater should aspire to be an imitation of the "racist works by Eugene O'Neill and Tennessee Williams" ("Notes" 7).

9. Huerta explains that Valdez's *The Shrunken Head of Pancho Villa* performed in California in 1964 "became the first produced play written by a Chicano about being Chicano" ("Looking" 38).

10. For discussions regarding the aesthetic, cultural, and social significance of Baraka's work, see Neal 62–78; Watts, *Amiri Baraka* 259–90; and H. Miller 179–216; in the case of Valdez's plays, see Huerta, *Chicano Theater* 11–45 and *Chicano Drama* 26–44; and Broyles-González 3–35.

11. Elam's comprehensive analysis covers their one-act and extended plays from 1965 to 1971, concentrating on their plays' shared themes and elements, such as the influence of the social context, the content and form of the dramatic texts, and their performing spaces (17).

interrogate areas of commonality. Only in this way can we move beyond the potentially polarizing divisions of race and ethnicity" (4). Cross-cultural studies, Elam adds, should "challenge the internal and external social restrictions and cultural expectations often placed upon critics of color to study only their native group" (7). My investigation into the theater of Baraka and Valdez is indebted and informed by Elam's analysis, which comparatively studies points of convergence between Black and Chicanx theater and the parallel trajectories of both groups in their fight for historical, social, and cultural inclusion.

This chapter examines Baraka's *The Slave* and Valdez's *Bandido!* and how both plays imaginatively challenge prevalent historical narratives of their respective groups by reexamining significant historical events—the legacy of slavery and the aftermath of the Mexican–American War (1846–48), respectively—through their use of the revolutionary archetype in order to situate the history of Black and Latinx people within the larger US historical narrative. Baraka and Valdez were similarly influenced by revolutionary movements in Latin America and the Caribbean during the 1950s, particularly the Cuban Revolution; while *Bandido!* was produced decades later in 1981, Valdez's play recovers the revolutionary ethos, themes, and engagement with the history of the Southwest already present in Valdez's *The Shrunken Head of Pancho Villa,* a play produced in 1964, the same year as *The Slave.* An element that distinctively connects *The Slave* and *Bandido!* is their use of experimentation that reflects some of the characteristics associated with the aesthetics of postmodernism such as the challenge of hegemonic historical narratives, the marginalization and fragmentation of subjects, and in the case of *Bandido!,* the use of self-reflexivity to disrupt and undermine its own narrative. A comparative analysis of the plays' emphasis on the history of violence, oppression, and racism—and their aesthetic representations of revolutionary figures—reveals points of convergence in the playwrights' work that in turn reflect shared traits within the Black and Chicanx theater traditions.

NATIONALISM, REVOLUTION, AND HISTORICAL SUBJECTIVITY

Baraka and Valdez embraced nationalist aspirations for their respective groups and were attracted to revolutionary ideas during the early 1960s, an influence that, although clearly reflected in *The Slave,* is also present in *Bandido!.* Baraka and Valdez, as Elam explains, were not only artists, but they were also activists and social theorists of their respective movements (3). In their early social activism and plays, Baraka and Valdez shared a social and artistic vision that emphasized racial and ethnic consciousness based on militancy and nationalistic ideologies. During the late 1960s and early 1970s, Valdez acted as one of the intellectual theorists of *El Movimiento* (The Movement), the more militant and nationalistic branch of the Chicanx civil rights movement. Valdez's early writings focused on the development of a Chicanx identity embedded with nationalism, indigenous myths, and Catholic symbols.[12] After Valdez moved from Delano, he commented that *El Teatro Campesino*'s performances moved beyond farm workers' concerns and increasingly engaged with other broader social issues such as the Vietnam War and racial discrimination ("Notes" 10).

Both Baraka and Valdez were similarly influenced by the Cuban Revolution, which presented a powerful example of a successful armed uprising in the American continent. In the case of Baraka, he described his travel to Cuba in the early 1960s as a turning point in his militancy and revolutionary thinking. Baraka wrote about his experiences visiting Cuba and witnessing firsthand the results of the revolution led by "a group of young radical intellectuals" much like himself ("Cuba Libre" 38).[13] The Cuban Revolution was also an important event for Valdez. As Jorge Huerta explains, before his involvement with César Chávez, Dolores Huerta, and the Delano farmworkers' strike, Valdez traveled to Cuba in 1964 and became an open sympathizer of the revolution ("When Sleeping Giants" 25). While the aesthetic output and social activism of Baraka and Valdez converge ideologically around 1965, at the height of their work with the Black Arts Repertory in Harlem and *El Teatro Campesino* in Delano, respectively, their work then diverges stylistically and thematically in the 1970s. A constant theme in their work, however, is the influence of nationalist and revolutionary thought, similarly present in *The Slave* and *Bandido!*.

The Slave engages with the era of slavery through the representation of Walker Vessels as a revolutionary leader in a contemporary context who carries the legacy of armed resistance dating back to the antebellum era. *The Slave* innovatively reshapes special and historical chronologies by presenting Vessels at the beginning of the play as a field slave in the antebellum South. The play's events abruptly move to a race war between a Black and a white army at an unnamed city and in an unspecified future. Vessels, now the leader of a Black liberation army, returns to confront his ex-wife, Grace, and her current husband Bradford Easley, and to take his two daughters, who live with

---

12. Valdez, for example, states in his manifest-poem, *Pensamiento Serpentino* (Serpentine Thoughts), "To be CHICANO is to love yourself / your culture, your / skin, your language" (175).

13. On the influence of the Cuban Revolution on Baraka, see also Reilly 132, and Woodard 52–54.

their mother and remain upstairs sleeping for the duration of the play. Their altercation results in the shooting of Easley by Vessels. As the advancing Black army approaches the city and the shelling increases, the house is hit and Grace is fatally wounded. Before the house collapses, Vessels doubts the goals of his revolution and tells Grace that their two daughters are dead, possibly by his own hands.

Bandido! recreates the life and myth of Tiburcio Vásquez, a historical outlaw and alleged revolutionary figure, and revisits the plight of *Californios,* the Spanish-speaking population in California, after the Mexican–American War. Vásquez belonged to a prominent California family of Mexican descent and eventually lost his land and social standing after the war. Vásquez lived as an outlaw in California for years but was eventually captured. *Bandido!* covers key events in Vásquez's last two years before his capture and prison sentence for his involvement at a store robbery at Tres Pinos, in Northern California, where three white Americans were killed. The play moves back and forth from vignettes of Vásquez's life as an outlaw, his romantic life, and scenes at a San Jose jail before his execution. Before his capture, Vásquez confesses his intent to incite a revolution against the Anglo majority in California, but his plan fails to materialize due in part to his own ambivalence regarding the consequences of a violent revolution.

The Slave is often characterized as a representation of the racially charged politics of the 1960s, and *Bandido!* as a reflection of the conciliatory multiculturalism of the 1980s;[14] however, both plays grapple with the ambivalence of presenting, to different degrees, the idea of overt armed revolution, which remains an unresolved tension throughout the plays; and similarly, both plays creatively contest prevalent historical narratives regarding the passive acceptance of the social conditions of marginalized subjects. While *The Slave* was first staged in 1964 and *Bandido!* decades later in 1981,[15] Valdez's play returns to the revolutionary themes of his previous work during the 1960s, particularly *The Shrunken Head of Pancho Villa,* when both playwrights shared similar aesthetic and political views related to the struggles of Black and Mexican American communities against historical oppression. It is significant that the revolutionary theme contained in *The Slave* and *Bandido!* surfaces at a period in the playwrights' careers when they wrote plays targeted at broader mainstream audiences, a contrast to the period when they produced social protest plays that were performed for either predominantly Black or Mexican Amer-

---

14. See Watts, *Amiri Baraka* 82–83; and Broyles-González 235–36.

15. *The Slave* opened in the St. Marks Playhouse in Greenwich Village in December 1964 (H. Miller 205). *Bandido!* was first staged in San Juan Bautista, California, in 1981, and then at the Mark Taper Forum in Los Angeles in 1994 (Rossini 88–89).

ican audiences.[16] *The Slave* and *Bandido!* share some thematic and experimental elements and techniques characteristic of postmodernism, primarily their challenge of historical certainty through the use of the revolutionary archetype. Jon Rossini has described this trait as the "aesthetic of resistance" inscribed in *Bandido!* (92), which is similarly applicable to *The Slave*. Although *Bandido!* is considered a less confrontational play, or even containing "proassimilationist themes," as Yolanda Broyles-González maintains (235), Valdez's play articulates an explicit attempt to incite a Mexican American armed revolution in California against whites, just as *The Slave* stages a Black revolution against white oppression, albeit in an undetermined future.

    The Slave and *Bandido!* engage with history and the social position of people of color in the US through the use of aesthetic elements that take the quality of "postmodern" as described by some scholars. In *A Poetics of Postmodernism*, an earlier and often-cited analysis of historical narratives and historical subjectivity, Linda Hutcheon argues that a characteristic of postmodern narratives is the author's challenge of the past as an objective and monolithic reality rather than a constructed set of discourses. Hutcheon describes this type of narrative as "historiographic metafiction," in which authors both revise and undermine the past as it "reinstalls historical contexts as significant and even determining, but in so doing, it problematizes the entire notion of historical knowledge" (*Poetics* 89). A postmodern interpretation of history, however, does not render the past an undetermined reality; rather, it creates competing views that are open to multiple interpretations. *The Slave* and *Bandido!* reflect Hutcheon's characterization of history as malleable by challenging its objectivity in relation to the past history of their respective groups. With a similar perspective, Phillip Brian Harper has argued that the aesthetic works by some writers of color prior to the 1960s can be interpreted as engaging with elements of the postmodern experience, particularly their engagement with the concept of "marginality" and "fragmented subjectivity" (28–29).[17] More specifically to Chicanx theater, W. B. Worthen has identified similar postmod-

---

    16. Scholars have discussed the role of audiences in either *The Slave* or *Bandido!* by focusing on Baraka's attempt to create a Black militant consciousness and Valdez's attempt during the 1980s to avoid the confrontational rhetoric characteristic of *El Teatro Campesino*'s plays. See Watts, *Amiri Baraka* 83; Sollors, *Amiri Baraka/LeRoi Jones* 134; Hernández 50; and Broyles-González 172–73, 232.

    17. In studying the emphasis on the fragmented and decentralized self that forms part of the postmodern condition, Harper argues that the alienation, despair, uncertainty, and fragmentation characteristic of postmodernism have been present in the work of some pre-1960s authors of color, a period that falls outside the traditional timeline of postmodern texts, since their postmodernist tendencies "deriv[e] specifically from [their] socially marginalized and politically disenfranchised status" (3).

ernist tendencies in the work of Chicanx playwrights, including Valdez; he points out that the treatment and disruption of historical objectivity in Valdez's *Shrunken Head* and *Bandido!*, along with their engagement with Chicanx history, reflects some postmodern characteristics such as the subversion and fragmentation of historical events.[18] Similar to Worthen, rather than claiming that Valdez's *Bandido!*, and Baraka's *The Slave* for the purpose of my analysis, deliberately engage with the aesthetics of postmodernism, my analysis shows that some of the plays' thematic, narrative, and stylistic choices align with postmodern aesthetics as both plays challenge the historical marginalization of their respective groups.

ENACTING THE ERA OF SLAVERY AND REVOLUTION IN BARAKA'S *THE SLAVE*

Few other Black writers of the 1960s made a more deliberate connection between their artistic and intellectual output and their social and political project for Black liberation than Baraka, which led to a new renaissance in Black aesthetics that in turn allowed him to gain a mainstream critical recognition previously denied to Black playwrights. Baraka's career began as a music critic and poet writing for local venues including *The Floating Bear, The Naked Ear,* and *Jazz Review* while living in Greenwich Village in the 1950s. The emerging Black Arts Movement depended on a network of small and local productions and publishing venues, and Baraka contributed to these efforts as the founder of Totem Press in 1958, an independent publisher that supported Black artists.[19] Baraka's first book of poems, *Preface to a Twenty Volume Suicide Note,* was published in 1961 by Totem Press in partnership with Corinth Books; Baraka also published *Blues People* in 1963 with William Morrow, a mainstream publishing house.[20] Baraka's ideological shift from the Bohemian ethos and counterculture of Greenwich Village to social protest and Black

18. Worthen explains the use of the term "postmodern" in his analysis of contemporary Chicanx playwrights by noting that "the thematics of Chicana/o history plays are inseparable from their rhetoric, typically from the use of discontinuity and fragmentation, appropriation and hybridity, heteroglossia and pastiche. This formal complexity might appear to verge on the blank aesthetic of the 'postmodern'" (103).

19. Baraka's appropriation of the means of literary production would be replicated in the 1960s by other Black artists and writers who created independent publishing houses such as Broadside Press and Third World Press. See, for example, Smethurst 179–80, and Babb 126–27.

20. See, Baraka's *Autobiography* 170–71, 181. Morrow's publication of *Blues People* speaks of the resurgence of interest in Black writers by mainstream publishers that would increase in the late 1960s and early 1970s.

nationalism is marked by the productions of *Dutchman* and *The Slave*. The staging of *Dutchman* at the Cherry Lane Theater in 1964 represents one of the early instances when a Black play was reviewed and discussed in mainstream publications, receiving both critical recognition and condemnation for its provocative portrayal of race relations.[21] *The Slave* was staged shortly afterward at the St. Marks Playhouse before Baraka moved to Harlem to work with the Black Arts Repertory.

Baraka's plays and essays from the early 1960s serve as a counterweight to the prevalent narrative that the social gains of people of color in the 1960s and 1970s were achieved only through nonviolent resistance.[22] *The Slave* has commonly been studied as a radical and confrontational social protest play that raised racial and ethnic consciousness and nationalist sentiments through representations of armed confrontation;[23] however, *The Slave* is seldom invoked in contemporary critical or general discussions of the civil rights era of the 1960s and 1970s. The theater work of Baraka and James Baldwin was directly influenced by violent events such as the assassinations of Medgar Evers and Malcolm X. Within the context of the emerging Black arts theater and Baraka's early plays, Kimberly Bentson observes that the 1960s were a time of "transition and anxiety in American cultural history" that was "marked by acts of social violence and insurgency" with few parallels in contemporary American history (133). Baraka's Black nationalist rhetoric in *The Slave*, shared by emerging radical activists such as Eldridge Cleaver and Huey Newton, is articulated in *Home: Social Essays*, which denounces the conditions of Black urban communities and the nonviolent methods to solve racial and economic inequality advocated by Black civil rights leaders. Baraka defiantly argues that the "struggle is not simply for 'equality'" but "to completely *free* the black man from the domination of the white man" ("Black Is a Country" 84). Baraka frames his confrontational stance and social demands based in part on his firsthand experiences with inequality and discrimination in urban enclaves such as Har-

---

21. While Hansberry's *A Raisin in the Sun* and Baldwin's *Blues for Mr. Charlie* were staged before *Dutchman,* Baraka's play was the first to receive an Obie Award in 1964 (Baraka, *Autobiography* 190); Baraka's Obie Award was one of the early recognitions of a Black play by a mainstream cultural organization.

22. Some scholars have noted that the militancy of Malcolm X and other Black nationalist leaders contributed to the creation of ethnic studies programs at colleges and universities. Gates, for example, points out that "most of us writing today about black literature in the academy owe our undergraduate scholarships, our graduate fellowships, and even our positions and promotions at least indirectly to the Black Arts and Black Power movements" (*Figures* xxvii). See also Smethurst 1–2.

23. For discussions on *The Slave,* see Sollors, *Amiri Baraka/LeRoi Jones* 134–38; L. Brown 147–50; Neal 67–74; Watts, *Amiri Baraka* 78–84; and H. Miller 205–11.

lem ("Cold, Hurt" 94–95). Echoing the discontent and violent protests in some major urban areas such as Watts, Detroit, and Newark in the 1960s, *The Slave* mirrors Blacks' simmering frustrations and responses to a deep-rooted social marginalization and sense of despair.

The Slave challenges received histories regarding the era of slavery by creatively dislocating and extending the scope of the militancy of the 1960s and by presenting Walker Vessels both as a revolutionary leader and a slave—presumably a rebel leader—who carries on the legacy of Black armed resistance from the antebellum South. Some critics have focused on how Baraka engages with the era of slavery in an experimental form in other plays such as *Slave Ship* and *The Motion of History*;[24] however, almost no attention has been given to the experimental engagement with history already found in *The Slave*.[25] Baraka's play invokes the figure of the slave revolt leader, a figure that prior to the 1960s tended to be mediated in mainstream texts written by white historians and writers.[26] In his nonfiction, Baraka challenges the myth of the content slave and the attempt at myth-making in historiography and social discourses that present Blacks during slavery as passive subjects who "didn't mind being [slaves]" ("Street Protest" 98).[27] Baraka subverts white historiography on stage by invoking the tradition of Black resistance dating back to David Walker and armed resistance by slave revolt leaders such as Gabriel Prosser and Denmark Vesey. As Werner Sollors correctly points out, Baraka begins by naming *The Slave*'s main character Vessels in a reference to Vesey and his subversive potential (*Amiri* 135). Baraka's use of the slave rebel figure, however, is experimental and differs from other conventional and literary representations of armed resistance by Black authors such as Arna Bontemps's *Black Thunder*, a fictional recreation of the historical 1800 Gabriel's rebellion. In *The Slave*, Vessels is not the historical reincarnation of Prosser or Vesey propelled into

---

24. See, for example, Watts, *Amiri Baraka* 269–73, 445–49, and L. Brown 23.

25. In his analysis of *The Slave*, Lloyd Brown mentions the significance of Vessels's position as a "field slave" and as an archetypal figure of Black militancy (150).

26. After the 1831 slave rebellion led by Nat Turner in Virginia, Thomas Gray, a white writer, took upon himself the task of writing down Turner's "free confession" before his execution for public consumption. In *The Confessions of Nat Turner*, Gray offers a distorted portrayal of Turner's actions while describing him as "fiendish," "savag[e]," and guided by a fundamentalist vision of retribution and conflict enacted in religious scriptures (6). While Frederick Douglass's *The Heroic Slave*, Martin Delany's *Blake*, and Arna Bontemps's *Black Thunder* contain fictional accounts involving slave revolt leaders, these texts weren't recovered until the 1970s.

27. Baraka further rejects this view by emphasizing the tradition of armed slave resistance, since according to Baraka, "the records of slave revolts are too numerous to support" the "faked conclusion" that slaves coexist harmoniously with their masters ("Street Protest" 98).

the future; instead, Vessels's initial position in the play as an outspoken and discontent slave stands as a symbolic figure of resistance who projects the legacy of slave rebellions and violent suppressions into a hypothetical future.

The Slave's prologue presents Vessels as a character who attempts to articulate his grievances but fails due to his position as field slave, which reflects his social marginality. The prologue purposefully obscures chronological time as Vessels appears as an *"old field slave"* who is "much older than [he] look[s] . . . or maybe much younger" at different periods during the play (43, 44). Vessels initially takes the form of a seer, elder statesman, or a Black preacher, but as he attempts to express his thoughts, he grows *"anxiou[s]," "less articulate,"* and *"more 'field hand' sounding"* (45). Scholars agree on the cryptic nature of Vessels's opening speech;[28] nonetheless, his restlessness and belligerent intent while still a slave is evident when he remarks that "we are liars, and we are murderers. We invent death for others" (43). Vessels's condition as a slave makes him unable to articulate a coherent message; as a result, his inability to effectively communicate marginalizes him and, at the same time, connects him to the emerging restlessness and frustration among disenfranchised Blacks, which finds physical expression in an altered social context in the play's subsequent acts. Signaling the ineffectiveness of rhetoric, Vessels turns to physical violence as a tool to address his social grievances.

Vessels's initial position as a *"field hand"* is significant for Baraka in the context of slave hierarchies and class distinctions among Blacks since he believes that the source for Black liberation in past and contemporary times will be carried out by marginalized subjects rather than Blacks in relative positions of authority or class standing. In the introduction to *The Motion of History,* Baraka makes the distinction between slaves who were "house servants and petty bourgeoisie-to-be" and "field slaves," who represented the majority and the authentic revolutionaries (13).[29] Hence, Vessels's initial position as a marginalized field slave connects him to the majority of disenfranchised Blacks rather than to the Black middle-class leaders of the civil rights era, who in Baraka's view, asked Blacks to "renounce [their] history as pure social error" and look at "old slavery" and its legacy of social and economic disparities as a "hideous acciden[t] for which no one should be blamed" ("Nonviolence" 135, 137). Vessels's position as a field slave functions as a social critique of Black civil right leaders and their methods; thus, presenting a clear ideological contrast between his radical militancy and their nonviolent social activism.

---

28. For discussions on *The Slave's* prologue, see Sollors, *Amiri Baraka/LeRoi Jones* 137; Watts, *Amiri Baraka* 78–79; and H. Miller 209–10.

29. See also Baraka, "What Does Nonviolence Mean?" 137.

The Slave destabilizes dominant historical narratives of slave suppression on stage by presenting a decentered subject who carries the legacy of armed resistance and has the potential to challenge the status quo through open revolution. The play's first act propels Vessels into a contemporary city in the 1960s where he becomes the leader of a "black liberation movement" who is able to mount an effective military offensive against whites (58). As Larry Neal observes, Vessels in this imaginary context "demands a confrontation with history. . . . His only salvation lies in confronting the physical and psychological forces that have made him and his people powerless" (70). Vessels refers to the source of his actions when he maintains that he is fighting "against three hundred years of oppression" (72). Vessels, moreover, echoes the intent of former slave rebel leaders such as Nat Turner when he boasts that he "single-handedly . . . promoted a bloody situation where white and black people are killing each other" (66). Neal contextualizes the violence depicted in *The Slave* by arguing that, despite Western society's aggression toward the oppressed, "it sanctimoniously deplore[d] violence or self-assertion on the part of the enslaved" (71–72). Vessels's armed resistance—taken as a continuation of past instances of slave rebellion—figuratively subverts the historical record since an organized and open slave revolt in the US did not last more than a few days. *The Slave* attempts, as Baraka notes in his often-cited essay, "The Revolutionary Theatre," to take Blacks' revolutionary "dreams and give them a reality" (211). As a result, Baraka's play goes beyond the representation of the militancy and radicalism of the 1960s by creating a fictional counterview of the historical record of slave revolt suppressions.

Despite the inclusion of a race war in *The Slave,* the play shows the limits of a military and bloody confrontation between Blacks and whites on stage; instead, it concentrates on the tension between Vessels's revolutionary goals and his ambivalent feelings toward whites due to his former acceptance of racial pluralism.[30] Although the war in *The Slave* has been raging for months and has tangible consequences since it is noted that Vessels's "noble black brothers are killing what's left of the city," or rather "what's left of this country" (49), it is only alluded to intermittently rather than enacted. The war serves mainly as the background for the verbal abuse, physical violence, and aggression in the living room among Vessels, Grace, and Easley. As Baraka has pointed out, the animosity between Vessels and Grace derives also in part from his radicalization and own personal struggles to reconcile his Black

---

30. Neal correctly observes that *The Slave* "is essentially about Walker's attempt to destroy his white past. For it is the past, with all of its painful memories, that is really the enemy of the revolutionary" (70).

nationalism to his marriage to Hettie Jones, a white woman.[31] The emotion-
ally charged scenes and recriminations between the three characters expose
the simmering feelings of rage and racial animosity that remained under the
surface before the war.

The Slave presents a clash between a Black radical and a white liberal, in
the form of Vessels's confrontation with Easley, which symbolizes the former's
attempt to overcome his past and continue his revolution. Samuel Hay maintains that in *The Slave* and other plays of the same period, "Baraka repeats
Baldwin's theme [in *Blues for Mr. Charlie*] that burning all bridges to white
liberals is the first step toward liberation" (95). Vessels does not direct his
hatred against openly prejudiced whites but against Easley, a college professor with a "liberal education, and a long history of concern for minorities"
(52). Consequently, Vessels's shooting of Easley represents the end of possible
coexistence between Blacks and whites, echoing the radical view—embraced
by Malcolm X and other Black militants at the time—that white liberals could
not contribute to the struggle for Black liberation. Grace realizes, however,
that in trying to overcome his former relationships with whites, Vessels risks
destroying himself and his family. Even though Vessels's role as a revolutionary leader fulfills a long-awaited dream and struggle for liberation that has
extended for centuries—exactly what Baraka exhorts in "The Revolutionary
Theatre"—*The Slave* depicts the revolution's toll on Vessels and his inability to
successfully navigate his own racial allegiances.[32]

The Slave's ending ultimately negates Vessels's prospects for a successful
revolution—even within the fictional setting created by the play—and reveals
the fate of his family when he asserts that his two daughters are dead most
likely by his own hands. Following the death of Easley, the fate of his children
in *The Slave*'s final scenes becomes the focus of attention; however, Vessels's
actions and statements suggest that he arrived at Grace's house with the inten-
tion of ending his children's lives. Vessels mentions at different times that he
returned to Grace's house because he "want[s] those children" (65), but the
stage directions at the beginning of act one suggest that he could have already
taken their lives before confronting Grace. After the shelling increases and
the house is hit, Grace is fatally hurt. When Grace asks him to "see about the

31. Baraka comments that his increasing militant stance against whites opened a chasm
between him and Hettie Jones, which forms the basis of the confrontation between Vessels and
Grace in *The Slave* (*Autobiography* 195–96).

32. Years later, Baraka observed that Vessels's revolutionary goals in *The Slave* were hindered due to his inability to shed his past. Baraka mentions that going "through the whole process of breast-beating, accusations, and lamenting meant" that Vessels still had "a relationship
with his wife, with his past" (Reilly 134).

girls," he repeatedly tells her that "they're dead" (87, 88). Scholars are divided regarding the fate of the children, suggesting that they could have died in the burning building, Vessels could have taken their lives, or that the scene is vague and unclear.[33] Although the play's ending appears perplexing, Vessels's seemingly incomprehensible actions gain meaning by taking into consideration that he arrived at Grace's house with the premonition that his revolutionary fight may not succeed. During a moment of weakness or sincerity, Vessels confesses to Grace: "I was going to wait until the fighting was over . . . until we have won, before I took [the children]. But something occurred to me for the first time, last night. It was the idea that we might not win" (68). Baraka in later years conceded that some of his plays preceding Malcolm X's death, including *The Slave*, were "essentially petty bourgeois radicalism, even rebellion, but not clear and firm enough as to [be] revolution" (*Motion of History* 12). Based in part on Baraka's own acknowledgement that Vessels lacked revolutionary conviction, some scholars have described Vessels's fight as futile.[34] Vessels's actions and the fate of his children, however, achieve an important symbolic meaning in the context of his former self as a slave when during the antebellum period, some slaves took the extreme action of ending their children's lives in order to spare them their fate as slaves.

The ending of *The Slave* inventively engages with the era of slavery by drawing parallels with tragic episodes during the antebellum era such as the well-known case of Margaret Garner, a runaway slave who took the radical measure of taking her daughter's life before her capture as an alternative to slavery, a tragic episode masterly rendered in Toni Morrison's *Beloved*. Although the absence of Vessels's daughters during the play may suggest a metaphorical interpretation of these characters, his disturbing actions toward them are also pragmatic as Vessels reasons that the fate of nonwhites may be in jeopardy after a possible military victory by the white army. Vessels returns to Grace's house because he believes he is "rescuing the children" from an unspecified danger (69); his rescue takes the form of a desperate form of protection. Morrison's use of Garner's story continued a tradition in antislavery writing that called attention to slaves' attempts to gain their freedom;[35] in a similar manner, and in relation to calls for a Black revolution in the 1960s, Vessels's seemingly incomprehensible actions in *The Slave* dramatize the way

---

33. See H. Miller 210; Watts, *Amiri Baraka* 82–83; and Hay 95.

34. Watts inconclusively suggests that the ambiguous fate of the children is "more annoying than provocative," leaving the ending of the play without "any resemblance of meaning" (*Amiri* 83). See also Sollors, *Amiri Barak/LeRoi Jones* 136.

35. According to Gilroy, the "horrific" story of Margaret Garner was often used by some abolitionists to raise awareness for the antislavery cause (66).

in which oppressive race relations cornered individuals into taking desperate actions. As a result, the children in *The Slave* represent the unfulfilled aspirations of a Black revolution, just as Garner's daughter symbolizes slaves' negated freedom. In Baraka's rendering of this parallel episode, Vessels's dreams for liberation are shattered for him and his children as they ultimately perish, and he returns to his slave-like state at the end of the play.

Beyond reflecting Baraka's radicalization and frustration regarding the marginalized conditions of urban Blacks during the 1960s, *The Slave* craftily contextualizes its radical and militant message by merging Vessels's revolutionary aims with historical instances of armed Black resistance. The play's endurance rests in its reminder that the struggle for social recognition during the 1960s was carried out not only through acts of nonviolent resistance but also through the prospects of violent confrontation. Aesthetically, *The Slave* uses innovative techniques that reflect postmodern aesthetics in relation to the challenge and subversion of dominant historical narratives about the era of slavery. Vessels's discomforting revolutionary message that stresses militancy, nationalist aspirations, and radical actions in the face of racial oppression stands as a form of historical memory that reflects the contentious history of race relations—not only during the 1960s but also at different junctures in American history. The play's engagement with the position of marginalized subjects and their past history of resistance found in Black theater is similarly present in the Chicanx theater tradition.

MEXICAN AMERICAN REVOLUTIONARY ARCHETYPES AND SELF-REFLEXIVITY IN VALDEZ'S *BANDIDO!*

Similar to Baraka, elements in Valdez's theater trajectory reflect the connection between the reinvigoration of social protest movements, political militancy, and calls for self-determination among Mexican American communities in the Southwest and the subsequent recognition of Mexican American theater in the mainstream. The turning point in Valdez's theater career began when he arrived in Delano, California, in 1965 to work with César Chávez, Dolores Huerta, and other social activists fighting to improve the conditions of Mexican American laborers in the agricultural fields (Huerta, "When Sleeping Giants" 25). Valdez's early plays consisted of *actos* (skits), performed by Mexican American farmworkers in open and public venues, thematized workers' exploitation and discrimination by agricultural conglomerates such as the DiGiorgio corporation. Valdez moved from Delano in the 1970s in order to professionalize *El Teatro Campesino* troupe; Valdez's *Zoot Suit*, first staged in 1978 at the Mark Taper Forum in Los Angeles for Mexican American and mainstream audiences, was eventually produced on Broadway in 1979.[36] When Valdez staged *Zoot Suit* on Broadway, however, its critical reception was mixed; Valdez's subsequent collaboration with Universal Studios to film the play led to *Zoot Suit's* broader mainstream critical success (Bruce-Novoa, *RetroSpace* 88–89). *Zoot Suit* marks the first time that a Mexican American play gained access to mainstream venues and became part of mainstream critical discussions, after decades of exclusion.[37]

Critical discussions of Valdez's works are often divided within the framework of Valdez's collaboration with *El Teatro Campesino* in Delano and his subsequent projects; however, *Bandido!* has not been commonly explored as a continuation of the nationalist and revolutionary themes and creative engagement with history already present in his pre–*El Teatro Campesino* play, *The Shrunken Head of Pancho Villa*, which introduced the use of the archetypal revolutionary figure for the first time in Chicanx theater (Huerta, "Looking" 38). Scholars have pointed out that the characters of the two brothers in *Shrunken Head*, Joaquín and Belarmino, reflect—and physically appropriate—characteristics of two historical figures of resistance, Joaquín Murrieta and Francisco "Pancho" Villa.[38] The ethos of Villa, according to Valdez, is staged both in a "realistic" and "surrealistic" manner, as the brothers' father, Pedro, fought alongside Villa during the Mexican Revolution, while Belarmino acts literally as the missing head of Villa (*Shrunken Head* 154). The play is explicit in relation to Villa's symbolism as a "peasant outlaw" and as "revolutionary giant" (155, 160). As Worthen aptly points out, *Shrunken Head* "brings the history represented by Villa—which figures in the play almost purely in the register of 'representation,' as dream and symbol—into sharp dialogue with the contemporary situation of Chicano/a identity politics" (110). *Shrunken Head* shows an imaginative treatment of history and the revolutionary figure that is recovered and situated within an American historical context in *Bandido!*.[39]

---

36. Huerta, *Chicano Theater* 61; and Broyles-González 170–71, 189.

37. Miguel Piñero's play *Short Eyes* was also staged on Broadway and received the 1973–74 New York Drama Critics' Circle Award (Iglesias xv). For an overview of the development of the Puerto Rican theater tradition in New York City, see Kanellos and Huerta, *Nuevos Pasos* vii–ix.

38. See Huerta, Introduction to *Shrunken Head* 143–44 and *Chicano Theater* 53–54; and Worthen 111, 118.

39. Huerta points out that Valdez's experimental style in *Shrunken Head* "set the tone for all of [his] later works, none of which can be termed realism or realistic" (*Chicano Drama* 60). Similarly, the importance of history for Valdez was closely connected to Chicanx identity and this theme is present at different stages during his career. Reflecting on the role of history within the Chicanx Movement, Valdez explains that he and other Chicanx artists during the 1960s were "forced to re-examine the facts of history, and suffuse them with [their] own blood—to make them tell [their] reality" ("La Plebe" xxxi).

The emphasis on the history of the Southwest in *Bandido!* serves to reclaim past events of war and conquest and to situate early Mexican Americans within a geographical space denied to them in prevalent historical narratives.[40] Previously the largest group in the state, *Californios* were considerably outnumbered only a decade after the discovery of gold in 1848. They faced social and economic discrimination—and more importantly—they lost most of their land and social position despite the protections granted to them in the Treaty of Guadalupe Hidalgo. Before the 1860s, *Californios* owned the most valuable land in California, but "by the 1870s, they owned only one-fourth of this land," and by "the 1880s Mexicans were relatively landless" (Acuña, *Occupied* 104). As Valdez notes in the prologue to *Bandido!*, his play is based in part on the historical Tiburcio Vásquez, a *"bandido"* or outlaw (97). Vásquez traced his ancestry to the first *Californios* who arrived in the eighteenth century, and his loss of land and social status—and subsequent life as an outlaw—forms the basis and context for Vásquez's actions in *Bandido!*. In the play, Vásquez mentions that a "hundred years ago, [his] great grandfather founded San Francisco with [Juan] De Anza. Fifty years ago José Tiburcio Vásquez [his grandfather] was the law in San José" (110); however, he laments that he "cannot even walk the wooden side-walks of either city without a leash" (110). Vásquez's reversal of fortune represents the fate of *Californios* after the US annexation of the territory, and Valdez's play attempts to create a connection among past and present histories of social exclusion.

Bandido! challenges dominant narratives of the US westward expansion that exalts the economic success stories of white settlers by focusing on Vásquez as a marginalized subject. In the prologue to *Bandido!*, Valdez challenges such narratives by contending that the "American mythology" that constitutes the history of the Old West remains *"under constant revision"* (97). *Bandido!* presents an alternative interpretation to the meaning and symbolic significance of Vásquez despite, or because of, his dreadful ending since, as Valdez also notes, Vásquez holds the ominous distinction of being the last man to be publicly executed by hanging in California in 1875 (97). According to Jon Rossini, critics and reviewers who saw the 1994 staging of *Bandido!* were critical about what they perceived as "revisionary history" (89).[41] While the play can be interpreted as a distortion of historical events, *Bandido!* questions the mere notion of what constitutes an historical event and its supposed

---

40. Huerta correctly notes that with *Bandido!*, Valdez offers Chicanx people a historical "presence in the state of California" (*Chicano Drama* 30).

41. Rossini discusses in detail the negative reviews by theater critics of the 1994 staging of *Bandido!* (89–90). Similarly, Broyles-González argues that the plight of the historical Vásquez in *Bandido!* is "wholly distorted by omissions" (232).

neutrality. Valdez's intent is to take advantage of the malleability of historical accounts—as the play's introduction suggests—to create his own historical narrative and revolutionary archetype.

As a contrast to Baraka's loose amalgamation of figures of resistance in *The Slave*, *Bandido!* is based on the historical Vásquez; however, rather than simply contesting negative historical characterizations and presenting the "real" Vásquez, Valdez's play carves its own figure of resistance based on competing interpretations. Although the revolutionary dimension of the historical Vásquez has been disputed by historians,[42] the revolutionary figure in *Bandido!*—just as in *The Slave*—is used as a symbol of resistance able to embody what Huerta describes as Chicanx people's "struggle against oppressive forces" (*Chicano Drama* 31). Rossini rightly observes that Vásquez in *Bandido!* stands as a rebel archetype since Valdez "reject[s] the easy label of criminal and tak[es] seriously Vásquez's revolutionary potential" (92). The representation of Vásquez in *Bandido!* is more complex than a simple revisionist rendering of Vásquez's life on stage; rather, *Bandido!*'s portrayal of Vásquez reflects what scholars such as Juan Alonzo have identified as the reconceptualization of the figure of the nineteenth-century outlaw and bandit after the 1980s (135–39). *Bandido!* balances two seemingly contradictory accounts in relation to the historical character of Vásquez and presents two Vásquez figures: a bandit innocent of shooting three Americans who becomes a figure of nonviolent resistance, and an armed rebel who attempts to incite a revolution in California.

On the one hand, *Bandido!* rejects the simplistic characterization of Vásquez as a petty thief and makes him a symbol for *Californios* against the US expansion into the Southwest that similarly echoed the nonviolent actions of César Chávez, Dolores Huerta, and other activists during the Delano strike. In *Bandido!*, Vásquez acknowledges his "twenty years as a horse thief and stage robber," but contends that his "career grew out of the circumstances by which [he] was surrounded" (127). Vásquez's actions reflect the changing circumstances of Mexican Americans as he adds: "I was thirteen when gold was discovered. As I grew to manhood, a spirit of hatred and revenge took possession of me. I had many fights in defense of what I believed to be my rights and those of my countrymen" (127). In the play's early scenes, Vásquez acts as a scrupulous bandit who restrains himself from shooting victims dur-

---

42. In popular accounts, it is believed the historical Vásquez was aware of the symbolic meaning of his actions and told at least one reporter about his intent to incite revolution in California; however, according to John Boessenecker, Vásquez, before his execution, "made no claim of being a revolutionary and offered no excuses for his lengthy criminal career" and "never took any steps to carry out a revolt against the Anglo majority" (372).

ing his raids. Vásquez informs his band before the raid at Tres Pinos that his "first cardinal rule" is "no killing" (116). When Vásquez is captured and sentenced for his involvement in the robbery, his hanging takes the form of an act of arbitrary justice, while also suggesting the limits of passive resistance by Mexican Americans after the annexation of California.

On the other hand, *Bandido!* employs the rebel figure inscribed in the history of Mexican Americans in the Southwest to articulate a message of resistance. Valdez connects Vásquez's rebellious actions to early California outlaws such as Murrieta and other "Mestizo" revolutionaries such as Villa, already present in his militant play *Shrunken Head* ("La Plebe" xxvi–xxvii). As the play progresses, *Bandido!* imaginatively uses Vásquez's revolutionary potential—whether historical or fictional—to insert a militant message as Vásquez shares his plans to begin a revolution to liberate California from US control. After the raid at Tres Pinos, Vásquez is once again on the run when he reaches the San Fernando Mission. There, he finds refuge in the estate of Don Andrés Pico, a historical figure, who during the Mexican–American War "defeated the US Cavalry at the Battle of San Pasquel [*sic*]" (138).[43] During their meeting, Vásquez invites Pico to join him in fighting Americans one more time when he confesses: "I'm talking about a revolution. With a hundred well-armed men, I can start a rebellion that will crack the state of California in two, like an earthquake, leaving the Bear Republic in the north, and [a] Spanish California Republic in the south!" (137). Vásquez, however, is subsequently captured without enacting his plan. The scene is significant for its symbolism since Vásquez's desire to begin a revolution is explicit. Rather than resolving these two facets of Vásquez's life—an innocent outlaw and a revolutionary—*Bandido!* purposefully complicates these two competing narratives.

An element that differentiates *The Slave* and *Bandido!* is that Valdez's play self-reflexively exploits and interrogates the facts and myth of Vásquez's life as it accentuates and undermines the play's own historical significance through the use of melodrama, parody, and the inclusion of fragmented and competing narratives within the play.[44] Linda Hutcheon explains that "parody is a

---

43. The Battle of San Pasqual was a short-lived battle of the Mexican–American War fought between Stephen Kearny's troops and a group of *Californio lanceros* (California lancers) led by Andrés Pico. After a brief scrimmage, the battle turned into a standoff with Kearny's brief siege of the village of San Pasqual (Eisenhower 222–26).

44. Huerta argues that *Bandido!* is divided into two distinct sections and explains that "when we are with Vásquez in the jail cell, we are observing the real man; when the action shifts to the melodrama stage we are sometimes watching the Impresario's visions and sometimes we are actually watching Vásquez's interpretation" (*Chicano Drama* 30). Other scholars, however, have observed that the line between the melodrama sections and the realistic jail scenes becomes blurred and problematic as the play progresses; see, for example, Worthen 114 and Rossini 89.

complex genre, in terms of both its form and its ethos. It is one of the ways in which modern artists have managed to come to terms with the weight of the past" (*Theory of Parody* 29). *Bandido!* creates two parallel narratives through the "play within a play" device in which some of the play's scenes are a reenactment of a play written by Vásquez himself about his life and staged by Samuel Gillette, a theatrical "impresario," while Vásquez awaits his sentence in a San Jose prison (98, 100). Gillette's artistic vision, when reenacting Vásquez's life on stage, and the writing and rewriting of Vásquez's own story in *Bandido!* examine and parody the process of theatrical representation and historical certainty. Hutcheon describes parody as the "perfect postmodern form" since "it paradoxically both incorporates and challenges that which it parodies" (*Poetics* 11). Under this interpretation, *Bandido!* calls attention to Vásquez's significance while simultaneously undermining the veracity of such assertion.

Bandido! self-reflectively weaves Vásquez's competing nonviolent and revolutionary message as Vásquez himself directly writes and rewrites his own story while in jail, thus mediating a set of seemingly contradictory positions. After the first staging of Vásquez's play by Gillette, Vásquez complains about Gillette's emphasis on his private life as "melodrama," whereas Vásquez's alleged romantic exploits are accentuated through his relationship with Rosario, a married woman (109). Rather than resolving the tension between Vásquez's personal life and his public persona, Valdez's play self-reflexively exploits these apparent contradictions by making the play's characters enact and argue these opposing views onstage. Gillette expresses skepticism regarding Vásquez's desire to prove his innocence during the killings at Tres Pinos and to enhance his pacifist stance, while at the same time trying to incite an armed revolt that reflects his revolutionary aspirations. When Vásquez and Gillette are negotiating the terms for staging Vásquez's play in San Francisco, Vásquez tells Gillette: "If I'm to be hanged for murder, I want the public to know I'm not guilty" (110). Gillette objects to this request as he wonders: "Twenty years as a vicious desperado and never a single, solitary slaying?" (110). At the same time, Gillette agrees to buy Vásquez's revised play and stage it in San Francisco but with "none of this Liberator of California horseshit" since he would "be laughed out of the state if [he tried] to stage that" (140). Vásquez's own crafting of his story and Gillette's assistance as theater producer and businessman combine to mediate the play's layered message.

Despite its revolutionary message, *Bandido!* portrays an unsuccessful revolution as Vásquez questions his actions due to his ambivalence regarding his intent to incite a revolution and his dual cultural identity as he decides—before his execution—to avert an armed confrontation. Before Vásquez's capture, Cleodovio Chávez, one of Vásquez's band members, is attracted to the possibility of gathering a group of armed men and "slaughter[ing] every gringo [they] meet" since he reasons, "If they're gonna hang us, it might as well be for something good—not petty thievery" (145). In a subsequent scene, Vásquez averts the possible confrontation by sending a letter to Chávez, who has not been captured, asking him "not to get himself and a lot of innocent people killed" (150). The possibility for armed confrontation—which is set in motion in *The Slave*—is averted in *Bandido!* due to Vásquez's own dual cultural identification as a *Californio* and an American. A significant gesture in *Bandido!* is that although Vásquez was chased in his homeland and persecuted by US authorities, he considers himself a product of his mixed Mexican and American background. Vásquez displays what Ramón Saldívar has identified as an "in-between existence" present in Mexican American narratives since the formation of the US–Mexican border (*Chicano* 17). In *Bandido!*, Vásquez has the opportunity to stay in Mexico, but he returns to California; when asked about his motives, Vásquez responds that he has "never relished the idea of spending the rest of [his] days in Mexico" since California is "where [he] belong[s]" (138). The character of Vásquez signals a transition in Valdez's drama from presenting the memory and ethos of Villa, a Mexican revolutionary, in *Shrunken Head* as an archetypal figure to Vásquez in *Bandido!*, a Mexican American figure of resistance, who belongs to the history of the US and the Southwest.

The Slave and *Bandido!* use innovative dramatic techniques that reflect postmodern aesthetics used by post-1960s playwrights of color regarding the malleability and fragmentation of historical narratives to question historical representations of their respective marginalized groups. Both plays reclaim previously overlooked figures in dominant historical discourses and offer them agency to recreate and alter the historical memory of each group. The plays transform marginalized subjects, from a slave and an outlaw, respectively, into revolutionary figures to create a historical continuity between previous instances of armed resistance and revolt from the past to their 1960s context. Both revolutionary leaders engage, to different degrees, in a quest to gain their freedom and previously negated historical spaces—a Black nation and an independent California, respectively—which can be achieved through violent means. *The Slave* and *Bandido!* revolve around the haunting memory of race relations in the US and episodes of armed resistance by altering historical narratives, as Baraka's contemporary revolutionary figure carries the history of slave rebellions, while Valdez's play disrupts historical representations by allowing its revolutionary figure to write and rewrite his own legacy.

The Slave and *Bandido!* ultimately present unfulfilled revolutions even in their fictional settings and show a similar ambivalence regarding their revolutionaries' actions and intents toward whites. Despite its representation of a race war, *The Slave* is less radical than commonly assumed since Vessels struggles unsuccessfully to jettison his previous racial pluralism and his past relationships with whites. Vásquez in *Bandido!* similarly struggles to incite a revolt against whites due in part to his dual cultural identity. Although the staged dates of the plays appear to respond to different social and political historical periods, they interrogate and grapple with ever-present questions of race and ethnic identity in the US that continue to define American society in contemporary times. *The Slave* and *Bandido!* represent an instance, among others, in which the themes, tropes, and techniques used by post-1960s Black and Mexican American playwrights and writers converge to show their shared formal and aesthetic commonalities.

CHAPTER 3

Fighting for One's Country

World War II Soldiers of Color in the Fiction
of James Baldwin and Rudolfo Anaya

Black and Latinx authors have long been in dialogue with the themes and tropes of the American literary tradition, including the tension between art and social protest. In the US, this tension dates back at least to the publication of Harriet Beecher Stowe's *Uncle Tom's Cabin* in 1852. Stowe's novel came to represent a type of fiction that served as a model to raise social awareness regarding the inhumanity of slavery and to incite readers to mobilize for social and political change. Some of the earliest works of Black fiction, including Frederick Douglass's *The Heroic Slave* and William Wells Brown's *Clotel*, both published in 1853, were in deliberate conversation with Stowe's novel, and in subsequent decades, other novels such as Frances E. W. Harper's *Iola Leroy* continued to engage in the evolving protest novel tradition initiated by Stowe.[1] While the work of writers of the Harlem Renaissance is characterized by their emphasis on aesthetics and Black culture, their writings were also tied to a larger project of social uplifting; theorists of the movement including W. E. B. Du Bois and James Weldon Johnson, however, attempted to accentuate the aesthetics rather than the political.[2] Richard Wright famously rebelled against the prominence of aesthetics, favoring instead Black political militancy, in his

---

1. Barbara Christian has discussed Harper's *Iola Leroy* and Brown's *Clotel* as novels in conversation with Stowe's *Uncle's Tom Cabin* (19–32).

2. David Levering Lewis notes that writers and theorists of the Harlem Renaissance opposed the Black nationalism represented by Marcus Garvey (37).

oft-discussed 1937 essay "Blueprint for Negro Writing."[3] Some years later, James Baldwin in "Everybody's Protest Novel" returned to the debate regarding art and social protest in fiction and would famously repudiate the protest novel tradition by describing the novels of Stowe and Wright as pamphlet novels.[4] The emergence of the Black Arts Movements in the 1960s would once again swing the pendulum toward a social consciousness in Black arts and literature.

Past Latinx social protest writing, while not primarily engaged with the literary tradition of social protest, expands as far as the second part of the nineteenth century and is primarily found in Spanish-language print culture. New York City constituted the epicenter of Latinx protest and revolutionary writing in the 1890s, which was tied to revolutionary and independent movements in Latin American countries and the Caribbean; these writings are represented by the English- and Spanish-language essays, editorials, and poetry of José Martí, Francisco Gonzalo "Pachín" Marín, and Arturo Schomburg, among others (Luis xii). While these Latinx writers were excluded for the most part from mainstream publications and periodicals, their writings were printed in Spanish-language newspapers in New York City. Among these writers, Martí, similar to Douglass and other Black writers, engaged in the protest novel tradition. Martí translated into Spanish Helen Hunt Jackson's *Ramona*, published in 1884, in which Jackson famously attempted to recreate the success of Stowe's novel while trying to raise awareness of the plight and displacement of Native American populations by American and European settlers.[5] In subsequent decades, Jesús Colón, similar to Richard Wright was influenced by communism and the political militancy of the 1930s, engaged with the broader social protest tradition in the US in some of his newspaper writings of the 1940s.[6] Some of the writings of Martí and Colón represent instances when

---

3. Wright states, for example, that in "order to do justice to his subject matter, in order to depict Negro life in all its manifold and intricate relationships, a deep, informed, and complex [social] consciousness is necessary" ("Blueprint" 102). The title of Wright's first collection of short stories, *Uncle Tom's Children*, evokes Stowe's protest novel tradition.

4. Baldwin distanced himself from the protest novel tradition by describing Stowe as "not so much a novelist as an impassioned pamphleteer" ("Everybody's" 14). Baldwin also interprets Wright's *Native Son* as following in the steps of Stowe's novel since "Bigger [Thomas] is Uncle Tom's descendent, flesh of his flesh, so exactly opposite a portrait that, when the books are placed together, it seems that the contemporary Negro novelist and the dead New England woman are locked together in a deadly, timeless battle" ("Everybody's" 22). In "Many Thousands Gone," Baldwin more thoroughly attempts to distance his writings from Wright's *Native Son*.

5. For a discussion of Martí's translation of *Ramona* and Jackson's decision to follow the protest novel tradition started by Stowe's *Uncle Tom's Cabin*, see Gillman 244–49.

6. For example, in one of his newspaper columns Colón alludes to the "democratic revolutionary tradition" in the US represented by Thomas Paine, Elijah Lovejoy, and Eugene Debs (*Way It Was* 61).

Latinx authors engaged with the themes and tropes found in the American social protest tradition; however, just as in the case of Black writers, the resurgence of civil rights and protest movements in the 1960s would lead emerging Latinx writers to wrestle with the tension between art and social protest in their fiction.

The emergence of the Black and Chicanx civil rights movements of the late 1960s and early 1970s brought attention to the study of artistic works by authors of color, and conversely, individual artistic expression functioned in part as a window into the historical memory, traditions, and singularities of each group. Although art and social protest had a symbiotic relationship, some Black and Latinx authors after the 1960s such as James Baldwin and Rudolfo Anaya shared similar preoccupations regarding the dichotomy between artistic creation and social protest in their work. This tension was accentuated for Baldwin in light of his notoriety as a successful Black author, who at the same time acted as one of the most notorious spokespersons during the struggle for civil rights. To a lesser degree and outside the national spotlight, Anaya contributed to the Chicanx Movement in the Southwest as both an activist and artist. While the authors' experiences differed in degree, a comparative analysis of Baldwin's *Tell Me How Long the Train's Been Gone* (1968) and Anaya's *Bless Me, Ultima* (1972), written at the height of the struggle for civil rights, sheds light on the novels' parallels and the authors' aesthetic goals and social preoccupations.

This chapter explores the shared thematic elements in *Tell Me How Long* and *Bless Me, Ultima* in relation to their treatment and engagement with art and social protest. While both novels describe the emergence of young artists of color in marginalized communities, they also incorporate the experiences of soldiers of color during World War II to bring attention to the war as an important antecedent of the fight for civil rights of the late 1960s and early 1970s. Several critics have explored either *Tell Me How Long* or *Bless Me, Ultima* and the emergence of their protagonists as artists, while others have focused on the novels' lack or indirect treatment of social protest elements;[7] however, the tension between art and social protest in these narratives has not been explored by scholars in relation to their treatment of the experience of soldiers of color during and after World War II. I argue that through the war experiences of the protagonists' older brothers, *Tell Me How Long* and *Bless Me, Ultima* similarly highlight the contributions of soldiers of color to the war effort as they faced the dilemma of fighting a war for their country only to be denied full citizenship rights at home. I examine the relationship between the

---

7. See Bigsby 113–29; L. Scott 20–47; D. Miller 121–48; R. Saldívar, *Chicano Narrative* 103–26; Fernández Olmos 13–24; and Caminero-Santangelo, "Jasón's Indian" 115–28.

discrimination experienced by soldiers of color during the war and the social militancy it sparked among social activists and returning veterans. *Tell Me How Long* describes the heroic service of Black soldiers in battle on the Italian front and the different forms of institutionalized racism and discrimination experienced by Black soldiers that has an historical antecedent in the 92nd Infantry Division, known as the Buffalo Soldiers. *Bless Me, Ultima* focuses on the effects of the mobilization period in Mexican American communities in the Southwest and the psychological effects of the war and the lack of institutional support for Mexican American veterans as they returned to civilian life.

My analysis of *Tell Me How Long* and *Bless Me, Ultima* contributes to the ongoing efforts by scholars to highlight the often-neglected contributions and sacrifices of soldiers of color during the war effort—in this case through an analysis of fictional representations of the war—since their service, according to historians, has often been overlooked in representative historical narratives of World War II.[8] Baldwin and Anaya represent only two examples among the many authors of color who fictionalized the mobilization period or the experiences of Black and Mexican American World War II soldiers.[9] The points of convergence and parallels in the artistic and social trajectories of Baldwin and Anaya—and their shared emphasis in their fiction on the influence of World War II on soldiers of color and their communities—reflect some of the commonalities among Black and Latinx writers after the 1960s. While it is important to emphasize the distinctiveness of each group's histories, cultures, and aesthetic works, it is equally valuable to call attention to some of their shared histories of social marginalization and how writers of color fought against those histories at important moments in US history.

BALDWIN AND ANAYA AS RELUCTANT SPOKESPERSONS FOR CIVIL RIGHTS

Much has been said regarding the tension between art and social protest in Baldwin, a trait that marked his social activism and writing career.[10] Already in the late 1950s and early 1960s, critics debated Baldwin's distinct roles as

8. On the efforts to bring attention to the role of Black and Mexican American soldiers during World War II, see Rivas-Rodriguez and Olgín 3; and Moore vii.

9. Representative works include Ralph Ellison's "Flying Home," Chester Himes's *If He Hollers Let Him Go*, William Gardner Smith's *Last of the Conquerors*, John Oliver Killens's *And Then We Heard the Thunder*, Villarreal's *Pocho*, Luis Valdez's *Zoot Suit*, and Américo Paredes's *The Hammon and the Beans and Other Stories*.

10. For discussions on the relation between art and social protest in Baldwin's work, see Standley 43–54; Leeming 216–52; Bigsby 113–29; and Baker, "Embattled" 62–77.

writer and activist; Fred Standley, for instance, observes that since the beginning of Baldwin's writing career, reviewers, commentators, and the general public saw Baldwin as "two James Baldwins," one the writer, and the other a spokesperson for civil rights (43). Baldwin struggled throughout most of his career with a need for artistic individuality and the pressure to serve as a spokesperson for Blacks.[11] Early in his career, Baldwin thought about the craft of writing primarily as an artistic endeavor, and his early notoriety grew when he chastised his mentor Richard Wright in "Everybody's Protest Novel" for being overly political in his fiction.[12] In some of his essays, Baldwin portrayed himself as an artist rather than an activist, and he described his main social responsibility as to "get [his] work done" and be "a good writer" ("Autobiographical" 9). Baldwin's statements regarding the incompatibility between art and social protest, however, mask his relentless social activism.

Since the start of his writing career, Baldwin emerged as an exceptionally engaged civil rights activist and supported, at different periods, the nonviolent and militant factions emerging in the late 1960s. In *No Name in the Street*, Baldwin recounts his early trip in 1957 to Southern cities at the center of civil rights unrest, where he met Martin Luther King Jr. in Atlanta for the first time.[13] In subsequent years, Baldwin met other civil rights figures such as James Meredith and Medgar Evers.[14] At this time, Baldwin became an active supporter of King's vision and sociopolitical strategy and acted in a leadership role during the March on Washington in 1963 (*No Name* 138–39). During the 1960s, Baldwin remained actively engaged by making trips to various cities, attending meetings and fundraisers, and serving as a chronicler of the movement (Weatherby 140). In time, however, Baldwin began to doubt the effectiveness of King's nonviolent strategy and became attracted to the confrontational tactics of emerging militant leaders such as Malcolm X and Huey Newton.[15] His creative work at this time reflected an ideological shift toward a more confrontational stance; *Blues for Mr. Charlie*, for instance, stands as a militant play based in part on the murder of Emmett Till and was dedicated to Evers after his assassination. The death of King in 1968 marked the end of Baldwin's active engagement with civil rights causes as he gradually faded from the spotlight and relocated permanently in France.

---

11. See Field 53 and Weatherby 181.

12. For a discussion of the well-known confrontation and subsequent chasm between Baldwin and Wright created by the former's essay, see Campbell 62–70.

13. In *No Name in the Street*, Baldwin describes his firsthand experience with Jim Crow segregation in Montgomery, Alabama (50–81). For another account of Baldwin's first Southern trip, see Leeming 135–47.

14. See Weatherby 208–9 and Leeming 216–19.

15. For Baldwin's views on Malcolm X, Newton, and the Black Panther Party, see *No Name in the Street* 92–100 and 169–78.

Similar to Baldwin, Anaya's early writing career was closely connected to the social activism among Mexican American communities in the Southwest in the late 1960s and early 1970s. In an autobiographical piece, Anaya describes the relation between his artistic work and Mexican Americans' fight for civil rights as he was attracted and influenced by social and political activists, including César Chávez, Reies Lopez Tijerina, and Rodolfo "Corky" Gonzales, and followed their steps by "organiz[ing] the first teachers' union in the Albuquerque school system" and opposing the Vietnam War ("Autobiography" 378–79). Anaya saw the Chicanx Movement as a galvanizing force that brought Mexican American artists and activists together, thus helping them to define their identity and a "sense of worth and destiny" (380). In Anaya's own account, his contribution to the movement in the late 1960s was primarily as a writer behind the scenes while working on his first novel, *Bless Me, Ultima*, which was embraced by most Chicanx activists and Mexican American communities in the Southwest as a fitting aesthetic expression that contributed to their social struggle.

In the early 1970s, Anaya expressed his ambivalence regarding the demands that the Chicanx Movement placed on emerging Mexican American writers and artists. Although Anaya acknowledged that his work achieved recognition due in part to the Chicanx Movement, he remained uneasy about the "pressure put on Chicano writers to be political" (Dick and Sirias xii). In later years, however, Anaya's fiction engaged explicitly with social and political themes; for instance, Anaya's second novel, *Heart of Aztlán*, contains a social critique regarding the economic conditions of Mexican Americans in urban areas (Anaya, "Interview" 3–4). Anaya's ambivalence continued for the remainder of the decade; in a 1979 interview, for example, Anaya stated, "We can proceed from one cliché, that all work, every act of life, is political, to the other side of the board that says art exists for itself, in and of itself. Somewhere in the middle I would find my place. I have never set out to write a political work" (Anaya, "Rudolfo" 18). Anaya and Baldwin searched for artistic independence and repeatedly contested the notion that artists were constrained by the demands from their communities; however, similar to the way these writers use their personal experiences to enrich their craft, their narratives also reflect the struggles of their respective marginalized groups and how their communities' fights for civil rights were influenced by World War II.

WORLD WAR II AND EARLY FIGHTS FOR CIVIL RIGHTS

World War II represents a critical social and political moment in the struggles for civil rights by people of color. Jacquelyn Hall, for instance, has argued that World War II stands as one in a series of struggles for civil rights that began in the "radical milieu of the late 1930s" and continued through "the New Deal Order," which combined to form part of the "long civil rights movement" (1235).[16] Other historians have also focused on the racism and discrimination experienced by Black and Mexican American soldiers during the war years and how protests to end discrimination in the military influenced the civil rights movements of future decades.[17] Black soldiers during World War II experienced entrenched institutionalized racism and discrimination while in service of their country. The roots of the discrimination against Black soldiers in World War II dates back to the military racial policies of previous wars; when World War II began, some Black leaders referred to the mistreatment of Black soldiers during World War I to oppose their participation in the war;[18] thus, Blacks faced the dilemma of enlisting and fighting for a country that had systematically violated their rights and freedoms. Once enlisted, Blacks served in segregated units, and with a few exceptions, their tasks consisted of maintaining the infrastructure of the war effort.[19] Black soldiers' personal recollections and testimonials of their conditions while in uniform shed light on the army's racial policies.[20] An equally disquieting aspect of the racism experienced by Blacks while serving was the bias of the military justice system.

---

16. According to Hall, the social protest movement against racial discrimination in the labor market and the military during World War II represents a link in a series of historical events that "accelerated" the rise of the "classical" phase of the civil rights movement of the 1960s and 1970s (1235).

17. Richard Dalfiume, for instance, has described the emergence of a Black militancy during World War II as the "forgotten years" in the fight for civil rights, since the protests against the discriminatory practices experienced by Blacks during the war laid the groundwork for the Black civil rights movement of later years ("Forgotten Years" 106). See also Neil Wynn, Kimberley Phillips, Christine Knauer, Maggie Rivas-Rodríguez, B. V. Olgín, Richard Griswold del Castillo, and Steven Rosales.

18. For accounts of the racist and discriminatory practices against Black soldiers during World War I, see Dalfiume, *Desegregation* 7–21; and Booker 11–31.

19. Bryan Booker notes that Black soldiers primarily served as the hard labor for the war infrastructure by building roads, bridges, airfields, installing pipelines, driving supply trucks, fueling vehicles and aircrafts, loading and uploading supplies, and cooking meals (60). For other descriptions of the systematic segregation of Blacks in the armed forces during World War II, see Franklin and Moss 386–99; and M. Levine 167–69.

20. For instance, a Black soldier in Camp Barkeley, Texas, wrote a letter to a civilian aid describing segregated facilities and racist practices, such as requiring Black soldiers to sit at the back in local buses, and even how German POWs were allowed into the segregated restrooms for whites, which made him conclude in his letter that "seeing this was honestly disheartening. It made me feel, here, the tyrant is actually placed over the liberator" (qtd. in Wynn 118–19). For an overview of the army's racial policies, see also Booker 192–93. For a discussion on the segregation of Black soldiers, particularly vis-à-vis German POWs and during the deployment of Black troops in postwar Germany, see Fehrenbach 19–28.

Neil Wynn, for instance, observes that although Black soldiers represented only 8 percent of the American forces, "they accounted for 21 percent of all those convicted of crimes and 42 percent of those convicted of sex crimes" (53). A telling example of these practices was the case of Louis Till, Emmett Till's father, who "was charged with rape and murder while serving with a transportation company in Italy" and executed abroad in 1945 (Phillips 170).

Latinx soldiers during World War II were also subjected to discriminatory practices, just as were Blacks, albeit to different degrees. Similar to Blacks, Mexican Americans in the Southwest at the outset of the war faced the dilemma of affirming their patriotism by joining the army while they were "treated as outcasts" in their own communities (Griswold del Castillo, "Paradox of War" 20). Black and Latinx soldiers served in disproportionately higher numbers in relation to their numbers vis-à-vis the entire US population;[21] likewise, Latinx soldiers were marginalized in the army; for instance, Steven Rosales points out that while Mexican American soldiers did not serve in segregated units, "discriminatory treatment often associated with racialized 'others' remained [their] de facto reality" (5).[22] Kimberley Phillips adds that although "many Mexican Americans and Native Americans served in integrated units," some Puerto Ricans were classified as "Puerto Rican Negroes" and were assigned to segregated units, which meant that "all of these groups faced discrimination and racial violence, and they debated the association of military participation with their pursuit of equal rights" (5). Indeed, Afro-Latinx soldiers found themselves in the paradoxical situation of fighting for freedom on the Pacific front while assigned to segregated units.[23]

The treatment of Blacks and Mexican Americans during the war years reinvigorated social activism among their groups and led to significant early civil rights victories. The origins of the March on Washington of 1963—one of the landmark events of the civil rights era—can be traced to the major social shifts brought by the war and early efforts by social activists such as A. Philip Randolph to protest racial discrimination in the early 1940s. Randolph's leadership was instrumental in the planning of the original march on Washington in 1942 that was halted only after President Franklin Roosevelt banned dis-

---

21. The consensus among scholars is that more than one million Blacks, and at least a quarter million Latinx people, served during World War II. On the numbers of soldiers of color who served in World War II and their disproportionate numbers in relation to the entire population, see Moore 29, Franklin and Moss 390, and Acuña, *Occupied* 323.

22. Similar to Blacks, military service for Mexican Americans "also meant continued exposure to discriminatory practices and segregated facilities at domestic military bases" (Rosales 55).

23. See Afro-Latinx Evelio Grillo's memoir *Black Cuban, Black American* in which Grillo recounts his experiences during World War II serving in a segregated unit.

crimination in defense manufacturing plants.[24] Randolph's relentless activism after the war was similarly responsible for one of the most substantial victories against racial discrimination when President Harry Truman ended racial segregation in the US Armed Forces with Executive Order 9981 in 1948 (M. Levine 175–76).[25] In addition, as a direct result of Blacks' service during the war, civil rights activism increased. According to Michael Levine, membership to the National Association for the Advancement of Colored People (NAACP) "soared from 51,000 in 1940 to 351,000 in 1945" (171).[26] Likewise, Mexican Americans fought a war abroad for freedom just to return to a segregated society structured around Jim Crow–style laws in the Southwest. Similar to Black veterans, when Mexican American soldiers returned from the war, they continued to experience segregation and structural racism in housing, the workplace, education, and public facilities in most of the Southwest.[27] The social and political activism of Mexican American veterans such as Dr. Hector P. García contributed to the activism that subsequently spread across the Southwest and other states. Under the leadership of García, the G.I. Forum was created in 1948 by returning Mexican American soldiers wanting to fight against discriminatory practices suffered by Mexican American veterans in Texas.[28] World War II, however, represents one among other major military conflicts including the Korean War and the Cold War that contributed to social gains by people of color in the postwar years.[29]

---

24. Under the leadership of Randolph, 22,000 Blacks rallied to protest employment discrimination on June 22, 1941. Trying to garnish the support from Blacks for his third term, Roosevelt issued Executive Order 8802, "prohibiting racial discrimination in federal government employment" (Moore 27–28).

25. Hall correctly notes that Randolph's militancy through demonstrations made racial discrimination part of "the national agenda for the first time since Reconstruction" (1248).

26. For discussions on the violence endured by Black veterans at home and the growth of political organizations such as the NAACP, see Wynn 83–97 and M. Levine 171–79.

27. On the segregation of Mexican American communities in the Southwest, see Acuña, *Occupied* 330; Griswold del Castillo, "Paradox of War" 11–15 and "War" 57–62; and Rosales 25–29.

28. Most famously, García protested and successfully resolved the case of Felix Longoria Jr., a fallen returning soldier who initially was denied the use of a funeral chapel in his hometown of Three Rivers, Texas, in 1945 (Rivas-Rodriguez 201).

29. Some historians have argued that the Korean War—rather than Truman's executive order—ended segregation in the armed forces, since this became the first time when the army integrated its combat units. For discussions on the Korean War's role on the army's racial policies, see Knauer 133–34; Rosales 73; and Heidi Fehrenbach 18–19. On the role of the Cold War in the fight for civil rights in the 1950s and 1960s, see Dalfiume, *Desegregation* 132–40; Hall 1248–49; and Phillips 152–62.

Baldwin's writings reflect his distress for the racialized violence experienced by Black soldiers and veterans at home despite their service.[30] Baldwin's *Go Tell It on the Mountain* contains a brief but disturbing episode that captures this racial violence through the image of a lynched and castrated Black soldier; the novel describes the "dead body of a soldier, his uniform shredded where he had been flogged, and, turned upward through the black skin, raw, red meat" (141). The image not only embodies the "nightmarish history" of race relations in America, as Horace Porter suggests ("South" 68), but also accentuates the racial hatred experienced by Black veterans who risked their lives fighting for their country only to die violently and inhumanely at the hands of their fellow citizens. Baldwin experienced firsthand the mobilization period and wrote about the discrimination experienced by Blacks in the army as a turning point in the fight for civil rights. Although Baldwin did not serve during the war, David Leeming observes that the "draft was a real possibility for him, though he would probably be deferred, as the oldest male child of a family consisting of a jobless father in ill health, a working mother, and eight hungry brothers and sisters" (37). Baldwin, however, encountered discrimination while working in the manufacturing industry, the exact type of discrimination that Randolph and other activists fought to end.[31] In *The Fire Next Time*, Baldwin refers to the systematic discrimination of Black soldiers who risked their lives for their country by observing that the "treatment accorded [to] the Negro during the Second World War mark[ed] . . . a turning point in the Negro's relation to America" (68). Baldwin goes on to describe the marginalized position of Black soldiers in the army that contributed to their social militancy after the war; he asks his readers to put themselves "in the skin of a man who is wearing the uniform of his country, is a candidate for death in its defense, and who is called a 'nigger' by his comrades-in-arms and his officers; who is almost always given the hardest, ugliest, most menial work to do. . . . And who, at the same time, as a human being, is far freer in a strange land than he has ever been at home. *Home!*" (*Fire Next Time* 68). Baldwin's vivid evocation of the racism experienced by Black soldiers, and the

---

30. According to historians, returning World War I Black veterans faced racial hatred and violence in the form of bloody race riots and gruesome lynchings, some of them while still in uniform. Debra Sheffer explains that "in 1918, eleven black veterans were lynched. In 1919, seventy-eight black veterans were lynched, with fourteen of those burned alive and several killed while still wearing their uniform" (184–85). See also Dalfiume, "Forgotten Years" 92; Phillips 7; and Wynn 13.

31. Campbell observes that after leaving school in 1941, Baldwin worked as a railroad hand at the US Army Quartermaster Depot at Belle Mead near Princeton, New Jersey, where he experienced racial discrimination (23–25).

lack of recognition or opportunities back home, constituted for Baldwin an important moment in Blacks' struggle for social equality.

Anaya also directly experienced the effects of World War II on Mexican American soldiers and their communities; he witnessed and was part of the exodus of working-class Mexican American families from small towns to larger urban cities in the Southwest accelerated in part by the job opportunities created by the war effort. In an interview, Anaya explains his close connection to the war while growing up by noting, "I grew up during World War II. Three of my brothers were in the service. When I started school, I remember the war was a topic. We used to save dimes and tin foil. The people that had sons or daughters in the service were very concerned. I remember when a serviceman got killed that the community would draw together" (N. García 13). Anaya also discussed the impact the war had on *Nuevomexicano* communities, as new opportunities became available for Mexican Americans after the postwar years, and the benefits of the G.I. Bill for some Mexican American veterans who were able to attend college (Crawford 105). While writing at the height of the civil rights era, Baldwin and Anaya further developed and thematized the significance of the war for soldiers of color and their communities.

THE SERVICE OF BLACK SOLDIERS IN COMBAT UNITS ON THE EUROPEAN FRONT

Baldwin's emergence as a leading writer reflects the struggle for literary recognition by pre-1960s Black writers who were assisted by social and cultural organizations that allowed them to write and get published in mainstream venues. Similar to some of his contemporaries, including Wright, Margaret Walker, and Ralph Ellison, Baldwin began his writing career by publishing in mainstream publications tied to social and cultural organizations. Baldwin wrote for *New Leader, Partisan Review,* and *Commentary* (Babb 118);[32] these publications were connected to larger cultural or political organizations that emphasized the inclusion of writers from previously excluded groups;[33] with

---

32. Baldwin's most famous essays, "Everybody's Protest Novel," for example, appeared in *Partisan Review* in 1949.

33. *New Leader,* a New York City–based magazine, had ties to socialist organizations; *Partisan Review* was associated with the Communist Party and the John Reed Club of New York; *Commentary* was created by the Jewish American Committee. Lawrence Jackson explores in detail the connection between some of these publications and pre-1960s Black authors (*Indignant* 7).

the assistance of Wright, for instance, Baldwin received a Rosenwald fellow-ship, which was part of the Rosenwald fund, a philanthropic organization with an emphasis on reaching Black writers (Jackson, *Indignant* 9–10). With the assistance of the Rosenwald fellowship, Baldwin was able to write *Go Tell It on the Mountain*, which was published by Alfred A. Knopf in 1953 with favorable reviews (Leeming 89). Baldwin also used part of the money from the Rosen-wald fellowship to move to Paris in 1948, following in the footsteps of Wright (Campbell 44). Baldwin wrote in France for years but returned to America in 1957 to participate in the fight for civil rights led by Dr. King.

The critical reception of *Tell Me How Long* after its publication was mixed, and this ambivalence has continued to the present.[34] Contemporary assess-ments of *Tell Me How Long* show a similar apprehension or praise regarding its aesthetic value and the way it compares to other Baldwin novels.[35] Some scholars have explored the novel's elements of social protest by focusing on Baldwin's attraction, after the mid-1960s, to the emerging Black militancy rep-resented in the novel through the character of Black Christopher.[36] William Weatherby, for instance, notes that Baldwin "wanted the novel to be topi-cal and reflect the change in the civil rights movement between the genera-tions of King and Stokely Carmichael" (279). Although the novel emphasizes Christopher's Black militancy, he remains an intermittent character who is not fully developed until the last section of the novel; Douglas Field rightly points out that Christopher appears only "for a dozen or so pages" (78). While *Tell Me How Long* engages with artistic creation in the form of Leo Proudham-mer's rise as a theater performer in a segregated society, an overlooked politi-cal aspect of the novel is the relationship between Leo and his older brother, Caleb, and how the latter's service abroad as a combat soldier during World War II is tied to Blacks' fight for civil rights.

Tell Me How Long depicts the emergence of a Black artist in a marginalized community confronting weak family ties, poverty, and instances of racialized violence. The narrative contrasts Leo's artistic aspirations growing up with his father's immigrant background and his mother's modest Southern roots. Leo remembers his family's poverty as a child when his father lost his job and his mother began to work as a maid, which ultimately places the family "on relief" (118). His childhood is marked by an episode between the brothers and white police officers in Harlem. After they are stopped and threatened without prov-ocation while walking back to their house, Caleb teaches Leo that policemen are "going to hate [him] as long as [he] live[s] just because [he is] black" (60);

---

34. See, for example, Puzo 155–58; and John Thompson.
35. Field 77 and Campbell 226.
36. See L. Scott 20–47; D. Miller 126–40; Berghahn 103–8; and Field 77–81.

this and similar episodes of white violence toward Blacks in the novel represent instances of social denunciation. As D. Quentin Miller points out, racism and violence toward Blacks by white officers show that "rage against white policemen is unmistakabl[y]" present in *Tell Me How Long* and is connected to "countless other depictions of police racism in Baldwin's work" (136). The systematic disenfranchisement and discrimination experienced by the brothers during their youth force them to eventually seek opportunities outside their community.

Leo's artistic aspirations equally clash with instances of racial prejudice in mainstream artistic circles that show the prevailing exclusion of artists of color during the postwar years. Leo's artistic rise puts him in contact with an elitist white society that is considerably more affluent and culturally sophisticated than his Harlem community. D. Quentin Miller correctly observes that Leo's actions make him seem as "someone who has betrayed the downtrodden of his race for the approval of the rich and powerful whites" (133); his artistic ascendance, however, is marked by a constant struggle to rise above racial stereotypes and social barriers. For instance, when Leo meets his white patrons and theater producers, Lola and Saul San-Marquand, for the first time at a formal gathering in a Park Avenue apartment, he is requested to play the piano; he acquiesces and "sing[s] a blues" since it is assumed that his skin color makes him a good singer and entertainer (100). Leo encounters multiple instances of veiled and open racism during his time as an apprentice at the San-Marquand's theater workshop located in a small town in Upstate New York. Based on his abilities and talent, Leo succeeds as a performer but is unable to gain full acceptance into mainstream cultural circles.

Tell Me How Long presents the dilemma for Blacks during the war as they were asked to serve and fight for a country that had historically excluded them. When Caleb is seventeen years old, he is implicated as an accomplice in a stabbing and robbery at a store, for which he serves several years on a prison farm in the Deep South. After he returns to Harlem, Caleb secures a menial job in the New York garment district, but due to the racism he experiences the first day at work—which his father endured at the same workplace for years—he leaves and eventually enlists in the army. When Leo is nineteen years old, and is in a position to serve, he initially refuses to enlist based on political principles; he reasons that he does not want to fight for a country that restricts the rights of Blacks and other people of color. While Leo is an apprentice at the theater workshop, he is asked by a new Black acquaintance, Matthew, if he would like to fight in the army; Leo thinks Matthew "must be joking" since he would "rather drop dead than fight for this miserable country" (177, 178). After

Caleb enlists, Leo is ready to be drafted, but he is deferred since his parents depend on him and he has a brother who is already serving. Although Leo consciously avoids voicing his opinions about the war to members of the army draft board, he harbors a strong resentment for the treatment of people of color not only at that time but throughout most of the country's history. Leo does not want "to fight for the people who had interned [the Japanese], who had also destroyed the Indians, [and] who were in the process of destroying everyone [he] loved" (347). While Leo remains skeptical of the army, Caleb sees it as one of his few alternatives to improve his position in society.

Caleb's experiences while serving are marked by the prevailing racial segregation in the army and the different attitudes toward Black soldiers during his deployment in Europe. Caleb enlists without conviction since he knows that the armed forces are segregated, but he also knows that they "can use [him] now"—regardless of his race—since the army "got a war to fight" (219). After his return from the war, Caleb explains to Leo that all of his friends were Black since the army "keep[s] the black and white separated" (392). Caleb, however, realizes that the racial prejudices prevalent at home were absent for the most part in Europe. When Caleb arrives in Rome, Italy, he is struck by the lack of race consciousness among some Italian women. He observes that they were "not at all like the [white] women" back home and "[didn't] look at [Blacks] like women" in New York, as if they were "scared to be in the same street with [them]" (394). Caleb describes how some off-duty white and Black soldiers mixed together socially in Italy while other white soldiers were openly hostile and unable to hide their frustration with Italians' more lenient attitudes toward race. Caleb's experiences resemble those of other Black soldiers who "commented on the feelings of freedom they experienced in Europe, which often significantly affected their attitudes upon their return home" (Wynn 53); similarly, Caleb's outlook is transformed by his experience abroad.

Caleb's portrayal as a combat soldier has major social implications as it highlights the value and bravery of Black soldiers and their growing militancy after the war. Caleb's experiences reflect those of the relatively few Blacks in combat units such as the Buffalo Soldiers. The fact that Caleb serves in a combat position is significant since the majority of Blacks who served were not allowed to carry weapons or serve in offensive units. As Christopher Moore notes, "Following Pearl Harbor, American military racial policy became simple: black soldiers were not generally asked to carry guns, but they were ordered to carry nearly everything else" (51). While *Tell Me How Long* lacks an overt reference to the Buffalo Soldiers, the description of Caleb's role in combat resembles the historical trajectory of the 92nd Infantry Division during the Allied invasion of Italy in 1943.[37] Although the novel is ambiguous regarding Caleb's role on the Italian front, he tells Leo that he saw "men dying all around [him]" and "bombs going off and howling and screaming and moaning and the fear of death and the shadow of death" (390, 391). Caleb notes that although he had "no right to kill," he "was shooting because [he] was a soldier, and people were shooting at [him]" (391). By making Caleb a combat soldier, *Tell Me How Long* contests the long-held misconception shared by whites that Blacks were unable to serve in combat units (Phillips 6). These soldiers also gained a new sense of their role in society; a testimonial from James Tillman, an Army Sergeant from the 92nd Infantry Division, refers to the larger significance of his service: "We had to prove that blacks would fight. . . . If we failed, the whole black race would fail. We were fighting for the flag and for our rights. We knew that this would be the beginning of breaking down segregation" (qtd. in Latty and Tarver 41).

Tell Me How Long contains a critique of the lack of social and economic support given to Black veterans as many of them continued to experience racism and discrimination at home, suffered the negative effects of combat, and were seldom recognized for their service. In *Fire Next Time,* Baldwin describes how "before and then during the Second World War, many of [his] friends fled into the service, all to be changed there, and rarely for the better, many to be ruined, and many to die" (34). Although some Black veterans took advantage of the G.I. Bill and other benefits, others were unable to receive educational or economic benefits due to their precarious social circumstances (Moore 321). During a discussion in *Tell Me How Long* between Leo and two Black men regarding the prospects for Black soldiers after the war, Fowler, one of Leo's acquaintances, thinks that his younger friend, Matthew, has a "great opportunity to go in the Army," enroll in school, and "make something of himself when he comes out" (178). Matthew, however, is reluctant to enlist since he is more realistic about the opportunities for Black veterans; he does not believe what he has heard "about this fine job [he is] going to get when [he] come[s] out [of] the Army" since he does not know any Blacks who "got fine jobs" (179). Matthew's skepticism reflects historical accounts related to the scarcity of opportunities for Black veterans in both Northern cities and those in the South living under Jim Crow.[38]

---

37. The Buffalo Soldiers gained ground and strategic positions and suffered setbacks from September 1944 to April 1945 while engaged in combat near Viareggio and Genoa, Italy (Moore 267–68). On the Buffalo Soldiers on the Italian front, see also Franklin and Moss 393–94; Hargrove 4–14; and Moore 259–72.

38. See Franklin and Moss 421; and Phillips 86–99.

Caleb, however, is able to turn his life around and advance his social position after the war. While in combat, Caleb is wounded and has a born-again conversion; when he returns to Harlem, he works as a "chauffeur for some broker," forms a family, and becomes an assistant pastor at The New Dispensation House of God in Harlem (379). Caleb's trajectory resembles that of some veterans who, despite discrimination and lack of job opportunities, were able to climb the social ladder with the assistance of local religious institutions (Franklin and Moss 413). The testimonial of James Tillman, the veteran Buffalo Soldier, closely parallels Caleb's experience; Tillman returned to a still segregated society, but he was changed, as he explains: "No one ever had any kind of celebration that included us as far as I know. . . . When I came home I couldn't even get a job. But while in the Army I vowed that if I lived, I would go back to my father's church, change my ways, and be thankful" (qtd. in Latty and Tarver 42–43). In *Tell Me How Long,* Caleb becomes "a respected man" who "has made something of himself . . . [and] made it out of nothing" (340). Although Caleb's fate after his return may not be representative, the novel's enduring image is one of a Black soldier who despite entrenched racism in the army honorably serves his country and is transformed by his service; thus, bringing attention to the war as a crucial episode in the "long" fight for social justice.

THE EFFECTS OF MOBILIZATION IN MEXICAN AMERICAN COMMUNITIES

The publication history of Rudolfo Anaya's *Bless Me, Ultima* is closely related to the history of the Mexican American independent publisher Quinto Sol, the long fight for literary inclusion by Latinx writers, and the Chicanx Movement. Pre-1960s Latinx writers in the Southwest and on the East Coast were unable to get published by mainstream publishers.[39] After graduating from the University of New Mexico, Anaya worked as a schoolteacher in Albuquerque and wrote *Bless Me, Ultima* during those years, and subsequently tried to find a New York or Boston publisher for his novel without success (Fernández Olmos 6–7). Octavio Romano's independent publishing house, Quinto Sol, was instrumental in offering to Mexican American writers opportuni-

---

39. For instance, while Jesús Colón wrote in the 1940s and 1950s, his book of essays, or "sketches," wasn't published by an independent New York publisher, Masses and Mainstream, until 1961. Other similar pre-1960s cases include the publication histories of Américo Paredes, Jovita González, and Mario Suárez.

ties that would change the trajectory of Latinx literature.[40] While reading the journal *El Grito*, Anaya came across a call for manuscripts from Quinto Sol (Fernández Olmos 7). *Bless Me, Ultima* was published in 1972 by Quinto Sol, won the Quinto Sol Award, and became the first Mexican American best-seller (Martín-Rodríguez, *Life in Search* 33). Romano's explicit goal to promote Mexican American writers was the direct result of the reemerging social and political militancy among Mexican Americans across the Southwest in 1960s. *Bless Me, Ultima* as a cultural text represents the convergence of the political and the artistic during the Chicanx Movement.

Anaya's *Bless Me, Ultima* has remained one of the most widely read and analyzed Mexican American novels since its publication at the height of the Chicanx Movement. Critics have examined *Bless Me, Ultima*'s engagement with social protest, or the lack of it, since its publication.[41] A controversy ensued when the 1972 publication of *Bless Me, Ultima* coincided with the resurgence of social and political activism by Mexican Americans across the Southwest. Marta Caminero-Santangelo, for example, explains how some early critics felt *Bless Me, Ultima* was not "connected to the larger social and iden-tity issues at the heart of the Chicano movement of the 1960s and the early 1970s" ("Jasón's Indian" 115). Anaya has pointed out that within the Mexican American civil rights movement, there were some Chicanx activists who ques-tioned *Bless Me, Ultima* since they believed the novel had "no social value rel-evant to the working class" ("Autobiography" 383). The novel's apparent lack of political themes, however, was interpreted by other commentators at the time as part of its strength and "enduring legacy" (Fernández Olmos 20–21). Since then, other scholars have argued that the novel indeed contains an ideo-logical and political message. Horst Tonn, for instance, maintains that since *Bless Me, Ultima* engages with Mexican American myths, history, and culture, the novel resonates with the Chicanx Movement's search for identity as the "formation of an identity is inconceivable without sound knowledge of the past" (4).[42] Despite the robust critical engagement regarding *Bless Me, Ultima*'s omission or indirect treatment of political and social issues, not enough atten-tion has been given to the novel's depiction of Mexican American soldiers during World War II through the portrayal of Antonio Márez's three older

40. For assessments on the influence of Quinto Sol in Latinx literature starting in the early 1960s, see Martín-Rodríguez, *Life in Search* 16–22; and Cutler, *Ends of Assimilation* 56–71.

41. See Tonn 4–7; Fernández Olmos 20–21; Caminero-Santangelo, "Jasón's Indian" 115; and Kevane 34.

42. Caminero-Santangelo presents a similar interpretation when she explains that *Bless Me, Ultima* "fully participates in the imaginative project of the Chicano movement" by laying "the groundwork for an understanding of Chicanos/as as 'people'" ("Jasón's Indian" 124).

brothers, León, Andrés, and Eugenio.[43] *Bless Me, Ultima* contains narrative and thematic parallels to Baldwin's *Tell Me How Long* as both novels depict the formative experiences of artists of color within their communities and the experiences of soldiers of color during World War II.

Bless Me, Ultima is a bildungsroman or coming-of-age narrative that engages with individual artistic expression and self-discovery by presenting Antonio growing up in a *Nuevomexicano* community.[44] Since Anaya's narrative stops when Antonio is still a child, his adult profession is unclear; however, the fact that Antonio goes on to tell his story suggests that he embraced writing as a profession. Ramón Saldívar has discussed Anaya's novel not only as a bildungsroman but also as a *Künstlerroman* by focusing on Antonio's growth as an emerging artist.[45] Some elements in *Bless Me, Ultima* such as the setting and characters are based on Anaya's experience as an emerging artist of color, and Antonio's early attraction to writing reflects a similar interest in Anaya.[46] When Antonio begins his formal education at a predominantly white school in a nearby town, he is attracted to learning and language as he discovers "the magic in the letters" (58). As the novel progresses, Antonio develops a singular view of the world that combines a sense of place, cultural identity, and language that will influence his identity as a writer.

Bless Me, Ultima emphasizes the rich culture and folklore of a *Nuevomexicano* community in the Southwest that is embraced by Antonio during his formative years through the guidance of his family and Ultima. While Antonio's mother expects he will use his aptitude for language and writing to become a priest in their community—which creates a tension between artistic individuality and community ties—he learns about his family's ancestral connection to the land and traditions.[47] When Ultima comes to live with the Márez, she and Antonio begin a journey of discovery and deep appreciation for the role that Ultima's cultural traditions play in the community. Héctor Calderón, for instance, correctly observes that Ultima embodies a culture and knowledge

---

43. Representative analyses of *Bless Me, Ultima* mention World War II but only peripherally; see, for example, Tonn 7; R. Saldívar's *Chicano Narrative* 113; Calderón 39; and Cantú 45.

44. For critics who have discussed *Bless Me, Ultima* as a bildungsroman, or coming-of-age story, see Fernández Olmos 16–17; Kevane 35; and Caminero-Santangelo, "Jasón's Indian" 115.

45. R. Saldívar suggests this outcome when he observes that, with Ultima's death, Antonio "turn[s] to art in the form of the writing of [his own] story" (*Chicano* 122).

46. On the similarities between Anaya's background and Antonio's experiences in *Bless Me, Ultima*, see Anaya, "Autobiography" 359–65, "Rudolfo" 12–13, and "Magic of Words" 177; and Baeza 2–7.

47. In an essay, Anaya reflects on this tension when he observes that the writer is "the mirror of the community from which he takes his material, and yet he is apart from [the community]" ("Silence" 57).

that comes from "the prehistory of the Southwest" and "possesses the collective memory of the mestizo race. . . . She instills in Antonio a respect for the spirit of all living things and a faith in the eventual goodness of nature" (42).[48] Unlike Baldwin's protagonist in *Tell Me How Long,* who distances himself from his parents' cultural traditions and is determined to overcome his social exclusion, Antonio's family traditions and community enrich his aesthetic vision.

While Anaya's narrative recounts Antonio's artistic journey, *Bless Me, Ultima* engages with social protest by describing the effects of the mobilization during World War II and the toll on Mexican American communities caused by soldiers' casualties. The narrative begins when Ultima comes to live with the Márez family since people in her town are now "scattered, driven like tumbleweeds by the winds of war" that have taken "the young boys overseas" (3). Other families have felt the effects of absent men in Las Pasturas who went to fight abroad; Antonio describes the town's changed landscape and how his "mother and Ultima dressed in black because so many women of the town had lost sons or husbands in the war" and "were in mourning" (32). The war's aftermath in other Mexican American communities in New Mexico is similarly alluded to as some families bury their sons. Antonio remembers that "almost every day there [was] a tolling of the bells for a son that [was] lost to the war" (48). Based on the war's effect on his community, Prudencio Luna, Antonio's grandfather, declares that the "war is terrible" since it takes men "away from the field," while disapproving of the army for giving soldiers "guns and [telling] them to kill each other" (49). The war, however, is felt even closer by Antonio, as his three older brothers serve in the army and survive the war.

While *Bless Me, Ultima* does not contain a detailed depiction of Mexican American soldiers in combat, the narrative alludes to the experiences of Antonio's brothers as servicemen overseas. Mexican American soldiers often served in combat positions during the war and in contrast to Black soldiers, they did not serve in segregated units but experienced discrimination (Griswold del Castillo, "War" 50). Hierarchies in the army limited the opportunities for Mexican American soldiers to hold leadership positions. Critics have pointed out the peripheral position Antonio's three brothers and their war experience have in the narrative;[49] nonetheless, the fact that Antonio's brothers are enlisted servicemen calls attention to the way Mexican Americans expe-

---

48. Other critics have discussed Ultima as an embodiment of some Mexican American and Native American customs and the influence those traditions have on Antonio; see, for example, Fernández Olmos 17; Caminero-Santangelo, "Jasón's Indian" 119–20; and Kevane 41–44.

49. Tonn observes that since Antonio is a child, his sense about the importance of the war and its significance "remains more or less on the level of hearsay, random pieces of information and rumors infused with folk belief" (7).

rienced the war years. Antonio's brothers, for instance, have mixed reactions about their army service. León believes that "[the war] was all right" while Eugenio, who seems more disturbed by the war than his brothers, thinks that the war was "like hell" (63). As the narrative progresses, the depth of the war's toll on the brothers emerges through their actions.

Bless Me, Ultima presents the mental effects of the war on returning Mexican American soldiers through the fate of Lupito, a returning veteran from Las Pasturas, who is unable to overcome his emotional stress caused by the war.[50] As Steven Rosales points out, one of the several complications that "plagued the lives of returning Mexican American veterans" was "the many physical and emotional scars acquired while in uniform" (10). Shortly after the arrival of Ultima to the Márez house, the family hears that Lupito has killed the town's sheriff by shooting him in the head at point blank range for no apparent reason since, as Antonio explains, "the war made him crazy" (16). As a group of armed men from town chases Lupito on the outskirts of town at night, Antonio follows them without their knowledge and finds Lupito hiding under a bridge with visible signs of a mental breakdown. Antonio thinks of his "wild eyes" as "the eyes of a trapped, savage animal" (18). When the armed men find Lupito howling and out of control, he refuses to surrender and is shot by the townspeople. Lupito's harrowing episode reflects the human cost the war had on Mexican Americans and their communities.

Anaya's novel further engages with the social dislocation and the psychological effects of the war on Mexican American soldiers that also affect Antonio's brothers in different degrees. Similar to the connection between Leo and his older brother Caleb in *Tell Me How Long*, Antonio admires his three older siblings, who act as role models. While in Baldwin's novel the brothers share a close connection and set of experiences, in *Bless Me, Ultima* the relationship between Antonio and his brothers is marked by a physical and emotional detachment due in part to the distance that the war creates between them. When the brothers return to their community, they lack a sense of direction; Antonio describes them as "turgid animals who did things mechanically" and "spent the winter sleeping during the day and in town at night" (65). Antonio relates his brothers' actions to their altered mental state; he believes that, similar to Lupito, the "war-sickness was in them" since they act "like lost men who went and came and said nothing" (65). His brothers are affected to different degrees; León, for instance, shows more symptoms of "the sickness," since some nights "he howled and cried like a wild animal" (66). The brothers

---

50. For a discussion of the physical and mental conditions such as posttraumatic stress disorder (PTSD) experienced by Mexican American soldiers, see Rosales 162–75; and Ainslie and Domínguez 144–55.

struggle to reintegrate without institutional support and ultimately fail to find their way back into their community.

Mexican American soldiers encountered several obstacles as they returned to civilian life, and *Bless Me, Ultima* portrays how they were often unable to take advantage of military benefits such as the G.I. Bill. Shortly after Antonio's brothers return to New Mexico, he "hear[s] in whispers that they were wasting their service money" (65), and after a few months, they have borrowed money and have "gotten into trouble" (66). The brothers' stagnation is exasperated by their awareness of other opportunities outside their community. León, for example, thinks that "it's hell to have seen half the world [and] then come back to this" (66). His frustration illustrates the realities of several Mexican American veterans who struggled to adapt and advance socially or economically after the war. Rosales, for instance, explains that, "provided with few transferable skills and unwilling or unable to utilize their G.I. Bill and other entitlements due to discriminatory practices and other logistical issues within the Veterans Administration (VA), many Mexican Americans returned to unskilled manual or migrant farm work in the civilian sector" (9). Andrés personifies the dilemma of some returning veterans who were unable to benefit from institutional assistance such as the G.I. Bill that, despite its acknowledged race-neutrality, disproportionally benefited white soldiers.[51] After León and Eugenio leave town, Andrés stays home and has a desire to return to school. His options are limited since he has to get a job at a supermarket and go to school at the same time. In contrast to León and Eugenio, Andrés shares with Antonio an interest in education; he tells Antonio that "if there's one thing [he] learned in the army, it's that the guy with an education gets ahead" (73). Despite his veteran status, Andrés is unable to continue his education and ultimately leaves town for Las Vegas, New Mexico, to join his two brothers.

Tell Me How Long and *Bless Me, Ultima* contain similar assessments of the positive effects the war had on soldiers of color as they were able to serve their country and experience the world outside their communities. The attitude of the Márez brothers reflects the experience of Latinx soldiers who had the opportunity to travel overseas and interact with members of different racial and ethnic groups for the first time. Writing about the experience of Latinx servicemen overseas, Luis Alvarez explains that "despite the violence and horror of the war, Latino soldiers described their overseas journeys in positive terms" (84). In *Bless Me, Ultima,* the brothers' war experiences influence

---

51. For a detailed discussion on the limited effects of the G.I. Bill on Mexican American veterans, see Rosales 137–57.

their identity and sense of opportunity outside their community; although they leave their family and community behind, they are able to forge a future with a newly acquired perception of their position in society. Eugenio, for instance, believes that he and his two older brothers became "grown men" after they "fought a war" (66). Since the narrative concludes a few months after the brothers return from service, their subsequent fate after they leave town remains ambiguous; however, the final assessment in the narrative is that the "war had changed them," which allowed them "to lead their own lives" (67). As with Leo's brother in *Tell Me How Long*, Antonio's brothers gain a heightened social consciousness directly influenced by their service.

World War II stands as the central transformative experience of the main characters' brothers in *Tell Me How Long* and *Bless Me, Ultima*, which reflects their shared thematic elements. Both narratives call attention to the contributions by soldiers of color and the war's significance in their struggle for social justice. Both authors highlight the patriotism and sacrifices of Black and Mexican American soldiers despite institutionalized racism and their disadvantaged position in the army. As Baldwin and Anaya similarly struggled to separate art and social activism, *Tell Me How Long* and *Bless Me, Ultima* equally focus on their protagonists' artistic journeys while engaging with the discrimination, challenges, and opportunities experienced by soldiers of color during the war as a way to creatively tie their service to the fight for civil rights from the postwar years to the 1960s and 1970s. World War II influenced social activism among communities of color as returning veterans experienced a world outside their marginalized communities and gained a new social consciousness. At a time characterized by divisive rhetoric, the fiction of Baldwin and Anaya shows an instance of the convergences among Black and Latinx authors based on their shared social, historical, and artistic commonalities that unite—rather than divide—people and communities of color.

CHAPTER 4

Arguing for Inclusion

Cultural Identity and the Literary Tradition in the
Essays of Ralph Ellison and Richard Rodriguez

The development of the Black and Latinx literary traditions sheds light on the struggles of Black and Latinx writers as they fought to be recognized and participate in mainstream intellectual and cultural debates. From the beginning of both literary traditions, through their autobiographies, newspaper writings, and essays, authors including Frederick Douglass, W. E. B. Du Bois, James Weldon Johnson, José Martí, Arturo Schomburg, and Bernardo Vega, among others, influenced the country's ever-evolving conversations about race and ethnicity. The classification and roles of writers as intellectuals have changed over time; pre-1960s Black and Latinx literary scholars such as J. Saunders Redding, Sterling Brown, and Américo Paredes form part of each group's intellectual tradition; likewise, some pre-1960s writers such as Jesús Colón, Richard Wright, and James Baldwin formed part of the intellectual tradition of each group through their writings, and in the case of Baldwin by engaging in public intellectual debates. The fight for social justice and increasing militancy of the late 1960s brought to the foreground a new generation of Black and Latinx social activists including Malcolm X, Huey Newton, Rodolfo "Corky" Gonzales, and José Angel Gutiérrez, among others, who acted as spokespersons for their respective groups. While the Black and Latinx literary traditions are characterized by writers, social activists, and theorists who contributed to social, cultural, and political discourses, the 1960s signals the time when authors of color entered mainstream literary conversations and were recognized as equal participants in the country's intellectual life.[1]

Among the post-1960s writers who found themselves in the public spotlight, Ralph Ellison and Richard Rodriguez entered the public intellectual arena through their essays, interviews, and public statements after their critical recognition as writers.[2] Ellison's novel, *Invisible Man*, and Rodriguez's autobiography, *Hunger of Memory*, have generated since their publication a considerable body of scholarship.[3] While Ellison came to literary prominence in the 1950s and Rodriguez decades later, their careers during the 1970s and 1980s were similarly based on their nonfiction, essays, and roles as public intellectuals engaging with social and cultural aspects of American life. Famously, Ellison did not publish a second novel after *Invisible Man* during his lifetime; instead, his writings consisted primarily of essays published in two collections, *Shadow and Act* (1964) and *Going to the Territory* (1986), covering different aspects of American cultural, art, and society. Similarly, Rodriguez's writings after *Hunger of Memory* consisted of essays and nonfiction collected in two books, *Days of Obligation* (1992) and *Brown* (2002), which share thematic concerns found in Ellison's essays, particularly in relation to race, ethnicity, and culture.

The multiplicity of views, ideas, and insights on various subjects contained in the essays of Ellison and Rodriguez have been praised by scholars but have also proved controversial, particularly in the case of Rodriguez. Arnold Rampersad, for example, praises the craft and significance of Ellison's writing by stating that the essays collected in *Shadow and Act* are only surpassed by Du Bois's *Souls of Black Folk*, judging by the way Ellison's essays have influenced a generation of Black writers and artists in subsequent years (410).[4] While the critical praise of Ellison's essays has been shared by past and con-

---

1. For critical discussions focusing on the influence of Black and Latinx authors on social, economic, and political discourses prior to the 1960s, see R. Levine, *Martin Delany*; Foreman, *Activist Sentiments*; Spires, *Practice of Citizenship*; Lomas, *Translating Empire*; and Limón, *Américo Paredes*.

2. Scholars have engaged with the writings of Ellison and Rodriguez in their roles as intellectuals and public figures. In the case of Ellison, see Watts, *Heroism* 14–15; Warren, *So Black and Blue* 16–18; and Jackson, "Invented Life" 12–13. For descriptions of Rodriguez as a public intellectual, see Limón, "Richard Rodriguez" 389–93; Moya 101–3; and Torres 166.

3. For representative analyses of *Invisible Man* see Gates, *Figures in Black*; Baker, *Blues, Ideology, and Afro-American Literature*; Jackson, *Ralph Ellison*; Warren, *So Black and Blue*; and Rampersad, *Ralph Ellison*. In the case of *Hunger of Memory*, see R. Saldívar, *Chicano Narrative*; Moya, *Learning from Experience*; Cutler, *Ends of Assimilation*; and Milian, *Latining America*.

4. Ellison's essays have been studied at times by subject matter, particularly his engagement with music and jazz; see, for example, Porter, *Jazz Country*; and O'Meally, *Living with Music*.

temporary critics, some scholars have engaged with some of the problematic positions taken by Ellison, particularly in relation to race; Jerry Gafio Watts, for instance, has discussed Ellison's overreliance on individuality and his passive rejection of Jim Crow segregation in the South during the 1960s.[5] Scholarship on Ellison's essays, however, continues to be overshadowed by studies on *Invisible Man*.[6] In the case of Rodriguez's essays, the scholarship on his work has concentrated for the most part on critiques of some of his views related to Mexican American identity; assessments of Rodriguez's nonfiction in *Days of Obligation* and *Brown* have been influenced by his controversial opposition to bilingual education and affirmative action, among other topics included in *Hunger of Memory*.[7] Due in part to the storm of controversy generated by *Hunger of Memory*, Rodriguez's subsequent essays have received considerably less critical attention by Latinx scholars.[8]

While scholars have praised but also highlighted the shortcomings of both Ellison's and Rodriguez's essays, their essays have not been studied comparatively despite the striking similarities regarding their views on race, ethnicity, and literature.[9] My analysis comparatively focuses on Ellison's *Shadow and Act* and *Going to the Territory* and Rodriguez's nonfiction and essays in *Days of Obligation* and *Brown*. Moving beyond their seminal and often-discussed works, *Invisible Man* and *Hunger of Memory*, I explore how their writings and some of their statements as public intellectuals closely converge on key positions and arguments, particularly the influence and contributions of different racial and ethnic groups to the formation and development of American culture and the influence and praise of the pre-1960s American literary tradition. This chapter focuses on both authors' insights, as well as some of their short-

---

5. For a detailed analysis of Ellison's views in some of his essays that emphasize individual choice in contrast to the collective social and economic struggles of Blacks in the North and South, see Watts, *Heroism* 65–97.

6. Porter maintains that few critics have "thoroughly discussed [Ellison's] essays" and "critics and detractors, as well as some of his supporters, rarely seem interested in sorting through the nuances of his thought" (*Jazz Country* 2, 6). Recent studies on Ellison's writings show that scholarship on Ellison continues to center on his fiction. See, for example, Conner and Morel, *New Territory*.

7. For discussions on the contentious debate between scholars of Mexican American literature and Rodriguez related to his opposition to bilingual education and affirmative action, see Limón, "Richard Rodriguez" 392–94; Staten 103–4, 109; D. Cooper 104; Torres 164; and Guajardo 70–71.

8. In an interview, Rodriguez observes that his essays have received less critical attention than *Hunger of Memory* (Torres 186). For discussions on either *Days of Obligation* or *Brown*, see Aldama, *Brown on Brown*; and Ferszt, "Richard Rodriguez."

9. Milian's *Latining America* and Michael Nieto Garcia's *Autobiography in Black and Brown* have studied Rodriguez's views on race and ethnicity in relation to the writings of W. E. B. Du Bois and Richard Wright, respectively.

comings in relation to their views on race and ethnicity and the influence of cultural exchanges in American social and cultural life. In their role as public intellectuals, Ellison and Rodriguez remained skeptical of calls for racial and ethnic identification made by Black and Chicanx nationalists during the late 1960s and early 1970s; instead, Ellison and Rodriguez sought to prove that the country's culture and literature have developed through cultural exchanges among different racial, ethnic, and immigrant groups from the country's formation to contemporary times. They similarly maintained that broad racial identifications such as "white" and "black" hide a larger complexity due to the blending of different traditions and experiences from different groups. In their essays, Ellison and Rodriguez embrace a dual and pluralistic cultural identity, respectively, that emphasizes the mixing of cultures during the formation of an American cultural heritage. While both writers insightfully interrogate racial, ethnic, and cultural identifications, they similarly overlook the processes of racialization and otherness of people of color that have taken place since the formation of the country. David Theo Goldberg, for example, agrees that "racial mixing 'n matching" has influenced racial and ethnic identity formation in the US (57); however, contrary to Ellison and Rodriguez, Goldberg investigates how mixed racial identities have been "colored with the revitalized cosmetics of the racialized condition" (61).[10]

Ellison and Rodriguez were similarly influenced by their reading and interpretation of the American literary tradition and its role in the formation of their cultural identities. In their essays and pronouncements as public intellectuals, rather than interrogating and challenging the literary tradition—an increasingly prevalent stance among post-1960s authors of color—Ellison and Rodriguez emphasize instances of cultural exchange present in the works of canonical authors such as Mark Twain; moreover, they make use of their individual experiences reading the American literary canon to make a case for universality in their writings. Toni Morrison similarly analyzes the degree to which Blacks and Black culture have influenced the American literary tradition; however, in a marked contrast from Ellison and Rodriguez, Morrison identifies the tropes used by white canonical writers who repeatedly "silenced black bodies" in their fiction and explores how this exclusion and marginalization represent a "major theme in American literature" (33). Ultimately, while Ellison's and Rodriguez's views on race, ethnicity, and the literary tradition offer insights, their essays and public statements often neglect the long history

---

10. For similar critiques in the way race and identity have gone through processes of racialization and otherness in the US context, see Mills, *Racial Contract*; Alcoff, *Visible Identities*; and Taylor, *Race*.

of social and literary marginalization of people of color in the development of an American cultural and literary heritage.

My aim is not to minimize the differences between historical periods and nuances in some of the positions taken by Ellison and Rodriguez—the former an already recognized author during the civil rights era of the 1960s and the latter an undergraduate and graduate student who experienced the Chicanx Movement of the 1960s and 1970s as a college student in California— or the differences of their respective groups' histories, cultures, and literary traditions. In criticizing the rush to find points of convergence among different groups during the Chicanx Movement, Rodriguez himself warns that "Mexican-American political activists, especially student activists, insisted on a rough similarity between the two societies—black, Chicano—ignoring any complex factor of history or race that might disqualify the equation" ("Mexico's Children" 65). Although there are clear differences between the writings of Ellison and Rodriguez, their essays reflect shared attitudes, experiences, and misconceptions, particularly in relation to the marginalized position of writers of color that both writers continuously overlooked in their role as public intellectuals during the post-1960s decades.

ELLISON, RODRIGUEZ, AND THE EMERGENCE OF BLACK AND CHICANX NATIONALISM

Ellison and Rodriguez remained skeptical about calls for racial and ethnic identification from Black and Chicanx nationalists as well as the increasing militancy and confrontational stance of some of their leaders during the late 1960s and early 1970s.[11] Writers and social activists such as Amiri Baraka and Luis Valdez were inspired by nationalist ideologies and came to embrace racial and ethnic pride; they similarly challenged discrimination and racism against people of color in different social and political realms.[12] During those years,

---

11. For a discussion on the ideological clash between Ellison and Black nationalists, see Watts, *Heroism* 10–14, 60–64. For a discussion on Rodriguez's critique on the Chicanx Movement, see M. Garcia 160–64.

12. Writing on the legacy of Malcolm X, Baraka articulates part of his nationalist and confrontational vision when he explains, "America can give us nothing; all bargaining must be done by mutual agreement. But finally, terms must be given by Black Men *from their own shores*—which is where they live, where we all are, now. The land is literally ours" ("Legacy" 240). Similarly, Valdez urged Chicanx people to embrace their culture and language as a symbol of resistance against an oppressive mainstream American society and its cultural institutions by maintaining that "the nature of Chicanismo calls for a revolutionary turn in the arts as well as in society" ("Notes" 7).

and in subsequent decades, Ellison and Rodriguez positioned themselves as public figures whose views on race, ethnicity, and culture served to counter Black and Mexican American militancy. By the 1960s, Ellison was one of the few Black writers who was recognized as an equal writer in a society still dominated by racial prejudices and racist attitudes toward writers and artists of color; however, as Kenneth Warren rightly notes, Ellison's world, dictated by Jim Crow segregation, was coming to a close with the advent of the civil rights and Black Power movements of the 1960s and the emergence of leaders such as Martin Luther King Jr. and Malcolm X (*So Black* 7–8). In subsequent years, Ellison acted often as a speaker and lecturer and publicly criticized the Black militancy coming from the Black Power movement and the racial views of important figures such as Eldridge Cleaver and Malcolm X (Rampersad 507). Ellison's own views proved controversial; his open attacks on the militancy of Black nationalists were criticized by other Black writers and more liberal intellectuals.[13] Equally significant, in contrast to Baldwin, who actively engaged in the fight for civil rights during the 1950s and 1960s, Ellison conspicuously remained detached from social activism and kept civil rights leaders at a distance, despite his literary fame and relative influence as writer and public figure. As a response to those critics, Ellison at times alluded to the incompatibility of art and social protest by arguing that he was an artist, not an activist.[14] Although this statement reflects Ellison's views at the beginning of his career, in subsequent years, and during his increasing significance as a public figure, he continued to assert that his role as writer was to master his art and craft, not to engage in social protest.[15]

Sharing a similar attitude with Ellison, Rodriguez remained critical of the emphasis on racial and ethnic pride by social activists and writers during the Chicanx Movement of the 1960s and 1970s. Rodriguez has remained an open and confrontational critic of the Chicanx Movement, and part of the chasm between Rodriguez, a Mexican American writer, and Chicanx activists, artists, and scholars derived from Rodriguez's critical assessment of the movement and the movement's emphasis on ethnic pride and the embrace of a Mesoamerican past.[16] In one of his essays, for instance, Rodriguez openly rejects Chicanx ethnic solidarity by stating that he is not related to Aztecs ("American Writer" 10). Rodriguez's provocative opinions contrast with those of Chicanx

---

13. See Rampersad 354; Jackson, "Invented Life" 21; and Porter, *Jazz Country* 6.

14. After the unparalleled success of *Invisible Man*, Ellison explained in an interview, "I wasn't, and am not, primarily concerned with injustice, but with art" (Chester et al.).

15. See Rampersad 307; and Watts, *Heroism* 21.

16. In a series of interviews, Rodriguez has expressed his contemptuous views on the Chicanx Movement; see, for instance Torres 164–66; and Sedore and Rodriguez 26.

writers of the 1970s and 1980s such as Rudolfo Anaya, Tomás Rivera, and Gloria Anzaldúa, who emphasized a Chicanx identity, based in part on Mesoamerican and Aztec history and symbols, and positioned their works against a white mainstream and Western-dominated cultural, economic, and political order (Staten 104). Rodriguez's open contempt for the Chicanx Movement has resulted in critiques of Rodriguez's writings by past and contemporary scholars of Latinx literature, since by rejecting a project of Chicanx identity formation, Rodriguez dismisses the multiplicity of Chicanx experiences, the valid social, political, and artistic concerns of Mexican American activists and writers, and their historical marginalization.[17] Rodriguez's critical view of the emergence of the Chicanx Movement fails to acknowledge the discrimination, disenfranchisement, and marginalization that characterized the lived experiences of Mexican Americans in the Southwest prior to the 1960s.

Despite the opposition to and rejection of Black and Chicanx nationalism, Ellison and Rodriguez paradoxically benefited from the gains made by the work of militant Black and Chicanx writers, artists, and activists during the 1960s and 1970s, which opened opportunities for writers of color in public, academic, and cultural spaces.[18] While Ellison was a recognized novelist before the 1960s, his notoriety increased by serving as a speaker at mainstream cultural and literary organizations (Rampersad 444–45). While Rodriguez experienced the advent of the Chicanx Movement as a college student, in subsequent decades, Rodriguez—just as Ellison—benefited from the gains made by Latinx writers and activists achieving literary recognition after the 1960s, despite his fierce criticism of those same groups. Rodriguez's ascent as a public intellectual was due also in part to the struggles for inclusion at mainstream cultural institutions by writers of color that allowed Rodriguez to disseminate his writing related to his experience growing up as a Mexican American in Sacramento. In their roles as public intellectuals, some of the views of Ellison and Rodriguez on race and ethnicity appealed to more moderate and conservative members of the mainstream literary establishment;[19]

---

17. Moya correctly observes that some Black and Mexican American "neoconservative" public intellectuals, including Rodriguez, "seriously underread the degree to which a variety of economic and social forces in our capitalist society exert control over the material conditions of the lives of ordinary people" (114).

18. As Rampersad notes, the social turmoil of the late 1960s brought a demand for Ellison as a speaker, and with it came money and prestige (378, 445). Similarly, Staten points out that Rodriguez's writings gained recognition and "success based in part on the appeal that his opposition to multiculturalism [had] for a conservative white audience" (104).

19. For discussions on the appeal of Ellison or Rodriguez to moderate and conservative writers and members of cultural and literary organizations, see Rampersad 394–95, Staten 104, and Moya 101.

similarly, they seldom publicly questioned their role as the "minority view" while participating in cultural, literary, and scholarly events.

VISIONS OF CULTURAL DUALISM AND THE LITERARY CANON IN ELLISON'S ESSAYS

Ellison's recognition by mainstream cultural organizations and institutions after the publication of his first and only novel, *Invisible Man*, is almost without parallel in Black literary history as he became one of the few pre-1960s Black writers to receive mainstream critical acclaim. The start of Ellison's career resembles the careers of Richard Wright, James Baldwin, and other Black writers of the 1940s and 1950s as they began writing for Black and mainstream periodicals and received the support of social and cultural organizations. Wright published Ellison's early writings in his role as editor of *New Challenge*, a literary magazine supported by Dorothy West; likewise, Wright helped Ellison to secure employment at the New York Writers' Project, which allowed Ellison to continue his writing career (Rampersad 98, 110). Ellison wrote essays and fiction for other magazines such as *New Masses, Antioch Review,* and the *New Republic,* among others, and his subsequent years of writing resulted in *Invisible Man,* which was published by Random House in 1952.[20] *Invisible Man's* critical success among mainstream critics was unique and reached a new height when Ellison won the National Book Award in 1953, thus making him the first Black writer ever to win a mainstream literary prize. Ellison's subsequent public role as a preeminent Black writer and sought-after intellectual and speaker on race relations, Black culture, and literature is unparalleled, since before Ellison, Black authors had traditionally been excluded from mainstream public and cultural institutions.[21]

Scholars have praised Ellison's essays published after *Invisible Man* for their insights into the formation of Black culture but have also scrutinized them for their moderate views on race relations and his emphasis on artistic individuality rather than Blacks' collective struggles.[22] While the emphasis on Black nationalism began to fade after the 1970s and was even abandoned by

20. For detailed discussions of Ellison's early years as a writer leading to the publication of *Invisible Man,* see Rampersad 143–211; and Jackson, *Ralph Ellison* 304–25.

21. Although Ellison did not publish a second novel, for the rest of his career he remained one of the most sought-after Black writers and became a member of some of the most prestigious cultural organizations such as the Century Association and the American Academy of Arts and Letters (Rampersad 393, 371).

22. See, for example, Rampersad 408–10; and Watts, *Heroism* 65–97.

some of its most forceful proponents such as Baraka, Ellison's insights in his essays and public statements regarding the mixed and pluralistic origin of American culture and how it has been influenced by different racial and ethnic groups continued to be admired and scrutinized.[23] In essays from *Shadow and Act* and *Going to the Territory,* along with his public statements, Ellison makes a case for the mixed origin of American culture based on his personal engagement with history, culture, and the literary tradition. While Ellison's views on the mixed origin of American culture resonate in an increasingly multicultural contemporary society, his emphasis on individualism and universality in literature has limitations in the way it considers the historical marginalization experienced by Blacks and the position of Black writers in the literary tradition.

Ellison argued that American culture was an amalgamation of influences by people from different racial backgrounds and that the cultural character of the nation had been fluid rather than fixed. James Alan McPherson, for instance, observes that "at a time when many blacks, especially the young, [were] denying all influences of American culture, Ellison, as always, doggedly affirm[ed] his identity as a negro American, a product of the blending of both cultures" (174). A major reason for Ellison's opposition to the rise of Black nationalism during the 1960s was his belief, acquired at an early age and reinforced at Tuskegee University, that Black culture was an intrinsic part of American mainstream culture and not an entity separated from it.[24] Similar to some of his contemporary Black writers after the 1960s such as Baldwin and Albert Murray, Ellison explored in some of his essays the ambiguities and paradoxes encapsulated in racial categorizations. Ellison was not alone when he argued that whites and Blacks shared a cultural background and that their cultural identities were intertwined;[25] however, Ellison's singularity was his relentless emphasis in his essays and public statements regarding Blacks' prominent role in the formation of American culture and the influence of mainstream culture on Blacks, while at the same time failing to acknowledge

---

23. Maryemma Graham notes that Ellison's "perspectives on artistic and cultural issues of importance always commanded attention and often provoked controversy. Refusing to bend easily with fads and fashions, Ellison maintained a consistent and always independent view of matters close to the heart of the American experience" (Graham and Singh vii).

24. Watts maintains that Ellison was not a Black nationalist but an American nationalist "insofar as he believes that Negro culture is an American phenomenon and occupies a centrality within American culture" (*Heroism* 107).

25. Baldwin and Albert Murray in their writings had similarly argued for the cultural interdependence among whites and Blacks in the past and present. See, for example, Baldwin, *Notes of a Native Son;* and Murray, *Omni-Americans.*

the disadvantaged position of Blacks in a society that seldom acknowledged their cultural and artistic contributions.

Ellison grapples with the problem of racial categorizations, as he claims that since its inception, American identity has been characterized by cultural exchanges among individuals from different backgrounds. In one of his essays, Ellison states that when we "find some assertion of [cultural] purity, [we] are dealing with historical, if not cultural ignorance" ("Alain Locke" 443). According to Ellison, it is easier to use "false" categories such as "white" or "non-white" or "black culture" and "white culture" when engaging with cultural influences rather than wrestling with more complex notions of cultural mixing and blending from the time "Western pioneers confront[ed] the unknown prairie" ("What America" 108). Ellison points out that "perhaps the mystery of American cultural identity contained in such motley mixtures arises out of our persistent attempts to reduce our cultural diversity to an easily recognizable unit" ("Little Man"16–17). Ellison correctly identifies how broad categorizations such as "American culture" and "black culture" divide and obscure exchanges between Blacks and whites; for Ellison, there is a "pluralistic wholeness" that is the result of a mixing of influences and cultures from diverse groups; he identifies divisions and fragmentations, from both whites and nonwhites, as "the source of many of our problems, especially those centering upon American identity. In relationship to the cultural whole, we are, all of us—white or black, native born or immigrant—members of minority groups" ("Little Man" 16). Ellison, however, appears to minimize the social, political, and legal conditions that influence those cultural exchanges, and more importantly, the formation of racial and ethnic identities. Likewise, not all immigrant groups have been treated equally, and that unequal treatment has influenced the acceptance of the cultural contributions of certain immigrant groups as part of American culture.[26]

Ellison, moreover, suggests that categorizations tied to racial and cultural identity such as "white" or "white culture" are inadequate since they mask the mixing and blending of ethnic and cultural influences throughout the formation of a distinct American culture; however, he avoids taking into consideration the social connotations of "whiteness" and its position as the default racial identification that has historically excluded people of color. For Ellison, the term "white" represents a broad category to describe individuals from different cultural backgrounds and identities that in the past were identified as Protestant Anglo-Saxons, Italians, or Jews. Ellison maintains that the place of

---

26. As Paul C. Taylor notes, the prevailing narrative is that the US is a nation of immigrants; however, a lesser acknowledged reality is that US immigration "has always been racialized" (185).

Blacks in America "is but a part of that larger conflict between older, dominant groups of white Americans, especially the Anglo-Saxons, on the one hand, and the newer white and non-white groups on the other, over the major group's attempt to impose its ideals upon the rest, insisting that its exclusive image be accepted as *the* image of the American" ("Twentieth-Century" 26). As a result, Ellison rejects the idea of a monolithic or static American cultural identity by offering as an example the influence of Jews in its formation, as he "consider[s] the United States freer politically and richer culturally because there are Jewish Americans to bring it the benefit of their special forms of dissent, their humor and their gift for ideas which are based upon the uniqueness of their experiences" ("World" 126–27). Ellison correctly questioned uncritical terms such as "white culture" at a socially volatile period in US history, not unlike contemporary times, when some people invoked the idea of distinct "white culture" and used it to exclude Blacks and other groups; nonetheless, Ellison omits from his analysis how the cultural contributions of non-Anglo-Saxon Protestants such as Italians and Jews are often minimized by the dominant white group.

In a similar manner by which Europeans from different backgrounds came together to create a distinct American cultural identity, Ellison argues that since the inception of the country—including slavery times—Blacks have contributed to its formation.[27] Ellison believed that Blacks and whites gained an American cultural identity distinct from the one of their African and European predecessors.[28] Ellison emphasizes in different essays the prominence of Blacks in the formation of the nation's cultural identity when he discusses diverse topics such as music, dance, and language; in relation to the influence of Blacks on American culture, Ellison states that "even the slaves, although thrust below the threshold of social hierarchy, were given a prominent place in our national iconography; their music, poetic imagery, and choreography were grudgingly recognized as seminal sources of American art" ("Little Man" 26).[29] In another of his essays, Ellison explains that as cultural exchanges

27. In an interview, Ellison states that the "history of the American Negro is a most intimate part of American history. Through the very process of slavery came the building of the United States" (Chester et al.).

28. As Watts cogently explains, for Ellison, "Black Americans were not Africans on the North American continent, nor for that matter were white Americans simply transplanted Europeans. Instead, black Americans were culturally part white, and white Americans were culturally part black. The history and politics of the United States had created a new, culturally heterogeneous people" (*Heroism* 13).

29. While Ellison's statements on slavery seem incongruous, Warren notes that Ellison's views of slavery were more critical than those held by white historians of slavery such as Stanley M. Elkins, who introduced the "Sambo" stereotype in studies of slavery, which was accepted by other predominantly white historians (*So Black* 61–62).

between Blacks and whites progressed, "inevitably these forms came together; there is always integration of artistic styles whether it is done out of admiration, out of need, or out of a motive of economic exploitation. It finds its way to the larger American public, and as such, everyone who is touched by it becomes a little bit Afro-American" ("Alain Locke" 445).[30] Ellison's public statements on the importance of the contributions of Blacks to American culture were significant, particularly in light of the entrenched racism of the 1950s and 1960s that Ellison experienced in Northern cities even after his literary success, not to mention the social and cultural realities experienced by the majority of Black artists and writers at the time.

The idea that cultural exchanges among whites and Blacks had created a distinct American culture has gained legitimacy in mainstream cultural and artistic conversations; however, Ellison emphasized cultural exchanges, and the inclusion of Blacks in narratives of the country's formation, at a time when Blacks lived under Jim Crow in the South and had few social and economic opportunities in the North. Ellison's bold claims regarding artistic individuality and the way these views were contested—not only by white conservatives but also by some liberal reviewers and fellow Black writers—are represented in his often-discussed exchange with Irving Howe in the form of essays written in mainstream magazines. After the publication of Howe's essay, "Black Boys and Native Sons," Ellison wrote a reply essay, "The World and the Jug," originally published in the *New Leader* in two parts in 1963 and 1964. In this essay, Ellison attempts to dispel the misconception that Blacks lack cultural agency and makes the argument for the preeminence of Black individuality within a segregated society. Ellison rejects Howe's idea that Blacks in the South were in complete racial and social subjugation; a more accurate portrayal, Ellison suggests, would show that despite Blacks' social and political marginalization, some Blacks could thrive artistically since "their ability to achieve freedom [was] limited only by their individual aspiration, insight, energy, and will" ("World" 116). Ellison's premise in "The World and the Jug" regarding Black individuality, based on his own literary and intellectual experiences, did not reflect the experiences of the majority of Blacks;[31] however, Howe and other

---

30. Ellison, moreover, contends in an interview, "I recognize no American culture which is not the partial creation of black people. I recognize no American style in literature, in dance, in music, even in assembly-line processes, which does not bear the mark of the American Negro" (McPherson 174).

31. Goldberg explains that contemporary theorists of race such as Charles Mills have demonstrated "how race is written into daily lives and experience in America. . . . Throughout US history, race has always been a central strand of state administration; a silent (and sometimes not so silent) barrier to kinship and adoptability; a condition of advancement and advantage, of power and privilege" (10).

readers of the 1960s expected Ellison to serve as a "spokesperson" for Blacks. While several scholars have praised Ellison's intellect and craft displayed in "The World and the Jug," some critics have questioned his views on Black and white cultural exchanges in his essay.[32] Some of his claims regarding Blacks' separate but equal position when it came to cultural exchanges in "The World and the Jug" remain evocative as well as problematic, especially at a time when Black leaders and citizens were organizing and protesting against racial segregation across the South and in state and federal courts. In one of the most incisive analyses of "The World and the Jug," Watts offers a thorough critique of Ellison's position on cultural exchanges between the two groups.[33] This tension, however, is not unique to "The World and the Jug" since in other essays and public statements, Ellison discusses cultural mixing through the prism of his own experiences, which differed considerably from the everyday concerns of other Blacks at the time.

Some of the insights and equivocations contained in "The World and the Jug" and other essays regarding cultural exchanges and Black individuality derive in part from Ellison's understanding and engagement with the American literary tradition. Ellison not only claimed that mainstream culture was influenced by Blacks but also that Black culture contained elements of white or European culture; in Ellison's view, Blacks were also culturally part white. Ellison made this argument by discussing his own dual cultural identity forged in part by his knowledge of American canonical works, which began in his early years and continued at Tuskegee University.[34] A major claim in "The World and the Jug" for the existence of cultural exchanges among Blacks and whites is his own experience reading works from the literary tradition despite Jim Crow segregation; he explains that "in Macon County, Alabama, [he] read Marx, Freud, T. S. Eliot, Pound, Gertrude Stein and Hemingway" (116). While Ellison's pronouncement obscures the fact that Macon County is the site of Tuskegee

---

32. For discussions related to the "The World and The Jug" on a variety of subjects, see Watts, *Heroism* 65–97; Jackson, "Invented Life" 13; Sundquist 218; Porter, *Jazz Country* 122–30; and Rampersad 401–3.

33. Watts contends, among other claims, that to "claim interracial cultural cross-fertilization within a society in which socially, politically, and economically based racial differences were so distinct may have appeared somewhat disingenuous" (*Heroism* 13).

34. While growing up, Ellison had access to a segregated public library in Oklahoma City where he read works including *The Last of the Mohicans* and *Huckleberry Finn* (Rampersad 29–30); he continued his interest in literature at the Tuskegee University library reading canonical works and by taking literature classes while majoring in music. Ellison was introduced to contemporary American writers while at Tuskegee through the guidance of the head librarian, Walter Bowie Williams, and literature professor Morteza Drexel Sprague, to whom Ellison dedicated *Shadow and Act* (Rampersad 60, 75–76).

University, and that perhaps not all southern Blacks would have had access to the same works of literature at their local library, Ellison relies on his knowledge of these works to describe his cultural identity when he states, "Indeed, I understand a bit more about myself as Negro because literature has taught me something of my identity as a Western man" ("World" 117). At a time when some Black writers began to exalt their racial pride, Ellison boldly claimed a dual cultural identity based on his reading of works from the Western tradition.

Ellison, moreover, makes the case in "The World and the Jug" and in other essays that other Black writers such as Wright and Baldwin possessed similar dual cultural identities as they were influenced by Black culture and the literary tradition. Ellison argues that Wright, Baldwin, and himself were influenced by canonical American authors and benefited from cultural exchanges despite living in a segregated society. According to Ellison, Wright "was as much a product of his readings as of his painful experiences, and he made himself a writer by subjecting himself to the writer's discipline—as he understood it. The same is true for [Baldwin], who is not the product of a Negro store-front church but of the library, and the same is true of me" ("World" 116); libraries and the literary tradition, Ellison believes, served as agents of cultural exchange between the two groups. In another essay, Ellison explains that part of his admiration for Wright, and the reason he considered him an equal as a writer, was based on their mutual admiration of Western literature and its influence on them.[35] Early in his writing career, Ellison maintained that a reason for Wright's mainstream critical recognition, in contrast to previous Harlem Renaissance writers, was the influence the literary tradition had on Wright (Rampersad 142). In "Richard Wright's Blues," for example, Ellison explains that one of Wright's distinctions was his dual cultural background as a Black writer who received influences from both European and Southern culture (78).[36] Ellison's argument that some Black writers were the product of a mixed cultural identity reflects Ellison's provocative understanding of cultural dynamics at a time when writers were uncritically categorized as white or Black by mainstream publishers and reviewers.

Part of Ellison's belief in cultural exchanges was that a number of canonical authors such as Twain and William Faulkner have been influenced by

---

35. Rampersad points out that Ellison and Wright shared a fascination for "Western learned culture" (97).

36. In other essays and in his remembrance of Wright, Ellison made a similar point observing that Wright was not only a Black writer but was also influenced by mainstream culture through his readings. Ellison states that in Wright, he "discovered a Negro American writer who possessed a working knowledge of modern literature" ("Remembering" 213–14).

Black culture;[37] nonetheless, Ellison interprets these exchanges in a positive light, contrary to Toni Morrison, who critically identified the erasure of the Black body in the fiction of those same canonical authors. In an essay, Ellison observes that in relation to the development of American fiction, "had there been no blacks, certain creative tensions arising from the cross-purposes of whites and blacks would also not have existed" ("What America" 109).[38] According to Ellison, Twain owed part of his success to Black influences since "without the presence of blacks, [Huck Finn] could not have been written. No Huck and Jim, no American novel as we know it" ("What America" 109). Ellison similarly believed that Faulkner had been deeply influenced by Black culture; during an interview, he notes that Faulkner's fiction "just goes to show that you can't be Southern without being black, and you can't be a black Southerner without being white" (Remnick 401). While the influence of Black culture on these canonical authors is well known today, Ellison made these claims at a time when the vast majority of Black writers and artists had been marginalized from the mainstream publishing industry, cultural organizations, and society at large. Twain and Faulkner, moreover, whose work Ellison cherished, did not advocate cultural exchanges and seldom acknowledged the influence that Black culture had in their work. Years later, Morrison made a similar claim in *Playing in the Dark* when she wrote that "American literature could not help being shaped by [the] encounter" with Black people (16); however, in contrast to Ellison, Morrison goes on to show how these encounters have been mediated by white writers in an unbalanced position of power that silence Black characters in literature. Morrison similarly uses the example of Jim in *Huck Finn* to show the subordinated position of Black characters and how these Black characters were "used to limn out and enforce the investigation and implications of whiteness" (52).[39]

Ellison's interest in literature allowed him to claim a dual cultural identity at a time when Black writers remained excluded from mainstream pub-

37. Scholars have explored the influence of canonical authors in Ellison's work, particularly Twain; see, for example, Jackson, "Invented Life" 11–34; Nadel 126–27; and Warren, *So Black and Blue* 64.

38. Ellison's perception of his own dual cultural identity is reflected in his well-known remark in "The World and the Jug" when he states that Richard Wright was a "relative," and others such as Faulkner and Hemingway were "ancestors" (140). Scholars, however, have pointed out how Ellison selectively approached his past and literary influences and minimized the mentorship of Langston Hughes and Wright. See, for example, Jackson, "Invented Life" 18–22; Watts, *Heroism* 68–69; and Rampersad 90–91, 98.

39. While Morrison also admired Faulkner's fiction and that of other canonical white authors, she theorized on how white writers and their writings and language "can powerfully evoke and enforce hidden signs of racial superiority, cultural hegemony, and dismissive 'othering' of people [of color]" (x); see also Spillers, "Who Cuts the Border?"

lishing opportunities and white-dominated intellectual spaces. Based on the influence of the literary tradition, and his understanding of its cultural and aesthetic value, Ellison remained skeptical of students' protests and their fight for the inclusion of authors of color in college courses during the late 1960s.[40] Throughout his career, Ellison not only opposed Black writers who emphasized in their work racial and ethnic pride, but he also refused to teach a Black literature course during his academic appointment at New York University (Rampersad 471). While Ellison condemned at times the obstacles faced by Black writers, he seldom questioned the standards and aesthetic values ascribed to the pre-1960s American literary tradition. Despite the limitations in Ellison's claim of a dual cultural identity, Ellison insisted on his recognition as an American writer belonging to both traditions.[41] Ellison remained a believer in cultural exchanges among Blacks and whites and the possibilities for emerging Black writers to be culturally enriched, rather than diminished, by embracing the American literary tradition.[42] Similar to Ellison, Richard Rodriguez delved into his formative social and academic experiences to arrive at a vision of cultural pluralism.

CULTURAL PLURALISM AND THE LITERARY TRADITION IN RODRIGUEZ'S ESSAYS

Rodriguez's literary trajectory reflects the marginalization of Latinx intellectuals throughout most of American literary history until the 1980s when some Latinx writers were able to participate in mainstream cultural and national conversations. As Latinx literary history shows, Mexican American writers from the Southwest, including Oscar "Zeta" Acosta, Tomás Rivera, and Roland Hinojosa, were published in increasing numbers by mainstream and small publishers after the 1960s; however, it was not until the 1980s when writers

---

40. Ellison contended that "the proponents of ethnicity . . . have helped give our streets and campuses a wordy, All Fool's Day, carnival atmosphere. In many ways, then, the call for a new social order based upon the glorification of ancestral blood and ethnic background acts as a call to cultural and aesthetic chaos" ("Little Man" 21–22).

41. Describing his dual cultural duality, Ellison explains, "I consider myself both and I don't see a dichotomy. I'm not an American because I arbitrarily decide so. I write in the American tradition of fiction. My people have always been Americans. . . . Culturally speaking, I inherited the language of Twain, Melville, and Emerson, after whom I'm named" (Geller 82–83).

42. According to Ellison, "We [Black] writers seem seldom to have grasped this process of acculturation. Too often we've been in such haste to express our anger and our pain as to allow the single tree of race to obscure our view of the magic forest of art" (Cannon et al. 112).

such as Rodriguez, Sandra Cisneros, Gloria Anzaldúa, and Cherríe Moraga, among others, began to enter mainstream cultural and literary conversations (Bruce-Novoa, *RetroSpace* 128–29).[43] Rodriguez studied literature at Stanford and UC–Berkeley; however, instead of entering academia, he became an essayist and freelance journalist writing for mainstream publications such as the *American Scholar, Harper's Magazine,* and PBS *NewsHour,* and in the process acquired the mantle of a public intellectual. Rodriguez's entrance into the mainstream public sphere came with the publication of his autobiography *Hunger of Memory: The Education of Richard Rodriguez,* originally published by David R. Godine in 1982. *Hunger of Memory* was widely reviewed in mainstream publications and became a literary success, particularly among mainstream readers and in conservative cultural and literary circles (Moya 101).[44] Scholars of Latinx literature have thoroughly critiqued the shortcomings in Rodriguez's views on Mexican American identity and assimilation in *Hunger of Memory;*[45] nonetheless, Rodriguez's writing remains relevant in the context of the struggle against literary invisibility of Latinx writers since Rodriguez's emergence as an essayist and public intellectual represented one of the early instances when a Mexican American writer gained a mainstream readership and participated as an equal in public and cultural spheres.[46]

In this section, I concentrate on how Rodriguez's views in some of his essays from his two collections, *Days of Obligation* and *Brown,* show distinct similarities with some of Ellison's positions related to the mixed origin of American culture as a result of cultural exchanges among different racial and ethnic groups. While Rodriguez's collections of essays have received less critical attention than *Hunger of Memory* among scholars of Mexican American literature, other critics such as Werner Sollors remain attracted to the distinctiveness of Rodriguez's views related to the mixed origin of American cultural identity as an amalgamation of cultural exchanges from different

---

43. In their study of post-1960s Latinx literature, Dalleo and Sáez discuss the ideological differences between Latinx writers influenced by social protest movements of the 1960s and some Latinx writers from subsequent decades who were "seen as apolitical and even conservative" (2).

44. *Hunger of Memory,* for example, was reviewed in the *New York Times,* the *Washington Post,* and the *Boston Globe,* among others, a rare event at the time for a book written by a Mexican American.

45. For representative analyses of *Hunger of Memory* and assimilation, see R. Saldívar, *Chicano Narrative* 157–58; Moya 111–23; and Cutler, *Ends of Assimilation* 89–95.

46. *Hunger of Memory* became a representative Mexican American text in college courses despite its controversial views on bilingual education and affirmative action, which were outliers among other Mexican American writers and scholars; see, for instance, Moya 101; and Cutler, *Ends of Assimilation* 104–5.

groups.[47] Sollors, for example, points out that Rodriguez's writing "provocatively emphasizes his polyethnic Spanish-Indian-African background. His version of Chicano identity, far from claiming any racial 'purity' or any immediate access to 'Mexican' identity, may yet be seen as the vanguard of a future American melting-pot identity" (*Invention* xvii).[48] While Rodriguez makes a case for the pluralistic origin of American culture, based in part on his social and academic experiences that resonate in a contemporary multiethnic society, his views—just as Ellison's—fail to grapple with the historical marginalization of writers and communities of color during most of the country's history. Rodriguez's essays constantly overlook the power dynamics that Charles Mills and other scholars have identified when they theorize about the European presence in the American continent, not as an idealized coming together of distinct ethnic and racial groups but rather as a project of economic and racial domination (*Racial Contract* 20).

Rodriguez examines race and ethnicity in relation to cultural exchanges throughout the formation of an American cultural identity, which he interprets as an amalgamation of racial, ethnic, and cultural influences. On the problem of categorization in relation to race and ethnicity, Rodriguez interrogates claims of racial, ethnic, or cultural purity. He offers his family background as evidence when he notes that it is mixed with Spanish, French, Jewish, and possibly African ancestry ("American Writer" 10). Rodriguez also rejects broad racial and cultural binaries when he argues that categories such as "majority" and "minority," "native" and "immigrant" are simplifications of individuals' more complex ethnic and cultural backgrounds. Rodriguez echoes Ellison's claim that a term such as "American" is a broad categorization that obscures the various contributions of racial, ethnic, and immigrant groups in the development of the country's identity. Rodriguez, for example, explains that "lacking any plural sense of ourselves, how shall we describe Americanization, except as loss? The son of Italian immigrant parents is no longer Italian. America is the country where one stops being Italian" ("Asians" 164); Rodriguez here, and in similar instances in other essays, claims that describing a person of Italian background and ancestry simply as an "American" obscures

---

47. See, for example, Staten, "Ethnic Authenticity, Class, and Autobiography"; and Garcia, *Autobiography in Black and Brown*.

48. Sollors's interpretation of Rodriguez's views on race and ethnicity resembles the prevalent idea of *mestizaje* in Latin America that presents race and ethnicity as a mix of racial or ethnic groups but fails to take into consideration the racial history of European colonization. In contrast, Paul C. Taylor has focused on the origins of racism in the American continent dating back to Spain and the Iberian Peninsula and the conquering of the Moors and the expulsion of all Jews in 1492 that was carried over to the American continent (39).

individuals' more complex cultural identities; nonetheless, Rodriguez fails to interrogate why whiteness is gained by some immigrants from predominantly European countries, but is constantly negated to immigrants from other racial and ethnic backgrounds and geographical spaces.

The experience of growing up among families from different racial and ethnic groups in Sacramento leads Rodriguez to question discussions of race in America concerning whites and Blacks as reductive since they exclude other groups; however, his emphasis on racial and ethnic pluralism seems ahistorical. Rodriguez argues that in the late 1960s "when black and white America argued, I felt I was overhearing some family quarrel that didn't include me. Korean and Chinese and Japanese faces in Sacramento rescued me from the simplicities of black and white America" ("Asians" 166). Rodriguez returns to a similar idea in *Brown* when he explains, "I think of the nation entire—all Americans—as my people. Though I call myself Hispanic, I see myself within the history of African Americans and Irish Catholics and American Jews and the Chinese in California" (128).[49] Rodriguez's emphasis on the multiplicity of ethnic and cultural influences in American society seems to serve as a critique to claims of racial or cultural purity embraced by the adherents of American exceptionalism; however, in making this claim, Rodriguez, similar to Ellison, overlooks the reality that while Asian Americans form an integral part of California and the country, Indian Americans, for example, have fought against the processes of racialization and marginalization as exemplified by the Supreme Court case *United States v. Bhagat Singh Thind* of 1923 (P. Taylor 46); thus, Rodriguez's post-1960s pluralistic inclusion of different ethnic groups in California omits these groups' past racialized history within mainstream society.

Rodriguez maintains—as Ellison does—that historical events show that the country has been already culturally mixed since its inception, but Rodriguez similarly fails to acknowledge the unequal position of power and influence among different racial and ethnic groups during the formation of the country. According to Rodriguez, the early republic began as a confluence of cultures when the "the meeting of the Indian, the African, and the European in colonial America" formed the "founding palette," which leads him to claim that his "nature is already mixed" (*Brown* xii, xv). While this is an evocative image that posits the mixing of racial and ethnic groups as the essence of early settlements by Europeans in the American continent, Rodriguez's image fails to take into account the processes of displacement, violence, and subjuga-

---

49. Rodriguez adds, "My classmates at Sacred Heart School, two blocks from our house, belong to families with names that come from Italy and Portugal and Germany. . . . We [were] an American classroom. And yet we [were] a dominion of Ireland," since he was taught by Irish Catholic nuns ("Nothing Lasts" 206).

tion of indigenous and Black bodies put in place by European settlers. Rafael Pérez-Torres cautions that in discussions of cultural mixing in early American historical periods, it is necessary to acknowledge "the physical memory of injustice and inhuman exploitation" at the root of cultural exchanges among different groups (4). In most of his writings and public statements, Rodriguez appears reluctant to acknowledge the degree in which violence, power, and racial social stratification have influenced cultural exchanges in the formation of the US. Despite these oversights, Rodriguez similarly argues, as does Ellison, that mainstream American culture has been influenced by Blacks. Rodriguez, for instance, rejects the idea of Black history and culture as separate from mainstream American history since "to be an American is to belong to black history" ("Asians" 170). Ellison for his part makes a similar point when he states that "materially, psychologically, and culturally, part of the nation's heritage is [African] American, and whatever becomes will be shaped in part by the Negro's presence" ("What America" 111). Ellison and Rodriguez, however, constantly fail to historicize in their essays the unequal power dynamics in which Blacks contributed to American culture.

Just as with the problem of presenting Black history and culture as separate from mainstream America, Rodriguez warns about emphasizing ideas of cultural "diversity" when discussing the country's identity and cultural heritage since "diversity" contradicts the idea of a shared and homogeneous American cultural identity. At different instances, Rodriguez voices his opposition to the noun "diversity" since the term, Rodriguez argues, stresses racial, ethnic, or cultural difference instead of emphasizing cultural commonalities; as a result, he is critical of the term diversity, since it is "a liquid noun [that] admits everything [and] stands for nothing" ("Asians"169). Rodriguez, for instance, explicitly embraced America's cultural heritage symbolized by figures such as Jefferson, Franklin, and the seventeenth-century Puritans while negating his allegiance to Mexican historical figures ("Asians" 169).[50] Rodriguez's apparent rejection of his Mexican American background and his adherence to an American historical and cultural heritage have been criticized by Latinx scholars as an acquiescence to a hegemonic American historical narrative due in part to his desire to assimilate;[51] for instance, in his analysis of Hunger of Memory, Ramón Saldívar argues that "Rodriguez chooses to assimilate without ever considering whether he acted by will or merely submitted to an unquestioned grander scheme of political ideology" (Chicano 158).

---

50. In another essay, for example, Rodriguez provocatively acknowledges Jefferson, rather than Benito Juárez, as his cultural forefather ("American Writer" 5).

51. For discussions on Rodriguez's engagement with social class and assimilation, see Moya 115–23; and Cutler, Ends of Assimilation 89–95.

Saldívar's point is pertinent since Rodriguez's critique of the Chicanx Movement overlooks the major social, economic, and political forces that had kept people of color on the margins in the US for centuries. If not an attempt to assimilate, Rodriguez's embrace of America's historical and cultural heritage is possible through an ahistorical or selective reading of America's history of race relations.[52] Throughout his essays and interviews, however, in a manner that echoes Ellison's attempt to downplay the historical marginalized position of Blacks, Rodriguez appears reluctant to acknowledge that large numbers of Mexican Americans have experienced different circumstances that made them question and challenge their unequal place within American society and its institutions.

A significant parallel emerges in some of the essays and public statements by Rodriguez and Ellison as both writers argue that despite the marginalization of people of color, they were able to assert their individuality in part through the reading of canonical authors.[53] Both Ellison and Rodriguez offer their own background and experiences reading Western and American authors to proclaim their mixed cultural identities. Rodriguez credits his contact with the educational system as the entry point to American cultural and literary heritage, as he writes that while growing up, "I didn't like America. Then I entered the culture. I entered the culture as you did, by going to school" ("Asians" 172).[54] In an early essay, Rodriguez adds, "I entered high school, having read hundreds of books. . . . Reading also gave me a broad sense of the concerns of Western culture" ("Education" 138). This statement resembles Ellison's position in "The World and the Jug" when he discusses the relation between literature and his "identity as a Western man" (117). Due in part to his reading experiences, Rodriguez argues that despite being a member of an ethnic group, he is not alienated from mainstream American culture; interestingly, Rodriguez claims that the pre-1960s American literary tradition was already culturally mixed since, for example, it included primarily works *about* people of color and immigrants.[55] Rodriguez, following an expected line of

---

52. Perhaps, as Staten suggests, "instead of merely betraying a presumed Chicano identity, Rodriguez's life narrative mirrors the tensions and contradictions of the Mexican and Mexican American societies [in the United States]" (105).

53. Cutler has discussed the way Rodriguez uses the Western literary canon in *Hunger of Memory* as a form of "symbolic capital" and the role literature had in Rodriguez's process of assimilation (*Assimilation* 90–91, 103–10).

54. Rodriguez explains in another essay that his cultural identity changed by reading canonical works at school and at the library; he states, "My teachers became the new figures of authority in my life. . . . I trusted their every direction. Each book they told me to read, I read and then waited for them to tell which books I enjoyed" ("Education" 131).

55. Rodriguez remembers going to the Clunie Library in Sacramento and reading Baldwin, Alfred Kazin, Willa Cather, and Twain, and discovering that American literature was already multiethnic ("American Writer" 11).

argumentation, omits in his claims that the pre-1960s American literary tradition functioned in relation to the exclusion of writers of color and that the inclusion of a handful of authors did not compensate for centuries of cultural and literary invisibility.

Based on his past reading experiences, Rodriguez was troubled by the challenges to the pre-1960s American literary canon posed by students of color protesting for changes at college campuses starting in the late 1960s. Rather than welcoming the advent of ethnic studies programs and the reading of authors of color on college campuses, Rodriguez laments that "now the American university is dismantling the American canon in my name" and provocatively equates the reevaluation of the American literary tradition with "the severing of memory" and "the dismantlement of [the] national culture" ("Asians" 171). As equally complicated as Ellison's exaltation of openly prejudiced white authors such as Faulkner and his reluctance to teach a Black literature course, Rodriguez's claims of cultural pluralism contain glaring misconceptions such as his open critique of Mexican American literature. While a graduate student at UC–Berkeley working on his PhD in the 1970s, Rodriguez openly questioned the idea of Mexican American literature itself and the student-led and social protest movements that brought changes to the way Latinx authors began to be published by independent presses, taught, and read at college campuses beginning in the late 1960s.[56] In an essay that precedes *Hunger of Memory*, Rodriguez discusses the "problem" with teaching a "Chicano novel" course by explaining that "this new literature, [the students] assured me, has an important role to play in helping to share the consciousness of a people currently without adequate representation in literature. Listening to them I was struck immediately with the cultural problems raised by their assumption" ("Going Home" 24). Part of Rodriguez's resistance to teaching a Chicanx literature course reflects common critiques made by conservative scholars after the 1960s who feared that racial and ethnic identification were favored in detriment to aesthetic value.[57] Ultimately, Rodriguez, similar to Ellison before him, was equally unwilling to accept the valid demands of

---

56. In an often-discussed episode in *Hunger of Memory* when a group of Chicanx students ask him to teach a "minority literature" class, he remembers wondering, "I don't think there *was* such a thing as minority literature" (161). Tomás Rivera's early analysis of *Hunger of Memory* explores the limitations of Rodriguez's reasoning in relation to Chicanx literature ("*Hunger*" 5–13).

57. Rodriguez openly opposes the increasing emphasis of ethnic studies programs and the opening of the literary canon by claiming that "when the American university began to approve" the creation of Black studies programs, "and when blood became the authority to speak, I felt myself rejected by black literature and felt myself rejecting black literatures as 'theirs'" (*Brown* 27).

students of color for the teaching and reading of writers whose voices and stories had been excluded up to that time.

In their roles as public intellectuals, Rodriguez and Ellison aspired to an apolitical art based on universality; however, claims of apolitical art often evade social responsibility and dismiss the marginalized position of authors of color vis-à-vis a Eurocentric and English-speaking literary tradition.[58] Rodriguez found in universality a form to counteract what he perceived as post-1960s authors of color's emphasis on race and ethnicity rather than aesthetic merit. In relation to Chicanx literature, Rodriguez explains, "Neither did I seek brown literature or any other kind. I sought Literature—the deathless impulse to explain and describe. I trusted white literature, because I was able to attribute universality to white literature, because it did not seem to be written for me" (*Brown* 27). Rodriguez arrives at a similar position in which Ellison found himself when the latter argued in "The World and the Jug" that his attraction to white male authors was based on artistic merit rather than racial identification. Charles Mills, however, warns about arguments made based on "universality" noting that "whites have routinely talked in universalist terms even when it has been quite clear that the scope has really been limited to themselves" (110). While fiction may be studied through aesthetic and "universal" values, Rodriguez and Ellison in their essays and public statements seldom acknowledged that very few white writers, critics, and scholars had ascribed that same quality of universality to the works of countless Black and Latinx writers before the 1960s.

Ellison and Rodriguez articulate in their nonfiction and public statements how individuals from different racial and ethnic backgrounds in the US have influenced, in different degrees, American culture. In their essays, both writers similarly question broad racial and ethnic categories, such as "white" and "black," and explore how American culture and its literature have been at times the result of the merging and blending of influences. Based on their engagement with the literary tradition, Ellison and Rodriguez offer similar arguments for their mixed cultural identities. Along with their insights into American culture and its literary tradition, their essays also contain limitations; both authors were unwilling to acknowledge the legitimate grievances of social activists and students of color or their calls for change at college campuses starting in the 1960s, which were instrumental in the creation of ethnic studies programs and the opening of the literary canon—and increasing opportunities for writers of color—from which Ellison and Rodriguez

---

58. In her analysis of Rodriguez's writings, Moya cogently dismantles Rodriguez's claim of universality and characterizes it as a "false universality" since it is based on a "universal subject" that is "bourgeois heterosexual European male" (124).

directly benefited. In a country that has historically struggled to acknowledge the complexities and nuances of race, ethnicity, and cultural influences from different racial and ethnic groups, the essays of Ellison and Rodriguez remain relevant for their insights as well as for their limitations; they are testament to the contentious reinterpretation of the contribution of racial and ethnic groups within a predominantly white society that until the 1960s systematically minimized the contributions of people of color to American cultural and literary heritage.

CHAPTER 5

Struggles in the Fields

Communities of Color in the Narratives of
Alice Walker and Helena María Viramontes

Alice Walker and Helena María Viramontes attended college when the American literary tradition had not yet been transformed by students' demands for curriculum changes at colleges and universities. Walker's essays from the 1970s are informed by her search for representation of Black authors in the literary tradition; while studying literature at Spellman and Sarah Lawrence, Walker found something missing: the writing of Black authors, particularly Black women.[1] As a student, Walker was not asked to read Black writers since they were assumed to be unimportant; instead, she was directed "toward a plethora of books by mainly white male writers" (*In Search* 6).[2] Walker grew up in rural Georgia, but when she looked for the representation of her experiences in fiction, she discovered that at Sarah Lawrence, Southern literature consisted primarily of the works of William Faulkner and Flannery O'Connor while the works of Jean Toomer and Zora Neale Hurston were out of print or relegated to bookshelves at university libraries (*In Search* 132). Walker's expe-

---

1. In relation to Walker's search for Black authors, she explains that "mindful that throughout my four years at a prestigious black and then a prestigious white college I had heard not one word about early black women writers, one of my first tasks was simply to determine whether they have existed" (*In Search* 9).

2. Walker was interested in the literary tradition but was dismayed when she discovered that a "comprehensive" anthology of English and American poetry did not include a single Black poet (*In Search* 131).

rience is not unique since before the 1970s, writers of color were, for the most part, excluded from American literature courses that were dominated by white male writers.[3] While Viramontes's experience as a literature student at Immaculate Heart College reflects the lack of Chicanx literature available to students, it also marks the beginning of changes in the inclusion of writers of color in college curricula.[4] As a California native, Viramontes could not find the experiences of Mexican American farmworkers in California represented in the literary tradition.[5] Based in part on their educational and reading experiences, Walker and Viramontes sought to inscribe their respective communities of color—which have previously been marginalized—into the literary tradition.

Walker and Viramontes attended college at the height of the Black and Chicanx civil rights movements of the 1960s and 1970s, and their writing reflected the fight for social justice in communities of color. Walker experienced firsthand the reduced social and economic opportunities of Black sharecroppers and laborers in the South under Jim Crow segregation. Viramontes experienced the discrimination and marginalization of Mexican and Mexican American farmworkers in the agricultural fields of California at a time when César Chávez, Dolores Huerta, and other activists were fighting for farmworkers' rights. Starting during her college years, Walker participated in the increasing fight for civil rights and after graduation, she worked for the NAACP's Legal Defense and Educational Fund in Jackson, Mississippi (Byrd 10). While Walker and Viramontes were both involved in the civil rights struggles of the 1960s and 1970s, part of their legacies stem from the way their fiction aesthetically represents the social and economic marginalization of their respective communities of color. Walker's *The Third Life of Grange Copeland* (1970) and Viramontes's *Under the Feet of Jesus* (1995) represent two intricately crafted narratives that can be described as "art-novels," to borrow Mark McGurl's term, as both novels depict aesthetically the struggles of communities of color in the South and the Southwest in the decades leading to the changes brought by the civil rights struggles of the 1960s and 1970s, and in the process, Walker and Viramontes inscribe those stories into the literary tradition.

---

3. For a thorough analysis of the field of American literary studies prior to the 1960s, see Shumway, *Creating American Civilization*.

4. While attending college at the height of the Chicanx Movement, Viramontes was introduced in her classes to writers such as Angela Davis, Gwendolyn Brooks, and Nikki Giovanni, among others ("Elevated Thinking" 246).

5. While Tomás Rivera's . . . *And the Earth Did Not Devour Him* describes the experiences of Mexican American farmworkers, Viramontes explains that even as an English major, she "had read very little of Chicano or Chicana literature because it simply wasn't accessible to us" ("Faith" 253).

Some critics have focused on either *The Third Life of Grange Copeland* and the role of sharecropping in Southern Black communities or *Under the Feet of Jesus* and the power of agribusiness over Mexican American workers in the Southwest.[6] Similarly, scholars have studied either *Third Life* or *Under the Feet* in relation to each novel's stylistic or linguistic elements;[7] however, less attention has been given to the way both novels' aesthetic and stylistic elements influence the social justice themes found in both novels such as the economic dependency of either Black or Mexican American farmworkers, child labor exploitation, or health hazards affecting farmworkers of color in the decades before the 1970s; moreover, *Third Life* and *Under the Feet* have not been studied comparatively despite their compelling similarities. In this chapter, I explore the thematic, aesthetic, and stylistic parallels in *Third Life* and *Under the Feet*, and how the novels' shared social justice vision and goals are mediated through the novels' emphasis and use of language, symbolism, imagery, and narrative experimentation that are associated with American literary modernism. Both novels engage with literary aesthetics as Walker and Viramontes sought to inscribe their fiction, along with their communities, into the American literary tradition through their emphasis on craft and some techniques that have influenced the literary tradition dating back to Henry James. Both narratives emphasize the inner lives and struggles of families of color and rely on aesthetic techniques often associated with modernism such as narrative experimentation, which influences the way both narratives present white landowners, corporate agribusinesses, and even the rise of social justice movements in their respective agricultural communities. Likewise, both novels combine stylistic techniques with their representation of female characters, particularly Mem and Ruth in *Third Life* and Petra and Estrella in *Under the Feet*, and their experiences struggling against a social, educational, and economic system sustained by the oppression and exploitation of Black and Mexican American farmworkers.

While my analysis interprets *Third Life* and *Under the Feet* as engaging with some of the aesthetic tenets of American literary modernism, this is not to suggest that Walker and Viramontes saw themselves as deliberately engaging with the stylistic practices of modernist writers the way Ralph Ellison did in *Invisible Man*.[8] Instead, Walker's *Third Life* and Viramontes's *Under the Feet* are influenced by some of the aesthetic choices associated with various

6. See, for example, Butler; Mason; D. López, "Ghosts in the Barn"; and Vázquez.

7. See T. Davis; L. Cooper; and Moya.

8. On the influence of modernist writers such as T. S. Eliot on Ellison and his efforts to recreate those same modernist tendencies and techniques in his fiction, see Rampersad, Lyne, and Genter, among others.

forms of modernism and the practice of modernist writing present in the literary tradition; in the case of Walker, *Third Life* reflects modernist tendencies found in the work of Faulkner and Toomer;[9] as for Viramontes, the influence of modernist and aesthetic techniques derives in part from the influence of Gabriel García Márquez, who in turn was influenced by Faulkner.[10] My analysis participates in critical discussions that have focused on the shared experiences of Black and Latinx women novelists and their fight against historical and literary marginalization;[11] Gloria Anzaldúa, for instance, explains that for too long, the "fine arts and literature [did] not belong to women-of-color, and culture and the social system [have] enslave[d] [their] hands in clerical, factory, field or secretarial work" (xxiv).[12] The narratives of Walker and Viramontes show that Black and Latinx women novelists share a set of historical, social, and literary experiences that reflect the points of convergence and commonalities that unite writers and people of color.

THE LEGACY OF AGRICULTURAL EXPLOITATION IN THE SOUTH AND SOUTHWEST

A distinct aspect of sharecropping in the South prior to the 1960s is its close connection to slavery as a system of economic exploitation of Black bodies that began after the end of the Civil War and continued more or less unabated until the end of Jim Crow segregation. Sharecropping relied on laborers, mostly Black without land, to work a piece of land owned by white landowners and to pay for renting the land, tools, and equipment with the profits from crops; these economic arrangements often left Black sharecroppers and laborers increasingly in debt, which made them economically dependent on white

---

9. In her essays, Walker had written about her "slight attachment to William Faulkner" that she later came to question due to Faulkner's views on race, and the significance of Toomer's *Cane* in her own development as a writer (*In Search* 19, 133).

10. Before completing her MFA at UC-Irvine, Viramontes participated in a writing workshop taught by Gabriel García Márquez (Corpi 130); likewise, Viramontes has discussed the influence of Márquez's *One Hundred Years of Solitude* in her development as a writer ("Faith" 253–54).

11. See Suzanne Bost's comparative analysis of Cristina García's *The Agüero Sisters* and Walker's *By the Light of My Father's Smile* 203–10; Helane Androne's analysis of Morrison's "Recitatif" and Viramontes's "Tears on My Pillow"; Acampora and Cotten, *Unmaking Race, Remaking Soul*; Cotera, *Native Speakers*; and Romero, *Activism and the American Novel*.

12. Among the collected essays in Anzaldúa's *Making Face, Making Soul/Haciendo Caras*, she includes essays by Walker and Viramontes. Acampora makes a similar point when she argues that women writers of color in their work have "aesthetically transform[ed] the values that have been used to stain them as inferior, deficient, and defective" (2).

landowners and lenders. In his study on sharecropping, Edward Royce notes that "although planters undoubtedly relinquished some of their control over the labor force with the breakdown of the plantation system [after the end of slavery], sharecropping by no means entirely freed black laborers from landlord supervision and management" (182). Sharecropping evolved out of the system of slavery and kept a few of its most pernicious elements. A key similarity between the system of slavery and sharecropping was that whites remained in ownership and control of the land.[13] Adding to the precarious position of Black laborers, "planters still retained ultimate managerial authority. The black labor force in the South, consequently, remained subject to the decision-making power and supervision of the planter" (Royce 216). Equally significant, sharecropping contributed to a system of white supremacy that resulted in the complete economic, social, and political subjugation of rural Black communities throughout most of the Southern states;[14] as a consequence, sharecropping not only ensured Blacks' unequal position in economic terms but also formed part of a larger system of racial and social oppression.

Richard Wright's *Twelve Million Black Voices* shows how sharecropping in the Southern states remained a form of social and economic control for a vast number of Black rural communities well into the decades when Walker's family lived in the South. Growing up in the 1920s and 1930s in rural Mississippi, Wright witnessed sharecropping as a perverse system of economic dependency and social control of landless Black farmers and laborers by white landowners. Wright writes about countless numbers of Black families "trapped by [a] plantation system" and how the position of Black laborers and white landowners took the form of "an odd sort of father-child relationship" based on an "impulse to cruelty" rather than a "sense of intimate understanding" despite the close living proximity between Blacks and whites in the South (*Twelve* 49). Economically, Black sharecroppers and their families, according to Wright, carried the burden of losses due to bad crops, weather events, plagues, and injury, which often led them into debt spirals, perpetual economic dependency, and a deep sense of despair and to believe that their exploitation was a fixed aspect of Southern life (*Twelve* 40). Only after World War II, with the migration of Blacks to Northern cities and decades of social and civil rights activism, were Black workers able to enter other professions that subsequently diminished sharecropping as an economic system that had influenced the lives of Black farmers and their communities for almost a century. Walker's father

---

13. Royce observes that sharecropping "did not transform property relations" between white planters and Black laborers "nor did it liberate blacks from the agricultural labor market or from the need to hire themselves out to their former masters" (216).

14. For a discussion on the relation between sharecropping and Jim Crow segregation, see Royce 217–19.

had experienced sharecropping in rural Georgia, and she discussed sharecropping's toll not only in economic terms but also on the psyche of Black families.[15] In the afterword to *Third Life*, Walker discusses her family's difficulties and her desire to write about the conditions endured by Black sharecroppers in Georgia; she attempted to "speak up about violence among black people in the black community at the same time that all black people (and some whites)—including me and my family—were enduring massive psychological and physical violence from white supremacists in the southern states" ("Afterword" 314).[16] Walker's father and countless other Black sharecroppers were affected by the oppressive economic system that influenced the relationships among family members and members of their community.

The conditions of Mexican and Mexican American farmworkers in the Southwest after its annexation to the US share parallels in relation to the development of a system of agricultural production based on the exploitation of communities of color. Ramón Saldívar dates the abuses of Mexican and Mexican American farmworkers in the Southwest as far back as the Treaty of Guadalupe Hidalgo in 1848, making a connection between parallel systems of economic exploitation of communities of color in the South and the Southwest; he points out that "agricultural products grown by black slave labor and cheap Mexican wage labor on land expropriated from the Indians and Mexico thus paid for the growth of American agriculture and industry in the nineteenth century" (*Chicano Narrative* 17). The economic marginalization of Mexican and Mexican American farmworkers in the Southwest, similar to Black sharecroppers in the South, continued unabated well into the twentieth century. Marshall Ganz, a social activist who was involved in the fight for civil rights in Mississippi and then in California during the 1960s, notes that the history of Mexican and Mexican American farmworkers in California had been a history of marginalization and political disenfranchisement, which resembled the conditions faced by Black sharecroppers in Southern states under Jim Crow.[17]

The legacy of the labor struggle between Mexican American farmworkers and white landowners and agribusinesses led by César Chávez and Dolores Huerta in the grape fields of Delano, California, informs Viramontes's writing.

---

15. Walker writes about "the evil greedy men who worked [her] father to death" and how her father, in turn, lashed out against his own family (*In Search* 21). See also, Walker's interview with John O'Brien 40–45.

16. Walker herself experienced violence that was "embedded in [her] father's need to dominate my mother and their children" ("Afterword" 316).

17. Ganz goes on to explain that when he arrived in California in 1965 to work as a social activist, he "saw farm workers who faced challenges not unlike those faced by their southern counterparts: no voting power, low wages, and, as people of color, subjected to California's own legacy of racial discrimination, which began with the Chinese immigrants" (viii).

As Rodolfo Acuña explains, the struggle in the fields against grape growers in the San Joaquin Valley during the 1960s and 1970s was fought not only by Mexican Americans but by other groups such as Filipino agricultural workers, who were fighting for living wages at the time (*Occupied* 268). Chávez, Huerta, Gilbert Padilla, and other labor activists fought to unionize Mexican American farmworkers in an attempt to create leverage against large-scale agribusinesses such as the DiGiorgio Corporation that profited in the millions in part by paying low wages to farmworkers (Acuña, *Occupied* 269–70). Leading to the Delano strike, farmworkers' labor conditions were deplorable; farmworkers' salaries were extremely low, they lacked adequate facilities such as working toilets, and some agricultural towns consisted of "one-room shacks without gas" that housed several workers who were charged high rent (Ganz 107–8). Led by Chávez and Huerta, Mexican American farmworkers picketed the fields and marched to Sacramento; they won arduous legal battles against a few agribusinesses that were instrumental in the creation of legislation for the improvement of wages and working conditions in California.[18] Viramontes experienced the conditions of Mexican American farmworkers in California that led Chávez and other social activists to organize in the 1960s.[19] Although Viramontes grew up in East Los Angeles, and her father worked on construction sites, her family spent summers picking fruit in Northern California to earn extra money (Kass), and she dedicated *Under the Feet* to the memory of Chávez. Based in part on the experiences of Walker and Viramontes with the economic marginalization of Black sharecroppers and Mexican American farmworkers, respectively, both writers sought to thematize the long history of social and economic oppression of Black and Mexican American families in agricultural communities in *Third Life* and *Under the Feet*.

MODERNISM, MODERNISMS, AND WRITERS OF COLOR

Few literary movements have influenced American literature more than modernism; nonetheless, modernism has taken different forms from its height in the 1920s and 1930s to its influence in subsequent decades. Rather than one modernism, there are several with distinct characteristics, including high

---

18. Unfortunately, the fight for farmworkers' rights in the fields of Delano represented just one instance of a widespread system of farmworkers' exploitation across the Southwest and other states. According to Acuña, Chávez's organizing efforts and legislative victories changed the working conditions of relatively few Mexican American farmworkers, since "Chavez at his zenith represented less than 10 percent of the nation's farm workers, limited to the states of California, Arizona, and Florida" (*Occupied* 276).

19. As Barbara Curiel rightly points out, "Published only two years after the death of César Chávez in 1993, Viramontes's novel is informed by the legacy of his political strategies" (30).

modernism, European modernism, Latin American modernism, late modernism, American modernism, and rural modernism, to name a few. Critics who have studied modernism in relation to authors from the Harlem Renaissance and in relation to American and European fiction describe two distinctive elements that emerge from the scholarship of modernism related to its ideological and aesthetic dimensions.[20] The first element relates to the ideological and historical elements of modernism as they relate to the emergence of the modern world at the turn of the twentieth century, the rise of the city, the destruction created by World War I, and the war's effects on individuals' psyche; for instance, individuals' alienation, distrust of previous ideologies, and religious certainties, represent major themes in T. S. Eliot's "The Waste Land." A second element of modernism relates to its aesthetic, stylistic, and linguistic choices; form and narrative experimentation; and the premise that poetry and fiction should be studied as works of art or aesthetic endeavors. Examples of this are the works of Eliot, Gertrude Stein, and William Faulkner, among others. The engagement with what has become known as modernist tendencies or style in the American literary tradition precedes the twentieth century and World War I, as some of these premises were famously advanced and theorized by Henry James in his essay "The Art of Fiction," published in 1888. James's vision of fiction as an artistic endeavor famously equates "the artist who paints a picture and the artist who writes a novel" (30). Mark McGurl, for instance, traces the development of the "modernist novel" as an attempt to create an "art-novel" based in part on James's vision of the novel as "fine art" (*Novel Art* 2).

The aesthetic tenets of modernism presented in the works of James and Eliot influenced American writers such as Toomer, Faulkner, and Ellison, and some of those modernist tendencies and premises are similarly present in the narratives of Walker and Viramontes. Toomer's *Cane,* for instance, equally shares the emphasis on narrative fragmentation found in "The Waste Land" and responds to the call for fiction as a highly crafted piece of art.[21] Although Faulkner witnessed the historical and moral dismantling of the modern world along with Eliot, Faulkner engages with aesthetics of modernism but presents

---

20. While Baker sees high modernist and Harlem Renaissance writers as hardly sharing the ideological dimension of modernism (*Modernism* xvi), George Hutchinson argues that the break between modernist writers such as Eliot and Black writers like Toomer is a false binary since the emphasis on democratic, cultural, and racial values—all ideological elements of modernism—were shared by both groups of writers (*Harlem* 14, 29–30). Blurring the lines between the ideological and aesthetic tenets of modernism, Michael North argues that the work of high modernist writers such as Eliot and Stein contains Black cultural and linguistic influences (25–26).

21. Sollors discusses Toomer's *Cane* as representative of "aesthetic modernism" and as a work that fuses "poetry, prose, and drama" and "a text that appeals to all senses by presenting strong visual images and musical and rhythmic effects that evoke smells and powerful feelings of pain and suffering" ("Jean Toomer's *Cane*" 20).

a discontinuity regarding the ideological aspect of modernism as his novels engage with the South and rural settings.[22] McGurl makes a similar point when he argues that Faulkner thought of the novel as a higher form of art, responding to James's call for fiction as a "fine art"; however, the major concerns in Faulkner's novels are not related to high culture or the intellect but rather depictions of "low life" (*Novel Art* 6). Decades later, Ellison continued the modernist tradition by engaging with Eliot's high modernism either by adopting or subverting some of its ideological and aesthetic tenets.[23] While scholars have discussed in detail modernist tendencies in pre-1960s Black writers, and scholars of Latinx literature have increasingly looked at late nineteenth- and early twentieth-century Spanish-language texts printed in the US for modernist influences,[24] less critical attention has been given to how some stylistic elements found in modernist writers have influenced post-1960s authors of color such as Walker and Viramontes.[25] *Third Life* and *Under the Feet* reflect their authors' preoccupation with what Henry James describes as the search for form since "questions of art are questions . . . of execution" (41); as writer-artists, Walker and Viramontes strive to create highly crafted works of art that rely on early literary models and emphasize the aesthetic elements of their compositions.

CYCLES OF ECONOMIC DEPENDENCY IN THE FIELDS OF GEORGIA

Some aspects of Walker's publication history are representative of the way post-1960s Black women writers fought to be included within the mainstream literary tradition that had kept them on the margins for centuries. Walker's

22. According to David Davis, one of the "modern" elements in modernist novels was their engagement with the phenomenon of the modern city, but the particularity of a Southern writer like Faulkner was that he made use of the stylistic experimentations in modernism and incorporated them into rural settings (89).

23. As Rampersad notes, Ellison admired "The Waste Land" as a highly crafted form of artistic expression, and Ellison himself, on different occasions, discussed *Invisible Man* in the context of Eliot's high modernism (76–77). William Lyne, however, argues that while "*Invisible Man* fits squarely into the Jamesian modernist tradition—the tradition of the well-made, artistically conscious novel," Ellison subverted those modernist models (322).

24. Cutler argues that the robust tradition of Spanish-language print culture in the US at the turn of the twentieth century was closely connected to "hemispheric literary movements," including Latin American modernism, which preceded European and American modernism ("At the Crossroads"). See also Lomas, *Translating Empire*.

25. One notable exception is John Christie's *Latino Fiction and the Modernist Imagination* that explores the development of post-1960s Latinx literature in part through Latinx authors' engagement with modernism and postmodernism. Christie, for example, identifies the short fiction of Cisneros and Viramontes as works that "establish their cohesiveness through associations and juxtapositions as modernist fiction does" (18).

literary career began with the 1968 publication of her poetry collection *Once* by Harvest Books, a subsidiary of mainstream publisher Harcourt.[26] The publication of *The Third Life of Grange Copeland* in 1970, also by Harcourt, coincided with the gains made by student-led protests to include writers of color in the college curricula and the mainstream publishers' response to this newfound demand. The publication of *Third Life* also relates to the time when women of color were beginning to enter academia in increasing numbers, and the works of female writers of color were first being studied and recognized by mainstream cultural institutions. Walker's *The Color Purple*, published in 1982, became the first novel by a Black writer to win the Pulitzer Prize and the National Book Award in 1983 in the extended histories of both literary prizes (Byrd 20–21); however, breaking into academic and cultural institutions that had traditionally marginalized the work of Black women writers continued to be a constant struggle as Black women writers experienced resistance even from Black male authors.[27] Walker became one of the first Black female writers to gain continued literary success and critical attention, which were both major literary achievements considering the long history of literary neglect of Black female writers dating back to Phillis Wheatley.

Criticism on *Third Life* has either emphasized the influence of the social and economic systems on the novel's characters or has explored its aesthetic and stylistic elements.[28] Barbara Christian, for example, correctly notes that *Third Life* shows "the tight control the white bosses have over black sharecroppers and how this control, although seemingly focused on a work relationship, finds its way into the relationships between black men, black women, and black children" (184–85). Other scholars have concentrated on Walker's engagement and emphasis on language while analyzing Walker's poetry in relation to her fiction, the influence of Toomer in Walker's nonfiction, and some of the shared stylistic elements in the writing of Walker and Ernest Hemingway.[29] While most analyses of *Third Life* focus on either its social and economic themes or the novel's stylistic elements, less attention has been given to the way the novel's critique of sharecropping and its effects on the Copeland family, particularly on Mem and Ruth, are influenced by stylistic and narrative

---

26. Walker's second poetry collection, *Revolutionary Petunias*, published in 1973, was nominated for the National Book Award (Byrd 16).

27. Valerie Babb notes that Walker's emphasis on the experience of Black women in her novels encountered resistance and was criticized by authors such as Ishmael Reed since it was "not unexpected that novels challenging presumptions [were] subjected to censure, but moving black and female experience from the margin to the center generated particular vitriol" (159).

28. See Butler 197–98 and Mason 297–301.

29. See T. Davis, "Poetry as Preface to Fiction"; Matthew Fike's analysis of Walker as rewriting of some of *Cane*'s passages in Walker's "In Search of Our Mothers' Gardens"; and Brogan, "Hemingway Talking to Walker."

elements, such as its use of language, imagery, symbolism, narrative experimentation, and shifting points of views, which are at the center of Walker's
vision of her work as an "art-novel" based in part on modernist premises.

Part of *Third Life*'s experimentation with narrative is its focus on the
Copeland family members and their overlapping and cyclical trajectories that,
rather than emphasizing geographical space and historical time, call attention
to the long history of Southern sharecropping. *Third Life* takes place in Green
County, Georgia, in the early decades of the twentieth century leading up to
the 1960s; however, geographical space and historical time are purposefully
obscured; instead, place and time are pieced together from the characters' life
experiences, as sharecropping was embedded into the social and economic
fabric of the rural South. Early episodes in the narrative show the cyclical
nature of male characters' economic dependency. The novel begins with Uncle
Silas's journey to the North; then, it is Grange who leaves for the North, and
subsequently Grange's son, Brownfield, follows their path and heads north.
Grange and Brownfield take the same route and not only stop at the same
place but are romantically involved with the same woman, Josie. Grange and
Brownfield find themselves, at different times, trapped by the same cycle of
sharecropping, poverty, and debt. The narrative also creates a parallel between
the system of slavery and sharecropping as an oppressive force that dictates the
choices of members of the Copeland family. Mem compares the living conditions of her family to those during "slavery times" (110). Captain Davis, the
white landowner, shows a paternalistic view of Black laborers working his land;
he thinks it is a shame that he needs to "look after" Black sharecroppers and
considers Brownfield's family as part of his own "family" (105, 118). The narrative's spatial indeterminacy suggests that the echoes of the paternalistic views
taken by slaveowners have morphed—rather than disappeared—after slavery.

Walker's novel mediates its depiction of child labor with aesthetic elements, as exemplified by the description of Daphne working in the cotton
fields—and her poisoning by handling arsenic—which relies on imagery,
symbolism, and shifting character perspectives. While working in the cotton
fields, Daphne, the oldest Brownfield's daughter, does "the tricky, dangerous
and disgusting business of handmopping the cotton bushes with arsenic to
keep off boll weevils" (71). The boll weevils, while only a passing reference,
symbolize the destruction of crops that contributed to Black sharecroppers'
economic debt and dependency on landowners. Daphne's handling of poison-
ous chemicals is presented through Brownfield's perspective in part to accentuate the effects on his psyche; as Brownfield witnesses the scene, his "heart
. . . actually start[s] to hurt him, like an ache in the bones, when he watche[s]
[Daphne] swinging the mop, stumbling over the clumps of hard clay, the hot
tin bucket full of arsenic making a bloodied scrape against her small short leg"

(71). Daphne's poisoning episode relies on impressionistic imagery rather than a reportorial denunciation as Brownfield sees Daphne "drenched with sweat, her tattered dress wringing wet with perspiration and arsenic; her large eyes reddened by the poison" (71). After Daphne spills arsenic on her body, "she breathe[s] with difficulty through the deadly smell. At the end of the day she trembled and vomited and looked beaten down like a tiny, asthmatic old lady" (71). From Brownfield's perspective, witnessing Daphne's poisoning and health deterioration at a close distance makes him realize that they are trapped in an uncaring economic system that is not far removed from the logic of the plantation economy during the era of slavery; he laments that he "could not save his children from slavery" since "they did not even belong to him" (72), thus continuing to blur the lines between slavery and sharecropping.

Third Life relies on imagery, in the form of drawings, language, and writing to thematize the history of racism and colonialism that Ruth experiences through the educational system as she discovers at school "The Tree of the Family of Man," an annotated textbook depicting the pseudo-scientific hierarchy of races. This episode encapsulates Ruth's encounters with racism in a segregated school in the South during Jim Crow. While in sixth grade, Ruth receives a secondhand textbook and discovers that it has previously belonged to Jacqueline Paine, a white student in an all-white school, who had written her name on the textbook; hence, Jacqueline's simple act of writing her name and originally owning the textbook points toward Ruth's second-class status as a student within the educational system. When Ruth inspects her used textbook, she discovers a drawing titled "The Tree of the Family of Man," which places whites of European descent at the top, with people of color in the middle, and a Black person at the bottom (239). This episode relies on Ruth reading Jacqueline's marginal notes on the drawing, and consequently Jacqueline's thoughts. Jacqueline's writings and annotations on the drawing that depicts the pseudo-scientific hierarchy of races shows the pernicious racist ideology promoted in textbooks, a learning tool that in this case also serves to foster racism. Jacqueline writes, for example, under the picture of a Native American, "*We saved them from disease and wild primitive life. Taught them useful activities as pictured above. They have also been known to make beads*" (239); while only a two-sentence annotation, Jacqueline's writing succinctly summarizes how a white-controlled educational system perceives Native Americans as "primitive" and in need to be "saved." Even more damaging, under the drawing of "a man, in black, with fuzzy hair, fat grinning lips, and a bone sticking through his nose" (239), Jacquelin simply writers "*A nigger*" (240). This episode thematizes images and writing as tools that naturalize racist ideologies that were sanctioned and perpetuated by education systems well into the 1950s.

A similar episode in *Third Life* that thematizes language itself is Mem's loss of her ability to talk, which is presented as the first step in Mem's gradual mental and physical decline after her marriage to Brownfield. The narrative states that the way Brownfield "set[s] out to destroy" Mem is through "her speech" (74). Mem originally went to school to become a schoolteacher, but after marrying Brownfield, he "drag Mem away from schoolteaching" since "her knowledge reflected badly on a husband who could scarcely read and write. It was his great ignorance that sent her into white homes as a domestic, his need to bring her down to his level!" (73). Mem's linguistic ability, in the form of reading and writing, becomes a curse under a sharecropping system that relies on Black laborers' inability to acquire skills that would remove them from the cotton fields. Brownfield affects Mem's linguistic ability by verbally demeaning her; Brownfield, for instance, reacts angrily when he is corrected by Mem on his own speech and yells back, "why do *you* always have to be so damn proper?" (74). Brownfield also humiliates Mem when she speaks in public; however, this "was not what Brownfield was after, either. He wanted her to talk, but to talk like what she was, a hopeless nigger woman who got her ass beat every Saturday night" (74). Mem's mental and physical decline is accompanied by a linguistic regression as Brownfield succeeds at affecting Mem's diction "first to please her husband, and then because she honestly could not recall her nouns and verbs, her plurals and singulars, Mem began speaking once more in her old dialect" (75). Mem's linguistic agency is taken away to call attention to her subordinate family role.

Mem's physical decline at the hands of Brownfield, and the family's ruinous economic condition, is depicted in part through the imagery and symbolism of the sharecropping cabins to which Brownfield is forced to move by white landowners. Theodore Mason correctly observes that *Third Life* "uses the sharecropper's cabin as a charged metaphorical structure indicating the fundamental and irresistible entrapment of its occupants" (297). After their marriage, Brownfield moves Mem and their daughters "from one sharecropper's cabin to another" as a reflection of Brownfield's economic dependency (77). Brownfield is a product of a Southern agricultural system based on the exploitation of Black farmers that had oppressed him all his life, and by the time he marries, this economic system has already "completely destroyed" him (286). The cabin where Ruth is born offers an insight into the family's state of neglect and utter poverty through Brownfield's indifference and inability to heat the cabin; it is noted that the "walls had been covered, probably neatly one time, with paper bags. . . . But the bags hung down now, here and there, in rustling flaps; the wind had pushed them loose" (91). The cabin's windows are covered with cardboard, but when it rains, the cold water gets in. Mem's gradual physical decline parallels the ongoing deterioration of the family's dwellings. Due to her work as a maid, and aggravated by Brownfield's violence, Mem shows a "swelling of the womb" and is unable to "hold out against him with nausea, aching feet and teeth, swollen legs, bursting veins and head" (133). Mem's body is also affected by "the two pregnancies [Brownfield] forced on her in the new house," which, "although they did not bear live fruit, almost completely destroyed what was left of her health" (137). Mem's narrative of descent ends with her death as Brownfield shoots her, which results in his going to jail.

Ruth's prominence in the latter part of *Third Life*, as the only carrier of hope in the Copeland family, relies on stylistic elements presented earlier in the narrative as Grange returns to Green County to assist Ruth in her attempt to break the family's cycle of social and economic marginalization. As Grange undergoes a transformation by becoming the guardian of Ruth by offering a sanctuary, he replaces Brownfield as Ruth's father figure after the former returns to George from the North where he experienced the racism that he originally tried to escape. While Grange is unable to erase his past vicious treatment of his wife Margaret and their children, the difference between Grange—in the latter part of the narrative—and Brownfield is that Grange stops blaming white people for his actions. Grange purchases a farm, in part with money borrowed from Josie, and in a symbolic gesture begins to grow cotton, which represents his attempt at economic independence as a landowner. A similar evocative gesture is that Grange does not allow Ruth to pick the cotton, since she is "not some kind of field hand!" (165); hence, the narrative presents Grange's attempt to break the entrenched cycle of economic dependency that was depicted as immutable at the start of the novel. In contrast to Brownfield's dilapidated cabin, Grange, now as Ruth's guardian, builds a "log cabin" for her that becomes her playhouse and a metaphorical place of respite (174). Grange's transformation, and attempt at a new life, serves as the basis for Ruth's desire to break the cycle of dependency as she begins to learn about the world outside Georgia and the possibilities beyond working in the fields, cooking for a white family, or marrying a man.

Significantly, episodes of the social activism of the 1950s and the early 1960s are presented toward the end of *Third Life*; however, it is unclear what effect those events have on Ruth since the narrative remains focused on the members of the Copeland family. For instance, the fight for school desegregation, which had affected Ruth's education and that of countless Black students, is only mentioned in one sentence by Grange when he notes that "the court been tellin' everybody that the black schools ain't up to the white" (250). While Grange tells Ruth to remember that "there have always been black folks fighting for better" (251), the references to the fight to end segregation in the South remain underdeveloped. Likewise, Ruth initially finds out about the increasing acts of civil disobedience on TV as "each day there were pictures of students marching, singing, praying, led by each other and by Dr. Martin Luther King" (292). When Ruth witnesses a student march in town, its description remains intermittent and impressionistic; Ruth sees students marching with signs that read: "I AM AN AMERICAN TOO!" and "I WANT FREEDOM TOO!" (295). Ruth's experience witnessing the march relies on symbolism as "someone push[es] a piece of paper into her hands" with the image of "a white man and woman chained to a rock" called "racism" with the caption, "You Will Not Be Free Until We Are Free" (296). The narrative, however, is ambiguous regarding the influence that the march has on Ruth; similarly, one of the final scenes in the novel involves a group of Black and white students visiting Grange's farm and encouraging him to register to vote, but the narrative does not reveal whether Grange votes. *Third Life* suggests that while the increasing fight for civil rights in the South has influenced Ruth, her attempt to break the family's cycle of poverty and dependency remains in her own hands.

Third Life remains similarly ambiguous regarding Ruth's subsequent trajectory, but one certainty is the shooting of Brownfield at the hands of his own father and the latter's death by the local police. When Grange shoots Brownfield at the courthouse, the narrative suggests that Grange seals his fate since his act will be punished through the white-controlled legal system; Grange physically liberates Ruth from Brownfield's control, but in doing so, he gives up his own life. The final scene describes the shooting of Grange by the police next to the house he built for Ruth. The gruesome and indiscriminate violence used to end Grange's life calls attention to the endless cycle of racial violence exacerbated by the historical marginalization of Black communities in the South and its effects on the Copeland family. The oppression experienced by the family stands for the marginalization of countless families in the rural South before the diminishing of the sharecropping system; however, *Third Life*'s indictment of a ruthless agricultural system based on exploitation of Black bodies represents one aspect of a larger economic system that similarly affected Mexican American farmworkers and their communities around the same time, thousands of miles away.

LABOR CAMPS AND MEXICAN AMERICANS IN THE CALIFORNIA AGRICULTURAL FIELDS

The genesis of Viramontes's *Under the Feet of Jesus* reflects another way the fight against literary marginalization was fought by Mexican American women writers in the post-1960s era, as women of color began to attend Master of Fine Arts (MFA) programs after the 1960s but continued to struggle for the validation of their fiction.[30] The nationwide institutionalization of creative writing programs and the training of writers, or what Mark McGurl describes as "the Program Era," coincides with the growing inclusion of writers of color in university curricula in the late 1960s and early 1970s. Viramontes's experiences at different writing programs, however, show that some faculty members at those programs in their pre-1960s form still perceived the American literary tradition as primarily the domain of white male writers who served as models. For Viramontes, as a writer of color in training, she had to overcome open discrimination and the diminishing of her experiences as a Mexican American woman by some faculty. After Viramontes left the graduate program at California State–Los Angeles, she enrolled at UC–Irvine MFA program in 1979, but at one point she was discouraged by yet another professor who thought her writing was merely a lesser "imitation of Gabriel García Márquez" (qtd. in Kass). Viramontes completed her graduate degree, and *Under the Feet* became her MFA thesis and was published by Plume in 1994. It was only after Viramontes received her MFA that she became a faculty member at Cornell University (Sáez 364). The publication history of *Under the Feet* represents an example of the multiple obstacles that Chicanx authors have encountered from the beginning of the Latinx literary tradition.

Scholars have focused on the social justice themes in *Under the Feet* such as farmworkers' economic exploitation, restrictive and racialized immigration policy, and environmental degradation.[31] Other critics have analyzed *Under the Feet*'s engagement with language, literacy, imagery, or other stylistic elements;[32] however, similar to the way analyses of Walker's *Third Life* emphasize either the social or stylistic elements in the novel, criticism of *Under the Feet* similarly concentrates on either the aesthetic or social elements, with some exceptions.[33] Paula Moya aptly interprets *Under the Feet* in part through the lens of other works of American fiction that engage with economic marginalization in rural or agricultural areas, including Faulkner's *The Sound and the Fury,* John Steinbeck's *The Grapes of Wrath,* and Tomás Rivera's . . . *And the Earth*

---

30. When Viramontes attended graduate school at California State–Los Angeles, she "was told by a professor that she did not belong there because she was writing about Latino issues" (Kass).

31. See Shea, "'Don't Let Them'"; D. López, "Ghosts in the Barn"; and Vázquez, "Their Bones Kept Them Moving."

32. Lydia Cooper has discussed in a sustained manner how *Under the Feet* is "systematically masterful and so rich with allusion and symbolism" (367). See also Moya, *Learning from Experience*; and Yvonne Yarbro-Bejarano, "Phantoms and Patch Quilt People."

33. Moya focuses on the novel's main character, Estrella, and her empowerment in part through literacy and how Estrella uses language as a tool to interpret her reality and her "social world" (20). See also D. López, "Ghosts in the Barn."

Did Not Devour Him (175–76).[34] As part of her analysis, Moya also identifies *Under the Feet* as Viramontes's conscious attempt to inscribe her novel into the American literary tradition by connecting *Under the Feet* with the realism of Steinbeck; however, it is similarly possible to interpret *Under the Feet* through Faulkner's modernism or the modernist aesthetics that dominated the literary tradition prior to the 1960s. *Under the Feet*'s use of stylistic elements associated with modernism shares close parallels to Walker's aesthetic choices in *Third Life*, as both novels mediate the representation and experiences of families of color in agricultural or rural settings through narrative experimentation, thematization of language, symbolism, imagery, and shifting points of view. Moreover, *Under the Feet*, just as *Third Life*, relies on the possibilities of the writer-as-artist model with the goal of crafting an "art-novel" that would allow both writers to inscribe the experiences of their respective communities of color along the fiction of canonical white male authors.

The narrative structure of *Under the Feet* experiments with shifts in time by overlapping characters' past memories and characters' point of view in an attempt to stretch the confines of linear narrative that resembles the emphasis on narrative experimentation in modernist novels. *Under the Feet* blurs geographical specificity and chronological certainty; instead, the novel likely takes place around the 1960s and focuses on the extent of the marginalization of a Mexican American family in the "labor camps" of California (13), whose experiences stand for those of countless similar Mexican American families who have toiled in the Southwest for decades. Moya has drawn parallels between *Under the Feet* and Faulkner's *Sound and the Fury* in relation to narrative structure;[35] *Under the Feet*'s shifting points of view and experimental narrative can similarly be interpreted under Faulkner's modernism, as shown in *As I Lay Dying*. Events in *As I Lay Dying* are told intermittently through the shifting points of view of different members of the Bundren family as they ride to the town of Jefferson to bury their matriarch, Addie, and events are presented at times in a recurrent manner through the perspective of different characters.[36] The first section of *Under the Feet* weaves together different scenes through characters' points of view as the scenes move between Estrella's family settling at their latest bungalow and two cousins, Alejo and Gumecindo, cutting peaches from trees at a nearby farm; however, within

---

34. Similarly, Barbara Curiel analyzes *Under the Feet* as responding to Steinbeck's *The Grapes of Wrath* and "some of its central assumptions about social justice for migrant workers" (28).

35. Moya explains that in *Under the Feet* "the narrative perspective shifts among four main characters so that the world portrayed literally changes characters—often from one paragraph to the next" (187).

36. In her discussion of Faulkner as a modernist writer, Jolene Hubbs describes *As I Lay Dying*'s narrative as eschewing linear time and presenting different narrators' accounts (462).

this alternating shift in characters' perspectives, there is an additional shift in narrative when Estrella remembers her father leaving the family when she was a child. *Under the Feet* contains similar scenes when an object or a person brings back a memory from Estrella, Petra, or Perfecto, and the narrative seamlessly shifts to a past memory, as in the scene when Estrella is picking grapes and the sight of a "small girl . . . wailing" brings her back to the time when Petra took Estrella to the cotton fields for the first time (51).

Under the Feet, just as *Third Life*, contains a similar depiction of child labor and child workers' poisoning by exposure to chemicals on an agricultural field affecting families of color, albeit thousands of miles apart, that equally relies on impressionistic scenes, imagery, and symbolism. Child labor and chemical poisoning in the fields, with few repercussions to white landowners, is thematized in both novels as these harrowing poisoning accidents appear as common practice for as long as children have worked in those fields. David Vázquez insightfully argues that *Under the Feet* "suggests that toxicity and environmental degradation are structural aspects of farmworker life" and describes Alejo's poisoning as the "central crisis in the novel" (363, 373). As a biplane begins to fumigate a peach orchard, whether by accident or as common occurrence, it begins to "releas[e] the shower of white pesticide" onto the peach trees at the same time Alejo and others are collecting peaches (76). The biplane hovering over the peach orchard resembles a "gray shadow cross[ing] over [them] like a crucifix" (76), a suggestive image that brings attention to the lethal dangers of chemical poisoning and the threat of death passing above the farmworkers. The scene also juxtaposes Alejo's suffocating in toxic chemicals with sensory imagery as the "lingering smell was a scent of ocean salt and beached kelp until he inhaled again and could detect under the innocence the heavy chemical choke of poison" (77). The extent of Alejo's poisoning relies on metaphors and the imagery of fire to accentuate the extent of his illness as Alejo feels "a hole ripped in his stomach like a match to paper, spreading into a deeper and bigger black hole that wanted to swallow him completely" (77). The appalling dangers experienced by child laborers and farmworkers in *Under the Feet* is reminiscent of Daphne's poisoning in *Third Life*, which calls attention to the novels' shared thematic and stylistic strategies.

The description of Estrella's learning process thematizes language itself and similarly echoes *Third Life* in its emphasis on literacy and the critique of a school system that stigmatizes and marginalizes children of color.[37] Estrella's language learning is equally connected to a school system that fails to teach

---

37. Critics have interpreted the scene when Estrella begins to decipher language and letters on her own by comparing them with the tools in Perfecto's red tool chest; therefore, connecting this scene to Estrella's "maturation" through her mastery of semiotics and her "expanded notion of literacy"; see L. Cooper 369; and Moya 177–80.

her how to read and is unable to understand the conditions of migrant children working in the fields, since teachers seem to be waiting "for the next batch of migrant children" (25). When Estrella comes to school, her teachers appear more interested in her physical appearance and cleanliness; as Estrella tries to learn the alphabet at school, "some of the teachers were more concerned about the dirt under her fingernails. They inspected her head for lice, parting her long hair with ice cream sticks" (24). The scene also emphasizes the teachers' counterproductive effect on Estrella's learning as they "scrubbed her fingers with a toothbrush until they were so sore she couldn't hold a pencil properly" (24–25); as a result, in the teachers' attempt to remove the soil under her fingernails—a proof of her exploitation as a child laborer—they further impede her ability to learn. Estrella is also stigmatized by her economic condition and appearance as she is asked by one of her teachers "how come her mama never gave her a bath. Until then, it had never occurred to Estrella she was dirty. . . . And for the first time, Estrella realized words could become as excruciating as rusted nails piercing the heels of her bare feet" (25). Estrella, similar to Ruth in *Third Life,* discovers that the educational system acts as a force that reinforces the marginalization of students of color along with its educational goals.

The characters of Petra in *Under the Feet* and Mem in *Third Life* share compelling similarities as mothers who struggle against oppressive male figures and a ruthless economic system based on exploitation that gradually debilitates them physically and psychologically. In *Under the Feet,* Estrella's unnamed father is absent, and while not a perverse figure like Brownfield, Estrella's father also drinks, has love affairs, and sees Petra's attempt to leave him as an afront to his manhood; similar to Brownfield, Petra's husband, in a drunken fit, vows to find Petra and their children if she decides to leave him, and "kill them all" (13). Petra has been working in the labor camps for years and had to pick cotton even when she was pregnant; nonetheless, she cannot secure a living wage, properly feed her children, or buy the type of fruits and produce she collects in the fields. Petra's constant health struggles are symbolized by her use of garlic as a home remedy due to her inability to receive proper health care. Due to Petra's physical exhaustion, she has problems standing up and her legs have "purple and thick" veins that are "like vines choking the movement of her legs. Even the black straight skirt she wore seemed tighter and her belly spilled over the belt of waist, lax muscles of open births" (61). Petra's only recourse for her health problems is to eat "five cloves of garlic pickled in vinegar every day to loosen her blood and ease her varicose veins; without the garlic, her veins throbbed" (62). In addition, Petra is pregnant, and her physical condition gradually worsens, but she is unable to receive medical assistance or pay for it since she is trapped in a large-scale agricultural system that is primarily concerned with its economic bottom line and treats workers as disposable.

The depiction of the family's struggle against an immigration system that stigmatizes Mexican American farmworkers, even when Petra and her children are US citizens, exemplifies the way *Under the Feet* relies on stylistic elements and impressionistic scenes to portray the criminalization of Latinx bodies in the agricultural fields.[38] The Jesus altar statue, one of the major symbols in Viramontes's novel, relates to the family's immigration status, as Petra places her children's birth certificates that prove their US citizenship under the statue. Petra's constant fear regarding immigration raids in the labor camps is repeatedly alluded to rather than enacted, as the narrative emphasizes the family's inner struggles rather than the workings of the immigration system. The narrative intermittently references the presence of the Border Patrol in the characters' minds; for instance, while watching a baseball game in a nearby field at dusk, Estrella is startled by the "high-powered lights beamed on the playing field like headlights of cars," which she thinks point at her similar to the flashlights of a "border patrol" vehicle (59). At that moment, Estrella feels like a "perfect target" and like a "stunned deer waiting for the bullet," which prompts her to "fis[t]" the "pisca knife" she is carrying and run home (60). When she arrives home, Petra thinks that Estrella is in fact running away from "La Migra," but Petra seems resigned to these types of immigration raids and thinks that there is "no sense telling La Migra you've lived here all your life" (62). The episode concludes with Petra's advice to Estrella, "Don't run scared. You should stay there and look them in the eye. Don't let them make you feel you did a crime for picking the vegetables they'll be eating for dinner" (63). The sense of surveillance from the US immigration system experienced by Petra and Estrella exemplifies the way Viramontes's novel mediates the criminalization of farmworkers with its aesthetic elements.

Similar to the manner in which *Under the Feet* describes the presence of the border patrol in the narrative by relying on impressionistic scenes and imagery, the fight to unionize farmworkers in California is treated in a circumspect manner even as Viramontes dedicates the novel to César Chávez. The depiction of the farmworkers' agricultural boycott of the 1960s in *Under the Feet* resembles the way in which Walker's *Third Life* engages with the increasing marches for social justice in the South around the same time, as the focus in both novels remains on the families rather than the social move-

---

38. Yarbro-Bejarano focuses on the narrative techniques in the Border Patrol episode in *Under the Feet* and correctly notes that "at no point . . . are agents of the Border Patrol 'physically' present; instead, Viramontes's narrative art succeeds in portraying a state of mind" (78).

ments. While the influence of Chávez, Dolores Huerta, and other labor leaders during the Delano grape strike of the late 1960s ignited similar efforts
to unionize Mexican American farmworkers in other parts of California, the
push for unionization of farmworkers is only alluded to in a few sentences in
Under the Feet. During a group lunch break on an undistinguishable hot day,
Estrella receives a pamphlet; as some workers pass water, others "passed out
white leaflets with black eagles on them" (84), an allusion to the logo of the
red flag with a black thunderbird used by the United Farm Workers organization; however, the reference to those unionizing efforts ends there, while the
fight for labor justice took years to produce concrete victories in the California
fields. Estrella's reaction when she receives the pamphlet is to "fol[d] it in half
carefully and plac[e] it in her back pocket for later reading" (84), which pur-
posely leaves open the possible influence that the pamphlet—and the social
struggle it stands for—has on Estrella.[39] The depiction of the emergence of
the Chicanx Movement in Viramontes's novel echoes the way in which Ruth
in Walker's *Third Life* experiences the increasing mobilization by Blacks for
civil rights.

The family trip to the clinic and Estrella's use of the crowbar to gain
agency relate to stylistic choices that *Under the Feet* employs to achieve the
novel's aesthetic goals.[40] As a turning point in the narrative, the drive to take
Alejo to the clinic echoes other novels in the literary tradition that rely on
family journeys with sick relatives such as *As I Lay Dying* taking the body of
Addie Bundren to Jefferson, and the Joad family journey to California with
the body of Grandma Joad in *The Grapes of Wrath*. The crowbar scene contrasts Estrella's poverty and her marginalized position in relation to the nurse
at the clinic; the nurse's social standing in American society is a stark contrast
to what Estrella is not. While the nurse holds a "purse and car keys" and "had
on a fresh coat of red lipstick, and [a] thick scent of carnation perfume" (137),
Estrella becomes "aware of her own appearance. Dirty face, fingernails lined
with mud, her tennis shoes soiled, brown smears like coffee stains on her
dress where she had cleaned her hands" (137). The economic disparities and
the family's poverty are accentuated as Perfecto falls short of the ten dollars
charged for the consultation. This is the moment when Estrella understands
her marginalized position in society and decides to fight back with the crowbar as she smashes the nurse's desk. The crowbar, moreover, symbolizes vio-

39. Vázquez interprets this scene as Estrella's rejection of this type of resistance in the form
of Chávez's United Farm Workers union (383).

40. As Shea explains, the crowbar represents "more than the materiality of struggle" but
also "the power and leverage" that Estrella gains through her "ability to read, to interpret, and
to name" (140).

lence as the last resource for social justice; Estrella notes, "You talk and talk and talk to them and they ignore you. But you pick up a crowbar and break the picture of their children, and all of a sudden they listen real fast" (151). Estrella's newfound agency relates to the final barn scene, perhaps the most discussed scene and symbol in the novel, as Estrella finally commits, while the family is driving back to the bungalow, to "tear down the barn starting tomorrow" (153).[41]

The way in which *Under the Feet* concludes with Estrella's newfound agency resembles the way in which *Third Life* ends with Ruth ready to write the next chapter of her journey. Both mothers in the novels, Mem and Petra, are similarly unable to escape the crush of a male-dominated and profit-driven society and to provide for their children; both fathers are absent, and Mem and Petra experience the hardship that they hope Ruth and Estrella will avoid in their adult lives. *Third Life* and *Under the Feet* employ the figure of the substitute father, in the forms of Grange and Perfecto, respectively, in order to assist in the development of the novels' protagonists. Despite the distance between Georgia and California, both novels describe the shared family struggles in the agricultural fields that began after the Mexican–American War and the Civil War and continued unabated until improvements in the farmworkers' conditions were created by increasing workers' activism for social justice during the 1950s and 1960s. The depiction of these social justice themes in *Third Life* and *Under the Feet* are closely connected to their aesthetic choices that reflect past modernist tendencies. Walker and Viramontes succeeded at creating the "art-novel" that Henry James envisioned at a time when late nineteenth-century American writers were searching for an identity; as women writers of color, Walker and Viramontes responded to James's call by inscribing their respective communities of color into the literary tradition.

---

41. Among the several critical interpretations of the final barn scene in *Under the Feet*, my reading is closer to López's analysis of the barn scene as Estrella challenges the exploitation of farmworkers by US agribusinesses ("Ghosts" 333).

CHAPTER 6

The Decline of the City

Naturalizing the Black and Latinx Urban Underclass in
the Short Fiction of Edward P. Jones and Junot Díaz

The emergence of the Black and Latinx short story tradition reflects the fight against literary exclusion that has pushed Black and Latinx writers to the margins; however, for some pre-1960s Black and Latinx writers, the short story served as a lifeline and as a way to affirm their experiences in fiction. Antebellum Black newspapers and periodicals published or serialized short fiction that was subsequently printed as novellas or novels, such as Frederick Douglass's *The Heroic Slave*, Martin Delany's *Blake; or the Huts of America*, and William Wells Brown's *Miranda* (Babb 11, 27); likewise, antebellum Black print culture includes some of the early instances of short story tradition in the form of Frances E. W. Harper's short story "The Two Offers" published in the *Anglo-African Magazine* in 1859 (Ernest, *Liberation* 305–6); Black short fiction continued to appear in Black periodicals such as Pauline E. Hopkins's short story "The Mystery Within Us," which appeared in the *Colored American Magazine* in 1900 (Babb 45). The late nineteenth century marks a transition when Black short stories began to be published in mainstream publications; for instance, Charles Chesnutt's first short story, "The Goophered Grapevine," was published in the *Atlantic Monthly* in 1887 (Andrews, *Conjure* ix).[1] In subsequent decades, Black magazines and periodicals such as *The Crisis*,

---

[1]. A few Black authors such as Chesnutt, Paul Laurence Dunbar, and Langston Hughes were able to publish short story collections, a rare opportunity in a white-dominated publishing world; these early short story collections include Dunbar, *Folks from Dixie*; Chesnutt, *The Conjure Woman*; and Hughes, *The Ways of White Folks*.

Opportunity, and *The Messenger* published short stories by Black writers such as Langston Hughes, Zora Neale Hurston, and Rudolph Fisher; Hurston, for instance, received her first publishing opportunity when she moved to Harlem, and Charles Johnson published two of her short stories in *Opportunity.*[2] This trend continued in subsequent decades as writers including Richard Wright, Ralph Ellison, and James Baldwin wrote short stories in either Black or mainstream magazines at the start of their careers.[3] The efforts of pre-1960s Black short fiction writers reflect their limited opportunities to publish their work and gain literary recognition.

While the development of Latinx short fiction is similar to the development of the Black short story, as the former began and was sustained by Spanish-language newspapers and periodicals throughout the nineteenth century, the origin of Latinx short stories is distinct in relation to the genre itself and what constitutes a short story. The emergence of the Latinx short story relates to the way Latinx short fiction is intrinsically related to the forms of production and the historical exclusion of Latinx authors from mainstream publications and publishing. Spanish-language newspapers and periodicals in the late nineteenth century sustained short fiction in larger cities such as San Francisco and New York City.[4] Likewise, New Mexico had, particularly in the late nineteenth century, a thriving Spanish-language print culture supported by Spanish-speaking communities that published short fiction, as in the case of Eusebio Chacón's "El hijo de la tempestad" (The Son of the Storm) and "Tras la tormenta, la calma" (The Calm after the Storm) both published in 1892 in *El Boletín Popular* (The Popular Bulletin) printed in Santa Fe, New Mexico.[5] In the early decades of the twentieth century, Latinx short fiction was published in Spanish-language newspapers and publications supported

2. Hurston won second prize in an *Opportunity* literary contest for her short story "Spunk" in 1925, and a second *Opportunity* literary prize the following year for another short story, "Muttsy" (Lewis 113–14, 179).

3. Similar to Hurston, Wright's start as a writer came as a short story writer. While unsuccessfully trying to find a publisher for two novels, Wright was able to publish a short story, "Big Boy Leaves Home," in *The New Caravan* in 1936, which led to a book contract with Harper (Yarborough xviii). Wright's short story collection, *Uncle Tom's Children,* published in 1938 allowed him to continue his writing career.

4. John Alba Cutler has studied Latinx short fiction that appeared in late nineteenth-century Spanish-language periodicals. Cutler focuses on two examples, Carlos F. Galán's series of sketches "Recuerdos de California" (Memories of California) printed in San Francisco in 1881 and Nicanor Bolet Peraza's "Historia de un guante" (The Tale of a Glove) published in New York City in 1895 ("Toward a Reading" 125). Similar to some Black periodicals that serialized fiction at the time, José Martí serialized his novel, *Amistad Funesta* (Fatal Friendship) in the New York magazine *El Latino-Americano* in 1885 (Echevarría xxx).

5. Cutler notes that while most scholars have discussed Chacón's fiction as novellas, or even novels, Chacón's fiction could also be considered short stories ("Eusebio Chacón's America" 129).

by civil rights organizations such as the League of United Latin American Citizens (LULAC) and its magazine *LULAC News* published in English and Spanish in Texas.[6] As with some Black writers who began writing short fiction, some Latinx authors such as Américo Paredes started their writing careers publishing short stories in Texas newspapers in the 1950s;[7] despite his early success, Paredes's fiction written around this time was published decades later (Hinojosa 6), due in part to the lack of publishing opportunities for Latinx fiction before the 1960s.

The emergence of Edward P. Jones and Junot Díaz as short story writers in the 1980s and 1990s relates to the struggles of short fiction writers of past decades; however, it is also connected to the experiences of Black and Latinx writers in creative writing programs and publishing dynamics. While the short story genre in the American literary tradition began with Washington Irvin and Edgar Allan Poe, the short story collection genre after the 1960s closely relates to the emergence of MFA programs at colleges and universities. Mark McGurl has described the institutionalization of creative writing programs at colleges and universities that began at the end of World War II as "the Program Era";[8] writers of color, however, have traditionally been underrepresented in MFA programs, particularly at the most selective institutions.[9] Díaz has written about attending the Cornell creative writing program and the sense of invisibility experienced by the few authors of color.[10] The significance of such experiences closely relates to the short story genre and

6. *LULAC News,* for example, published J. C. Machuca's short story "Love and Duty" in 1936 and Alice Dickerson Montemayor's "Stolen Paradise" in 1938 (González, *Border Renaissance* 161, 166).

7. Paredes won a *Dallas Times Herald* short story contest in 1952 with a group of short stories titled *Border Country* (Morín 23). Mario Suárez wrote and published short stories in the *Arizona Quarterly* magazine in the 1940s, but he was unable to find a publisher, which led him to pursue a career as a journalist rather than a fiction writer (Lomelí 3).

8. In *The Program Era,* McGurl describes the rise of the creative writing programs after World War II from a handful of creative writing programs at universities, which gained in popularity in the 1960s and 1970s, to their eventual proliferation at the turn of the twenty-first century (23–25). For an extended critique on how MFA programs have traditionally diminished the experiences of writers of color, see Sáez, "Generation MFA."

9. Michael Hill, for example, calls attention to the small number of Black writers accepted into the Iowa Writers' Workshop up to the 1960s that included Margaret Walker, Herbert Nipson, Michael Harper, and John Edgar Wideman, and how James Alan McPherson's workshop experience starting in 1968 "resembles the journeys of his black forebears in that he was the only African American in the program when he attended" ("Timely" 124). Sandra Cisneros and Helena María Viramontes are two well-known Latinx women writers who attended MFA programs in the 1970s and 1980s, respectively.

10. Díaz explains that these programs are "too white," meaning "too white as in the MFA had no faculty of color in the fiction program—like none—and neither the faculty nor the administration saw that lack of color as a big problem" ("MFA").

MFA programs, as short story collections are commonly the culmination of an MFA degree, which in turn serves as a form of "academic credentialing via MFA programs" and one of the few career paths for authors of color to secure academic teaching positions (Sáez 378); however, these same narrow avenues for literary legitimation, created in part by the publishing industry and forces in academia, have resulted in mainstream recognition for only a few Latinx writers, including Díaz. While it is important to contextualize Díaz's writing in relation to the allegations of his mistreatment of women, Díaz's work is intrinsically connected to the Latinx literary tradition and the historical exclusion of authors of color in academia, publishing, and cultural institutions.[11]

In this chapter, I focus on two short story collections, Edward P. Jones's *Lost in the City* (1992) and Junot Díaz's *Drown* (1996), to explore their shared aesthetic and formalistic strategies in their representation of the struggles and challenges of Black and Latinx people in urban spaces. Both short story collections show that the challenges affecting people of color in urban enclaves such as poverty, social marginalization, broken families, and addiction date back to a legacy of racial discrimination and economic inequalities that persisted after the fight for civil rights of the 1960s and 1970s. Critics who have studied either *Lost in the City* or *Drown* have engaged with their characters' struggles and hardships.[12] Moreover, several scholars have often described these two collections as containing realistic elements or as representative of "gritty" or "grim" realism;[13] however, *Lost in the City* and *Drown* move beyond realism by engaging with thematic and stylistic elements found in literary naturalism such as the influence of environment, human agency, the sensational or grotesque, poverty, violence, and addiction, all tropes or themes found in the naturalistic fiction of Frank Norris, Stephen Crane, and Jack London. Both collections, however, do not simply employ these tropes, but they subvert the tradition by taking on the bleakness that permeates their stories to call attention to the legacy of racial and economic marginality among urban communities of

11. For a view that acknowledges the voices of women who have been affected by Díaz's behavior while also raising larger questions about race and gender in society, see Alcoff, "This Is Not Just about Junot Díaz." For a representative analysis that highlights the need for accountability for male writers in positions of power and the role of publishing and academia, see Gil'Adí, "'I Think about You, X—.'"

12. James Coleman explains that characters in *Lost in the City* make use of their "connections to the South and its black tradition of strength and survival," which allow "them to survive or makes survival a possibility" in the North (6). In the case of *Drown*, Silvio Torres-Saillant observes that the stories in *Drown* "unveil a contemporary yarn of misery, uprooting, and endurance" (131).

13. For critics who have referred to *Lost in the City* as "realistic" fiction or as engaging with "realism," see Jackson and Jones 98; and Torday 350. For descriptions of *Drown* as a "gritty realist" work or "grim realism," see Dalleo and Sáez 78; and C. González 11.

color, which despite the social gains of the 1960s and 1970s has continued in subsequent decades.

Literary naturalism has a questionable reputation when it comes to the depiction of marginalized groups; however, some Black writers, particularly Richard Wright, subverted some of the tropes and themes found in naturalist novels to emphasize the legacy of racial discrimination. While in *Lost in the City* and *Drown* the struggles in urban settings are among people of color, characters confront at another level the legacy of urban segregation, failed urban policy, and white indifference, or denial, that in a naturalistic context takes the form of external forces acting upon individuals.[14] The stories "The Girl Who Raised Pigeons," "Young Lions," "The Sunday Following Mother's Day," and "Lost in the City" in *Lost in the City* incorporate some of the themes, tropes, and stylistic techniques of naturalist fiction to document the social and economic struggles of Black communities in segregated Washington, DC. While in Wright's naturalistic fiction, particularly *Native Son*, the overwhelming oppressive force acting upon individuals is racism and the legacy of segregation in Northern cities, characters in *Lost in the City* similarly struggle against social and economic forces. Their economic and social circumstances create hardships that they are often unable to overcome; thus, showing the physical isolation of some Black communities in DC and the stress it puts on families and family unity. Likewise, the stories "Ysrael," "Aurora," "Drown," and "Edison, New Jersey" in *Drown* portray characters of color affected by social and economic marginalization in urban areas of New Jersey, New York City, and the Dominican Republic. *Lost in the City* and *Drown* show that despite the significant social and political gains of the 1960s, the lack of economic opportunities and the legacy of urban segregation continue to affect working class communities of color, as well as how some post-1960s Black and Latinx writers continued to engage and subvert the literary tradition.

ECONOMIC OPPORTUNITIES IN INNER CITIES AFTER THE CIVIL RIGHTS ACTIVISM OF THE 1960s

While race and ethnicity continue to play a prevalent role in American society, the importance of income, social stratification, and economic stagnation are similarly connected to the struggles of the communities of color in urban

---

14. Dorothy Stringer correctly observes that the narrator in *Drown* "never discusses politics or economics proper, never uses racial, national, or ethnic terms for himself or people he loves, [and] never identifies either personal or institutional racism as such" (116).

cities. A significant number of people of color in urban areas continue to live under pressing economic conditions despite the social and political gains of the Black and Chicanx civil rights movements of the 1960s and 1970s that brought the gradual end of de jure and de facto segregation in the South and Southwest, respectively; despite these gains, other social and economic problems such as lack of jobs, substandard housing, and deficient schooling continue to affect people of color. Scholars have discussed and documented the economic decline of Black urban communities in the decades after the 1960s; William Julius Wilson makes a point that racial discrimination is not the only factor affecting Blacks in inner cities since economic factors such as the lack of employment accounts for some of the disparities in inner cities that only worsened in the 1970s and 1980s.[15] Pre-1960s civil rights leaders, intellectuals, and writers similarly argued that although some Blacks experienced certain social mobility in Northern cities, which created an emerging small Black middle class, the vast majority of Blacks remained at the bottom of the social ladder.[16] Their arguments stressed the importance of racial discrimination and the lack of economic opportunities. Even after his long and challenging campaign for civil rights in the South, Martin Luther King Jr. broadened the scope of his social activism to highlight economic disparities among racial groups, though those conditions persisted in subsequent decades.[17]

After King's assassination, other Black and Mexican American civil rights leaders and activists such as Ralph Abernathy and Rodolfo "Corky" Gonzales organized and came together in campaigns such as the Poor People's Campaign of 1968 in Washington, DC, which focused on economic disparities affecting Blacks, Latinxs, and other people of color. Similar to the case of calls by Black writers and activists for economic justice, pre-1960s Latinx writers

15. As Wilson explains, "Despite increases in concentration of poverty since 1970, inner cities have always featured high levels of poverty, but the current levels of joblessness in some neighborhoods are unprecedented" (*When Work Disappears* xiii). Taking a similar view, Cornel West argues that "to engage in a serious discussion of race in America, we must begin not with the problems of black people but with the flaws of American society—flaws rooted in historic inequalities" (6).

16. For W. E. B. Du Bois writing in 1940, it seemed "evident that economic planning to ensure adequate income [was] the crying need" of Blacks (*Dusk* 204). Wright's *Twelve Million Black Voices* chronicles the struggles not only of Black Southerners during Jim Crow segregation but also the precarious conditions in most Black urban enclaves such as Chicago due to de facto segregation policies in Northern cities.

17. In his often-mentioned 1967 speech, "Where Do We Go from Here," King points out that Blacks "liv[e] in the basement of the Great Society. [They are] still at the bottom, despite the few who have penetrated to slightly higher levels. Even when the door has been forced partially open . . . [,] [Blacks] are still impoverished aliens in an affluent society" (181).

denounced in their writings the marginalization of Latinx people, particularly Puerto Ricans, in New York City during the 1940s and 1950s.[18] "Corky" Gonzales, similar to King, emphasized the political along with the importance of education, housing, job development, and economic opportunities for Mexican Americans, particularly in urban areas.[19] Gonzales's demands reflected the economic realities for countless Mexican Americans in large cities in the Southwest and across the country.

Despite critical discussions regarding the decreasing significance of race and the emphasis on social class by post-1960s Black authors, Jones and Díaz engage in their short fiction with the economic struggles of people of color in inner cities based in part on their working-class backgrounds. Kenneth Warren has explored how pre-1960s Black literature engaged with Jim Crow segregation and how writers of subsequent decades such as Trey Ellis, Andrea Lee, and Michael Thomas emphasized social class, rather than race, in some of their novels. Warren takes on Ellis's ideas of the New Black Aesthetics, or NBA, to argue that a group of Black writers and artists in the late 1980s was "emerging as members of the rising professional managerial class for whom the doors of private schools at all levels" opened and that these writers "could appear simultaneously as the culmination of the past," that is, when Jim Crow segregation ended, "or a break with it" (*What Was* 121). While Warren avoids generalizations, the backgrounds of Jones and Díaz do not resemble the middle-class comfort described by Ellis. Jones and Díaz grew up in working-class urban communities of color that continue to struggle with the legacy of racism, segregation, and marginalization in Washington, DC, and Perth Amboy, New Jersey, respectively.[20] The class struggles of the urban underclass at the latter part of the twentieth century explored and thematized in *Lost in the City* and *Drown* remain just as prevalent as when King, Abernathy, and "Corky" Gonzales, among others, organized for economic justice.

---

18. In *A Puerto Rican in New York*, Jesus Colón calls attention to the marginalization of racial and ethnic groups in New York City in the 1950s by noting that while in the past it was Italians and Jews who were discriminated against, in subsequent decades it was Puerto Ricans and Blacks who were "relegated to the last rung of New York's social ladder" (10). See also Vega, *Memoirs of Bernardo Vega*.

19. See "Corky" Gonzales's statement during the Poor People's Campaign of 1968 where he calls attention to the economic dimension in the fight of people of color, "We Demand."

20. In interviews, Jones has mentioned growing up in poverty in Washington, DC, and being raised by a single mother, who lacked formal education, since his father was absent (Als, "Edward"). Díaz moved to the US at a young age and grew up in "a tough Latino neighborhood" (Stewart); moreover, Díaz's early experiences resemble Jones's background in some key respects such as his upbringing in an urban community of color and an absent father.

AMERICAN LITERARY NATURALISM AND
BLACK AND LATINX WRITERS

Literary naturalism emerged as an outgrowth of literary realism, as the for-mer emphasized the environment, the natural world, and the effects of those forces on individuals. Louis Budd situates naturalism in the late nineteenth and early twentieth centuries and argues that it centered around how "indus-trialism and urbanism, now clearly irreversible, were accelerating" and how "the conflict between capital and labor was getting bloodier at the seams of a hardened class structure" (42). The move from literary realism to natural-ism is accomplished through sensational effects, sentimental scenes, the influ-ence of natural and evolutionary forces, sexual deviance, and crime, among other themes (Newlin 5). While there are competing definitions regarding the characteristics of literary naturalism, scholars agree on the major practitioners of the late nineteenth and early twentieth centuries: Theodore Dreiser, Jack London, Frank Norris, Edith Wharton, and Stephen Crane, who incorporated in their works themes such as the urban city, social and economic dispari-ties, addiction, and the struggles of the poor, working class, and immigrants.[21] However, literary naturalism, and some of its ideology, reflected at times a dis-turbing dimension when the deviance, addiction, and innate violence depicted by these writers often fell on the outcasts, underclass, immigrants, and anyone who did not fit the White Anglo-Saxon Protestant (WASP) model or were simply the "other."[22] Literary naturalism, however, goes beyond stigmatization and othering as representative naturalist works such as Crane's "The Open Boat" and London's *The Call of the Wild* engage with people's struggles against nature, the environment, and the influence of forces on characters beyond their control, and in subsequent decades, some Black writers were influenced and engaged with these other aspects of literary naturalism.

---

21. Richard Lehan observes that while "the naturalists sometimes depicted the upper class, they more often descended the social ladder to portray the world of the poor and the out-cast. . . . The naturalists felt that the more attention that was given to lower or deviant aspects of life—to poverty, alcoholism, degeneration, and the dysfunctional family—the more 'realistic' the writing would be" (7).

22. For instance, Howard discusses how naturalist fiction was influenced by nativists who saw with alarm the rise of the city and its increasing "immigrant population[s], divided by lan-guage and culture from the native-born population," and feared "a foreign body—an Other—within the city and within the nation" (85). In addition, scientific racism, a "close cousin" of nativism, attempted to prove the inferiority of Blacks, immigrants, and other ethnic groups and how some naturalistic writers aptly took on those ideas (Howard 85–86).

While scholars have considered some Black authors such as Chester Himes and Ann Petry as influenced by literary naturalism, perhaps no other Black author is more closely associated with naturalism than Richard Wright, who adopted some of its conventions, themes, and subject matter.[23] John Dudley, moreover, argues that previous Black writers such as Charles Chesnutt, Paul Laurence Dunbar, and James Weldon Johnson, among others, can be considered naturalist writers as they "accurately depict[ed] and critique[d] the inequalities and shortcomings of a rapidly changing society" (258). Wright's *Native Son* engages with some of the themes in naturalism such as the influence of the environment in the form of the city of Chicago, which affected characters and created a sense of overwhelming social and economic forces affecting characters beyond their control. Richard Lehan, for example, describes *Native Son* as a "rewrit[ing]" of Dreiser's *American Tragedy* (1925) from the point of view of [the] black experience" and Bigger Thomas as a character "held in place by economic forces" who "is unable to escape his black environment" (222). Wright indeed emphasizes the environment; however, this overwhelming force in *Native Son* is not a blind cosmic force but the result of centuries of marginalization and exclusion that created a Bigger Thomas.

Wright had a direct influence on Jones, who in turn influenced Díaz, and similar to *Native Son*, *Lost in the City* and *Drown* subvert themes and tropes in naturalism by moving away from the stigmatization of racial and ethnic groups to the focus on the social and economic forces that affect individuals in contemporary urban communities of color. In interviews, Jones has discussed the influence of *Native Son* and *Uncle Tom's Children* in his writing.[24] Jones, moreover, had made the explicit connection between his fiction and Wright's works, particularly *Black Boy* and *Native Son,* and observing that in *Lost in the City,* he "write[s] in naturalistic fashion" (Jackson and Jones 102). Similar to the way Jones was influenced by Wright, Díaz has referred to Jones's work as a "model" (Céspedes and Torres-Saillant 900). While Díaz's statement serves to establish a literary affinity and an instance of intertextuality among some of the fiction of Jones and Díaz, a comparative analysis of *Lost in the City* and *Drown* shows the compelling shared traits in their thematic, narrative, and aesthetic choices that are closely associated to literary naturalism.

---

23. In Wright's autobiography, *Black Boy*, he mentions the influence of naturalist writers such as Dreiser and Crane (250, 278). Yarborough, among other scholars, has discussed the extent of these influences in Wright's fiction (xix).

24. Jones remembers reading in his youth Wright's short story "Bright and Morning Star," included in *Uncle Tom's Children*, "over and over again for the beauty of the language but also for the personal pain in it" (Graham and Jones 424–25). See also Jones's interview with Marita Golden 50–51.

THE LEGACY OF URBAN SEGREGATION
IN JONES'S *LOST IN THE CITY*

Instances in Jones's literary career reflect how the inclusion of authors of color in college and university classrooms after the 1960s opened opportunities for writers of color to attend MFA programs and publish their work, which in turn was increasingly read by college students, discussed by scholars, and achieved literary recognition in a still predominantly white literary establishment. After college, Jones attended the University of Virginia and received his MFA in 1981. While working as editor at a newsletter, Jones published in mainstream literary magazines some of his short stories that would become part of *Lost in the City*.[25] After *Lost in the City* was published by Amistad in 1992, Jones achieved literary prominence with the publication in 2003 of his neo-slavery novel, *The Known World*, which won the Pulitzer Prize for fiction in 2004. Jones's training in an MFA program and the mainstream critical recognition of his writing served as the necessary "credentialing," as described by Elena Machado Sáez (378), for writers of color to attain academic positions, and in the case of Jones, culminating with his appointment as professor of creative writing at George Washington University.[26] Jones's literary trajectory is significant since only a few decades earlier mainstream publishers, academic institutions, and cultural organizations marginalized Black authors; however, these rare instances of literary recognition often take attention away from the large number of writers of color who continue to struggle at MFA programs and for publishing opportunities in contemporary times.

While critics have emphasized the influence of the environment in Jones's short story collection in the setting of Washington, DC, and the thematic parallels between *Lost in the City* and Wright's *Uncle Tom's Children*, scholars have not studied *Lost in the City* as naturalist fiction.[27] I focus on "The Girl Who Raised Pigeons," "Young Lions," "The Sunday Following Mother's Day," and "Lost in the City" to explore how the stories' thematic concerns and stylistic and narrative techniques are informed by literary naturalism and the fiction of Richard Wright. Jones has discussed his emphasis on a realistic portrayal of Washington, DC, and his characters;[28] however, some of Jones's stories transcend realism and move toward naturalism through their emphasis on the environment, economic forces, and class stratification. "The Girl Who Raised

---

25. Jones's short story "The First Day" was published in *Callaloo* in 1982 and "Marie" appeared in the *Paris Review* in 1992.

26. For an expanded overview of Jones's background and body of work, see Coleman 1–8.

27. See Jackson and Jones 98; and Coleman 6–7.

28. In an interview, Jones explains his emphasis on realistic over imaginary settings stressing that "all the *places* that [he] write[s] about are real" (Als, "Edward").

Pigeons" explores the sense of isolation and despair created in part by limited economic opportunities within a Black community. Robert Morgan is raising his daughter, Betsy Ann, in DC as a single parent with the constant fear that he will not be able to protect her as he works long hours as a taxi driver. They are part of a fractured family; Clara, Robert's wife, died from a brain tumor shortly after Betsy Ann was born. As she grows up, Betsy Ann is caught one day stealing candy at a grocery store. Robert is distraught when he discovers "that his daughter had been somewhere doing bad while he was out doing the best he could" (18). Robert's relationship with his daughter is marked by overprotection and a deep sense of responsibility toward her, which he is unable to fulfill. When Betsy Ann is born, Robert, a nineteen-year-old single father, is offered the opportunity to place her in foster care. He is told by an acquaintance that a "young man like [him] shouldn't have to worry [himself] like this," but he rejects this idea (7). Robert's tenuous position is complicated by his economic condition, which impedes his efforts to properly care for Betsy Ann.

The symbolism of the pigeons in "The Girl Who Raised Pigeons" relates to stylistic techniques such as the use of objective language, which is characteristic of naturalist fiction. June Howard discusses the emphasis on objectivity and the importance of detail through a reportorial description of details and events, characteristic of literary naturalism; she points out that in naturalism "the detail signifies not only reality but the rigorous investigation of reality" (147). The emphasis on reality and objectivity in the story is achieved with a direct writing style and a reportorial depiction of the struggles, and moments of respite, of the working class. The image of the pigeons exemplifies the role of the writing style, as the pigeons serve as the means to describe the relationship between a father and a daughter through the use of direct language and declarative sentences.[29] A constant element in "The Girl Who Raised Pigeons" is the care and attachment that Robert and Betsy Ann have for the birds. Initially, the pigeons are described by their original owner, "Miles the barber," as his "children" (2), while also representing freedom through their ability to fly. When Betsy Ann initially receives two of them as presents, she places them at a coop on their house roof, but they return to Miles's roof because that is "all they know to do" (10). They are instinctively connected to their place of origin, similar to the way characters such as Miles and Robert are attached to their neighborhood. Likewise, the pigeons reflect the characters' state of mind and hopes for the future. When some of the pigeons die, Robert becomes distressed; at one time, Betsy Ann discovers a dead pigeon, but she tries to

---

29. Maryemma Graham notes in her interview with Jones that his "writing is simple," to which Jones adds that he has "never been one for any fancy words anyway" (Graham and Jones, "Interview" 428).

protect her father by hiding it. As she tells their landlord, Miss Jenny, "Don't tell Daddy [a]bout that dead pigeon. You know how he is: He'll think it's the end of the world or somethin[g]" (14). Jones's use of direct language blends human interactions with seemingly minor events in everyday life to create a sense of fragility within the city's confines.

The bird imagery in "The Girl Who Raised Pigeons" represents the natural world but also the birds' hopelessness at the mercy of natural forces in the form of predators, a motif also used in Wright's *Native Son*. Jones's story vividly describes the pigeons' helplessness when they are trapped and eaten by rats, which serves as a metaphor to represent the struggle of individuals against their environment. The ominous presence of rats resembles the beginning of *Native Son*, which uses a similar image to symbolize the deplorable state of Bigger Thomas's living conditions in his segregated Chicago South Side neighborhood. Rather than a description of the events, the climactic scene in Jones's story recounts the aftermath after the death of the birds. One day Robert goes to the coop and discovers the pigeons' "bodies with holes so deep he saw white flesh, essence[;] it was the sight of dozens of detached feathers that caused his body to shake, because the scattered feathers, more than the wrecked bodies, spoke to him of helplessness" (22). The pigeons' inability to protect themselves against this danger reflects Robert's own inability to protect Betsy Ann in their neighborhood. Although he does not identify the pigeons' aggressors, the narrator mentions that when Robert "saw the tracks, he realized immediately that they had been made by rats" (22). The dead pigeons, which were used as symbols of hope, create a marked impression on Robert as he discerns "a kind of orderliness to the trail, even with its ragged bits of pigeon life, a fragment of feather here, a spot of blood there" (22). The juxtaposition of order and chaos reflects Robert's position as a resident of a city that is both organized and chaotic. Despite its bleakness, the story contains a glimmer of hope as two pigeons survive and fly away. The opening story in *Lost in the City*, however, foreshadows the calamities experienced by most characters in subsequent stories.

"Young Lions" further emphasizes the characters' hardships within the inner city as its protagonist, Caesar Matthews, lacks economic opportunities, which lead him into a path of violent crime and domestic violence such as that found in some of Wright's fiction. When the story begins, Caesar and his partner, Carol, abruptly reach a critical point in their relationship when he asks her to become his accomplice in a robbery. Although "Young Lions" revolves around the planning and execution of the robbery, the story pieces together Caesar's troubled past. Caesar is a young Black male who grows up in a broken family. At an early age, his mother dies, and his father, Lemuel, is unable to properly look after him despite his stern guidance. After his father discovers that Caesar is not attending school, he waits for him one night, slaps him, and throws him out of the house. Lemuel believes that he is "just slaving away [his] life to raise up . . . [a] goddamn no-account" (68). When Caesar moves to a friend's house, he discovers that his friend, Sherman, robs people for a living; Caesar, however, "was not particularly surprised or disappointed" because beyond "the cocoon of family[,] . . . he was learning [that] anything was possible" (69). The story accentuates the scarcity of economic opportunities for young Black males in the inner city. The relationship between Caesar and Carol, along with their economic hardships and instances of male physical abuse, is reminiscent of Wright's short story "Long Black Song," in which Silas and his wife Sarah struggle economically and Silas physically abuses his wife, thinking she is having an affair; both short stories shed light on the social and economic marginalization of Black male characters who in turn physically abuse their partners.

The description of Washington, DC, in "Young Lions," and other stories in *Lost in the City*, emphasizes the urban city's overpowering influence on individuals and the disparities created by social class that reflects a trope in naturalist novels. As James Giles points out, the emergence of literary naturalism in the latter part of the nineteenth century was in part a "response to the phenomenon of the new American city" (323). Similar to the contrasting representations of wealth and poverty in urban cities in naturalist novels such as Dreiser's *Sister Carrie* and Wright's *Native Son*, "Young Lions" differentiates among sections of DC, divided by social class and wealth; one well-known section of the city consists of government buildings and tourist attractions frequented mainly by middle-class residents and tourists; another section is composed of broken homes, poverty, and limited opportunities mostly populated by poor and working class Black residents.[30] The city outside the boundaries of the characters' neighborhoods appears as a foreign and hostile territory. Caesar, for instance, "had never come down to the world below Constitution Avenue, except for those times when relatives came from out of town. . . . He knew that his father worked in one of the government buildings, but he didn't know which one" (66). The disparities between these two worlds highlight inequalities related to race; yet, social class also plays a role, as Jones's story differentiates between working- and middle-class Black characters; for instance, while Caesar is following a woman close to the White House, he sees a Black father with his family visiting the building and taking photographs;

30. Kennedy and Beuka correctly point out that in *Lost in the City*, "Jones largely ignores the white world and the much-photographed public space that enshrines and monumentalizes the national narrative" of prosperity (11–12).

both are Black; nonetheless, they live worlds apart, which implies that class and economic factors, not only race, influence Blacks' relation to the city.

Among the stories that compose *Lost in the City,* perhaps "The Sunday Following Mother's Day" more closely engages with the sensationalism and pessimism found in literary naturalism. Jones's story illustrates how a single sudden act—in this case a seemingly senseless murder—negatively affects the victim's family. The story opens with Samuel Williams's stabbing of his wife, Agnes, one morning in their house for no apparent reason. The narrative revolves around the murder's aftermath and the fate of the couple's two young children, Sam and Madeleine. When Samuel is convicted and sent to jail for twenty-five years, the children grow up with an aunt. As Samuel's release from jail approaches, he begins to write to them in an attempt at reconciliation. Madeleine initially reciprocates and writes back, but Sam rejects his father's attempt at reconciliation and wonders, "Why would anyone in the world write to the man who killed [his] own mother?" (132). Despite this tragic event, both siblings grow up in relative stability and are able to form families of their own. As Samuel attempts to reconnect with his two grown children, the narrative explores the characters' inability to overcome Samuel's past actions, which permeate the story with a sense of hopelessness and despair.

The tragic and indelible scene in "The Sunday Following Mother's Day" centers on an episode of extreme violence, Samuel's stabbing of his wife, which echoes the violence and sensationalism in some naturalist novels such as Norris's *McTeague.* Samuel's murderous act is also described using the reportorial or objective language associated with naturalist novels that emphasize the facts rather than the motives. The narrator in Jones's story describes Samuel's stabbing in a reportorial manner: "When Madeleine Williams was four years old and her brother Sam was ten, their father killed their mother one night in early April. If their mother sent forth to her children a cry of help, or of good-bye, they did not hear it" (117). The murder is also depicted in a matter-of-fact style that obscures the motives, and more importantly, the narrator does not delve into the lasting consequences of Samuel's actions on his two children. After the murder, Samuel calls his sister to confess by simply stating, "I stabbed her a lot" (117). When his sister arrives at the crime scene, she finds the victim in the bedroom "dead, head down, sitting on the floor with one leg under her in a giant pool of drying blood" (118). This murder echoes Norris's *McTeague,* in which the eponymous character also murders his wife in a school where her body is found by a student the next day, drenched in a pool of blood. McTeague's murderous act has commonly been interpreted by critics in relation to Norris's emphasis on atavistic and hereditary traits thought to be found among the poor, marginalized, and immigrant populations at the turn of the twentieth century (Howard 91); however, Jones, rather than emphasizing the atavistic or deviant, engages with the consequences of those seemingly senseless acts.

Stories in *Lost in the City* engage with drug addiction as an overwhelming force that affects characters and creates naturalist narratives of decline, or as Howard describes them, "plot[s] of decline" (98). Alcohol addiction represents a force acting upon individuals in naturalist novels such as in Crane's *Maggie* and Norris's *McTeague* that result in characters' social and economic decline. Addiction plays a similar role in "Young Lions" through the character of Sherman, Caesar's accomplice. Sherman's life has been affected by drug addiction; when the story begins, Sherman is in the hospital recovering from a heroin overdose. Similar to Caesar, Sherman lacked family support; when he is ten years old, Sherman leaves home, drops out of school, and by the time Caesar meets him, Sherman had never "ha[d] a real job" (69). Sherman's narrative of decline is described as an almost inevitable consequence precipitated by his social condition and the overpowering force of addiction. The devastating effects of drug addiction serve as the main trope in "Lost in the City," the story that gives its name to Jones's short story collection. Lydia Walsh, a successful lawyer, wakes up one day to find out that her mother just died at the hospital. "Lost in the City" mixes scenes of Lydia's reminiscences of times with her mother and her present unfulfilled and solitary life, along with her cocaine addiction. As James Coleman rightly notes, "Lydia seems to have absolutely no sense of a positive direction to move in and no sense of anything that can save her" (6). In the brief window into Lydia's life that the narrative provides, her main yearning is to get "lost in the city" (148).

Lost in the City is permeated by a sense of despair and is populated by characters who are struggling to overcome their oppressive environment. Critics, however, have often emphasized the glimmers of hope spread throughout some of Jones's stories. Daniel Torday, for example, observes that "while all of Jones'[s] characters live in a fated world, they don't hesitate to fight it" (362);[31] ultimately, there are hardly any positive outcomes for the characters in the stories, who at most times appear overwhelmed by external forces and their environment. Under a naturalistic interpretation of *Lost in the City*, the sense of hopelessness that permeates Jones's stories reflects what Wright attempted in *Native Son*; Wright used and subverted some of the tropes of naturalism, including its pessimism, to call attention to the social and economic struggles

---

31. Similarly, Coleman emphasizes hope, rather than despair, in *Lost in the City*. Coleman maintains that "female and male main characters in the fourteen stories are 'lost in the city,' imperiled in their Washington, DC, environment in one way or another, but they are not always, and perhaps never, imperiled and 'lost' beyond hope" (6).

of the working class that were not created by cosmic forces but by the real and ever-present social and economic disparities in Black urban communities.

LATINX URBAN NATURALISM IN DÍAZ'S *DROWN*

Junot Díaz's literary career, similar to Jones's, relates to the protests of students of color in the late 1960s for the inclusion of writers of color in courses at colleges and universities that influenced the way Black and Latinx texts were published, studied, and read. Díaz graduated from the MFA program at Cornell in 1995, published *Drown* as his first short story collection in 1996, and became a faculty member at the Massachusetts Institute of Technology. Similar to Jones, some of Díaz's short stories included in his first short story collection first appeared in mainstream publications.[32] In another parallel with Jones, Díaz's moment of literary recognition came with the publication of his first novel, *The Brief Wondrous Life of Oscar Wao* in 2007, which also won the Pulitzer Prize for fiction in 2008, a historically elusive recognition from the literary establishment to a Latinx writer, since this was only the second time that a Latinx writer had won this award in its century-long history; prior to Díaz's novel, only Oscar Hijuelos's *The Mambo King Plays Songs of Love* published in 1989 received the Pulitzer Prize for fiction in 1990.[33] The historical exclusion of Latinx authors in mainstream cultural institutions adds a layer of complexity to the current reconsideration of Díaz's writing due to the allegations of sexual misconduct toward women; it is partly the dearth of Latinx authors and the lack of proper representation in publishing and academia that further amplifies the visibility of a handful of Latinx writers. Díaz's literary trajectory, nonetheless, exemplifies not only past but current struggles by Latinx writers to navigate predominantly white cultural and academic institutions and gain access to publishing opportunities in meaningful numbers.

A number of critics have discussed Díaz's engagement with discrimination, immigration, and other struggles of people of color in the inner city in *Drown* and its depiction of the inner city in relation to Piri Thomas's *Down These Mean Streets*, an autobiographical narrative that depicts Thomas's experiences as a Black Puerto Rican growing up marginalized and racialized in Spanish

---

32. "Ysrael" and "Fiesta, 1980" were published in *Story* magazine; "Drown" and "How to Date a Browngirl, Blackgirl, or Halfie" first appeared in the *New Yorker*; "Edison, New Jersey" was published in the *Paris Review*.

33. For a discussion of Hijuelos's novel and his place in the Latinx literary tradition, see Juan Flores, "Life Off the Hyphen."

Harlem during the 1950s.[34] Indeed, their writings share parallels, and Díaz has mentioned the influence of *Down These Mean Streets* in his fiction (Céspedes and Torres-Saillant 900). While critics have engaged with the depiction of the inner city in *Drown* through Thomas's autobiography and some of their shared themes, including racial discrimination, violence, and drug abuse, they have not engaged with *Drown* in relation to literary naturalism or Jones's *Lost in the City*. My analysis focuses on "Ysrael," "Aurora," "Drown," and "Edison, New Jersey" and their depiction of the struggles of communities of color in the inner city through the lens of naturalism; similar to Jones's *Lost in the City*, Díaz's stories subvert some of the themes, tropes, and narrative techniques found in naturalist fiction to emphasize the legacy of marginalization of people of color in segregated urban communities that accounts for the bleakness and pessimism in *Drown*.

"Ysrael," the opening story in *Drown*, emphasizes the sensationalist and the grotesque also present in naturalist narratives through the facial disfigurement of its central character.[35] The main trope or metaphor in "Ysrael" is the eponymous character's facial disfigurement, which echoes an almost identical trope present in Stephen Crane's novella, "The Monster"; in Crane's work, the facial disfigurement of Henry Johnson, a Black coachman working for a doctor, leads to Johnson's ostracism from town, even though his facial injury is the result of his courageous act of saving the doctor's son from a house fire. The sensationalist and the grotesque are used in "The Monster" to create a sinister effect, not only caused by Johnson's facial injuries but also by the townspeople's reactions to the uncanny and the unknown, which represent a shared symbolic trait in both "The Monster" and "Ysrael."[36] Richard Perez insightfully interprets the mask that Ysrael wears as representing the "real and symbolic other that haunts" characters in the story (94). The masks used by Ysrael and Henry Johnson in "The Monster" similarly symbolize the violence against the marginalized at the hands of the stories' main characters and the townspeople. In Díaz's story, Yunior "peg[s] Ysrael with a rock" in a previous encounter (14), and Yunior's older brother, Rafa, physically assaults Ysrael toward the end of the story by smashing a "bottle on top of his head" (18). Their actions

---

34. For critical discussions of *Drown* in relation to some of the themes in Thomas's *Down These Mean Streets*, see Paravisini-Gebert 165; Sandín 101; Perez 94–95; and Dalleo and Sáez 85–86.

35. Critics have studied "Ysrael" through the prisms of masculinity, disability studies, colonialism, and migration; see, for example, C. González 14–17; Perez 93–110; Irizarry 58–62, and Minich 51–57.

36. Howard has discussed the grotesque and sensationalist in naturalist narratives, including the role of the reader as "spectator," as they relate to "the structural elements of the genre and to its recurrent discomforts" (37, 116).

echo the way Henry Johnson is chased out of town in part by townspeople throwing rocks at him the day Johnson ventures into town; a significant difference between the two narratives is that the violence on Ysrael, a Dominican character, is inflicted by two other Dominican characters, while the violence against Henry Johnson in "The Monster" comes from the white townspeople. The story of "Ysrael" sets the tone for the following stories in *Drown,* as the tables are turned and Yunior, the former aggressor, becomes "the other" once Yunior migrates with his family from the Dominican Republic to the US.

The theme of drug addiction in "Aurora" parallels the way in which some characters in Jones's *Lost in the City* struggle with addiction and its influence. Most of the stories in *Drown* are narrated in the first person from the point of view of Ramón de las Casas, or Yunior. Critics have discussed whether the narrator of the stories is Yunior or if other unnamed characters narrate some stories;[37] my analysis focuses on Yunior as the same narrator in "Ysrael," "Aurora," "Drown," and "Edison, New Jersey" and as an ambivalent character marked by adverse economic circumstances similar to other male characters in *Lost in the City.* In "Aurora," Yunior is now a teenager and a drug dealer, and his partner, Aurora, is a recovering addict out of juvenile jail; their relationship is marked by drug use and male physical violence.[38] Among the various social problems affecting communities of color in urban areas, drug addiction in "Aurora" is portrayed as part of the urban landscape. The drug trade is described in an open and direct manner as Yunior and his friend, Cut, sell drugs to other teenagers. During a regular day, they would "hit the crowd at the bus stop, [and] pass by the trailer park across Route 9 . . . [d]ropping rocks all over. Ten here, ten there, an ounce of weed for the big guy with the warts, [and] some H for his coked-up girl" (50). The story also presents the use of drugs in Black and Latinx neighborhoods as an overwhelming force that affects not only teenagers but the larger community. Yunior mentions that he has "friends in Perth Amboy and New Brunswick who tell [him] they deal to whole families, from the grandparents down to the fourth-graders" (51). Just as in *Lost in the City,* drug addiction also emerges in "Aurora" as a larger force that leads to broken relationships, social isolation, and narratives of decline.

---

37. David Gates observes that Yunior "may or may not be" the narrator in some stories. Similarly, David Cowart explains that Yunior "may or may not be the pool table deliverer" in "Edison, New Jersey" and that he is clearly not present in other stories (193). In contrast, Bridget Kevane reads all the stories as derived from Yunior's experiences (72–73).

38. For a thorough analysis of Díaz's writings as replicating the violence toward women that Díaz himself claims to write against, see Gil'Adí, "'I Think about You, X—'"; Yomaira Figueroa-Vásquez interprets Díaz's fiction and its depiction of violence toward women as a reflection of colonial oppression that affects both survivor and perpetrator (67–87).

"Drown" exemplifies the way Díaz's stories engage with the urban city as an overwhelming force or as an uncaring environment that leads to narratives of decline that characterize naturalist fiction. "Drown" focuses on poverty, broken families, and the lack of viable economic opportunities for young Latinxs in urban communities despite the prevalent narrative of upward social mobility in America. "Drown" concentrates on the friendship between two high school friends, Yunior and Beto, who become estranged when Beto leaves for college and Yunior remains in the neighborhood; the narrative is explicit regarding male sexual attraction, and scholars have discussed "Drown" through the lens of either masculinity, queerness, or homophobia.[39] "Drown" also explores poverty and family ties through the relationship between Yunior and his unnamed mother.[40] Social inequality, poverty, and their effects on characters are tropes in literary naturalism and also relate to the idea of readers as "spectators" of the hardships of the working poor; Jude Davies, for example, notes that representative naturalist works by Crane, Norris, and Dreiser "interpolate readers as fellow members of the middle-class and offer them access to the public, domestic, and laboring spaces of those who work manually or who are unemployed" (307). Family cohesion in "Drown" is fractured by the members' economic situation. Yunior's mother is absent for extended periods of time, working at a low wage "housecleaning job" (99). The interactions between Yunior and his mother are marked by the subtext of economic hardship; the family is further hindered by Yunior's absent father and the family's status as recent immigrants. Although the family escapes from poverty in the Dominican Republic, they are still poor relative to other segments of the US population.

"Drown" emphasizes upward social mobility as a way to escape an oppressive environment that is similarly depicted in Jones's "The Sunday Following Mother's Day." "Drown" explores the prospects of upward social mobility through education as one of the few avenues for advancement to the urban working poor, as Beto is able to attend college and leave the inner city.[41] While Yunior and Beto share a similar background growing up in the London Terrace apartments in an urban New Jersey city, their eventual trajectories follow opposite paths that represent an instance of social advancement through

39. For discussions of "Drown" through the lenses of masculinity or queerness, see Dalleo and Sáez 85–89; C. González 43–47; and Irizarry 64–69.

40. As Danny Méndez notes, "Díaz's characters come from families who are well acquainted with poverty" (119).

41. Dalleo and Sáez correctly point out that "education is the means of Beto's abandonment of the barrio" (86). For analyses that discuss Beto as an example of upward social mobility, see Frydman 140; and Dalleo and Sáez 85–86.

educational opportunity; however, their ability to move out is not based only on academic aptitude but also is shaped by negative social experiences. Before going to college, Beto "was delirious from the thought of it" while Yunior "hated every single teacher on the planet" (91, 101). Although they are equally capable, Beto is "the one leaving for college" (94). Yunior's lack of interest is formed in part by his negative experiences at school; Yunior remembers a teacher comparing students to space shuttles as the teacher explained: "A few of you are going to make it. Those are the orbiters. But the majority of you are just going to burn out. Going nowhere" (106). In "The Sunday Following Mother's Day," despite the family tragedy, one of Samuel's children, Madeleine, is able to move upwardly and leave DC. Madeleine attends Columbia University, marries a lawyer, and reaches middle-class status. Both short stories present poverty and social stagnation as ever-present forces influencing characters with little chance of success.

"Edison, New Jersey" further explores social stratification among different communities within the US as it describes a small wealthy class—mostly white—at the top of the social ladder sustained by a working class composed of people of color and immigrants that resonates with similar tropes in Wright's *Native Son*. "Edison, New Jersey" explores the subtle but rigid social disparities among different communities that prove hard to bridge, as Yunior, working as a deliveryman at a furniture store, constantly interrogates his social position and how it affects his everyday life.[42] Díaz's story dispels the misleading belief of equal economic opportunity in American society as the narrative accentuates the economic disparities among poor and affluent communities. Although the wealthy and the working class share a geographic region, "Edison, New Jersey" reflects a society divided by social and economic boundaries dictated primarily by education, profession, and income. Yunior is aware that different neighborhoods correlate with wealth and the type of furniture he delivers as he notes that "if someone is just getting a fifty-two-inch card table delivered . . . [,] [t]hose are your Sportswood, Sayreville and Perth Amboy deliveries. The pool tables go north to the rich suburbs—Livingston, Ridgewood, [and] Bedminster" (122). In the latter cases, usually the customers are "doctors, diplomats, surgeons, presidents of universities, [and] ladies in slacks and silk tops who sport thin watches you could trade in for a car" (122). In *Native Son*, Bigger Thomas lives not only in a racially segregated city but also a stratified city divided by income with affluent dwellers of the Gold Coast on the North Side and economically struggling Black communities on

---

42. In an interview, Díaz alludes to these challenges within communities of color when he notes that "if you're poor in the United States, chances are you're going to be poor for a very long time" (Céspedes, Torres-Saillant, and Díaz 893).

the South Side. Under the thin veneer of social homogeneity, members of different racial and ethnic groups in "Edison, New Jersey" and *Native Son* quickly become divided by physical and economic boundaries.

Just as in Dreiser's *Sister Carrie*, "Edison, New Jersey" emphasizes the constant search for material possessions and economic gain in a society obsessed with financial success that only a few people can achieve. In Dreiser's novel, Carrie Meeber comes to Chicago from rural Wisconsin with dreams of financial success, and while Chicago does offer opportunities, she is mesmerized by the goods and merchandise displayed at the Chicago downtown stores. In "Edison, New Jersey," Yunior is aware of pervasive social inequalities but still daydreams about possessions that his present job as a low-wage worker makes almost impossible to obtain.[43] While working at the register at the furniture store, he calculates "how long it'd take [him] to buy a pool table honestly," considering that a "top-of-the-line, three-piece slate affair doesn't come cheap," and discovers that it would take him "two and a half years if [he] give[s] up buying underwear and eat[s] only pasta" (128). Yunior observes that in some cases, income is commonly tied to inherited wealth; he associates wealthy individuals with "court case [last] names" such as "Wooley, Maynard, Gass, [and] Binder," but he relates Latinx last names to "convicts" and individuals "coupled together on boxing cards" (130). His way of righting this wrong is by stealing small items from customers' houses while delivering pool tables and sometimes failing to ring up purchases at the store. When he uses the stolen money to buy presents for his girlfriend, Yunior confesses that "this is the closest [he has] come to feeling rich" (125). While *Sister Carrie* allows its protagonist to achieve her goal of financial success, a rare narrative of ascent among naturalist novels, Yunior mainly just survives economically, which relates to the limited prospects for social advancement of a significant number of people of color in urban communities.

Lost in the City and *Drown* show the permutations and evolution of the American literary tradition as authors of color have continued to incorporate and subvert some of its aesthetic, stylistic, and thematic conventions. Depictions of the underclass, working class, and immigrants, along with their struggles, have an antecedent in literary naturalism, and similar to naturalist narratives, the opportunities for characters to ascend the economic ladder in *Lost in the City* and *Drown* are limited due to rigid social stratification. The unvarnished depiction of the challenges and aspirations of the disadvantaged, underclass, and working class relate to the way in which Richard Wright, and

---

43. As Dalleo and Sáez rightly note, the narrator of "Edison, New Jersey" is particularly "obsessed with material goods" (79).

other Black writers, subverted some of the conventions and tropes of literary naturalism to present—in an unembellished manner—the effects of historical, social, and economic exclusion to a readership that was predominantly white and middle class before the 1960s. *Lost in the City* and *Drown* show that the economic challenges identified by Black and Latinx civil rights leaders after the 1960s continue in contemporary times. Despite suggestions that after the end of Jim Crow segregation Black writers created a different type of fiction that moved away from the overwhelming significance of race, Jones and Díaz show that unmitigated poverty, limited educational opportunities, and lack of health and social services remain ever-present issues faced by a large number of communities of color in urban areas.

Black and Latinx Writers in the Twenty-First Century

The Visibility of the Few and the Exclusion of the Many

In the preceding chapters, I studied comparatively instances when Black and Latinx authors between the 1960s and the turn of the twentieth century thematized in their novels, short stories, plays, and essays the social, economic, and cultural marginalization of their respective groups and communities in different geographical regions and historical periods. Black and Latinx authors grappled within their aesthetic and intellectual works with the legacy of the civil rights movements of the 1960s and 1970s. My study focused on the parallel thematic, stylistic, and formalistic strategies shared by a number of post-1960s Black and Latinx authors and the concerted ways in which they have challenged dominant historical, social, and cultural narratives regarding the place of people of color in American society.

While the resurging social activism and militancy of the late 1960s and early 1970s among Blacks and Latinx people emphasized racial and ethnic pride, along with calls for cultural and artistic self-determination, some post-1960s Black and Latinx writers thematized the historical marginalization of their respective groups by engaging with some of the aesthetic, thematic, and formalistic elements and concerns found in the American literary tradition, its literary movements, and authors. The long history of instances of intertextuality between Black and canonical authors has been advanced by some scholars of Black literature such as Henry L. Gates and explored in earlier decades by writers such as Ralph Ellison;[1] nonetheless, the influence of the American literary tradition in post-1960s Black and Latinx authors has not been sufficiently explored. While each literary tradition presents and represents a distinct origin, development, and set of aesthetic and cultural characteristics, the Black and Latinx literary traditions contain shared historical, thematic, and aesthetic traits due in part to the way some Black and Latinx authors have engaged with pre-1960s American literature. The increasing number of authors of color in the literary tradition has begun to fulfill the vision of scholars such as Ramón Saldívar, who has called for a "reconstruction of American literary history" that would include the voices of those who "were and continued to be silenced" in order to arrive at "a truly integrated American literature" (*Chicano* 217–18).

My comparative study explores convergences and commonalities among some post-1960s Black and Latinx writers; nonetheless, since the beginning of each literary tradition, some of their works have converged in relation to their formal, aesthetic, and ideological goals. Some of these instances of shared experiences are present in the development of the Black and Spanish-language print culture through the "long" nineteenth century, the newspaper and political writings of Frederick Douglass and José Martí, the influence of mainstream publishers in the fiction of Charles Chesnutt and María Amparo Ruiz de Burton, and the role of communist organizations in the political writings of Richard Wright and Jesús Colón, among others. Due in part to the ways historical narratives, texts, and the artistic output of Black and Latinx authors have circulated since the 1960s, instances of cultural, artistic, and ideological exchanges among these writers have expanded. Increasingly, scholars of Black and Latinx literatures have focused on historical, social, and cross-cultural commonalities among writers from these and other ethnic groups in the US context. Additional possibilities for comparative studies of Black and Latinx authors are significant; some of these include the newspaper writings of Langston Hughes and Jesús Colón, the poetry of Sonia Sanchez and Lorna Dee Cervantes, the political writings of Huey Newton and Rodolfo "Corky" Gonzales, the fiction and poetry of Gwendolyn Brooks and Sandra Cisneros, and the novels of Toni Morrison and Ana Castillo.

A major thread in each of the preceding comparative analyses is the instances of literary marginalization experienced by authors from the beginning of the Black and Latinx literary traditions to contemporary times. Start-

---

1. See Gates, *Loose Canons* xi–xix; Jackson, *Indignant Generation* 1–14; and Ellison, "Remembering Richard Wright" 198–216.

ing around the second half of the nineteenth century, Black and Latinx writers similarly fought to publish their writings in local newspapers and periodicals that were supported by their respective Black or Spanish-speaking communities in different cities and regions. As the decades progressed, some Black and Latinx authors tried to publish their work in mainstream publications and publishing houses and gained a sustaining local or mainstream readership. Publishing dynamics changed starting in the late 1960s, only after students' protests and activism gave rise to the institutionalization of Black and Latinx literature at college campuses and reawakened the interest of mainstream publishers in authors of color.

My comparative analysis showed how post-1960s Black and Latinx authors built upon the legacy of past struggles against literary invisibility and broke some of the barriers that had hindered pre-1960s Black and Latinx authors. Some post-1960s Black and Latinx writers attended prestigious creative writing programs, gained academic appointments, and achieved mainstream critical recognition from literary and cultural institutions that had been denied for the most part to authors of color up to the latter part of the twentieth century. While the twenty-first century represents an unparalleled period of literary recognition for authors of color such as Colson Whitehead, Lin-Manuel Miranda, and Natasha Trethewey, among others, their current moment of recognition is partly the result of decades of struggles to be published and read by past writers of color such as James Weldon Johnson, Américo Paredes, James Baldwin, and Helena María Viramontes, to name a few. While the fight against cultural marginalization led by students and activists on college campuses that began in the late 1960s changed exclusionary practices in predominantly white academic and publishing spaces, the fight is clearly far from over.

Although some authors of color have attained a moment of literary recognition measured by the number of awards granted by mainstream cultural organizations (Pulitzer Prizes, National Book Awards, MacArthur fellowships, etc.), the mainstream publishing industry continues to lag behind when it comes to the publication, promotion, and compensation of authors of color.[2] The publishing industry, dominated by the "Big Five" publishing houses, looms as an often unapologetic, white-dominated industry, not only in leadership positions but also among its literary agents, editors, and marketing departments. Historically, the publishing industry has served as one of de facto gatekeepers that, while judging works based on aesthetic merit, has also functioned as a white-dominated space that has not been sufficiently inter-

---

2. In a *New York Times* article published in 2020, Concepción de León and Elizabeth Harris describe the disparities in book advances between white writers and writers of color ("#PublishingPaidMe").

rogated or scrutinized in critical discussions;[3] when it comes to the stories of writers of color, however, often the publishing industry, and its predominantly white editors and decision makers, assess the aesthetic and cultural merits of those stories. The result of this top-down system creates and promotes at times works of fiction that blatantly exploit the historical and cultural experiences of some communities of color.[4] The development of the Black and Latinx literary traditions, along with the history of exclusion by the mainstream publishing industry, demonstrates that the current practices of the publishing industry toward Black and Latinx authors are the result of decades, or even centuries, of literary marginalization. Likewise, as illustrated by the ever-present fight for cultural and artistic recognition by writers of color that has contributed to the development of the Black and Latinx literary traditions, it would be a mistake to rely solely on the mainstream publishing industry and its profit-driven model to righten this history of cultural exclusion. Independent publishing houses such as Arte Público have played an instrumental role over the past decades by offering opportunities to emerging Latinx authors when other doors were closed. It was Arte Público Press, for instance, that first published Sandra Cisneros's groundbreaking *The House on Mango Street,* despite Cisneros's credentials as a graduate from the Iowa Writers' Workshop. The publication of Cisneros's *The House on Mango Street* with Arte Público represented the start of her writing career; however, it also meant the lack of a promotional and advertisement apparatus from a mainstream publisher; in the case of *The House on Mango Street,* it was Latinx scholars reviewing and writing about it, and professors assigning Cisneros's novel in classrooms, that moved Cisneros's novel from the literary margins into the mainstream as it was reissued years later by a mainstream publisher.[5]

When it comes to the publishing and teaching of emerging writers of color, particularly women, meaningful changes in practices would not come from within the publishing industry but from mobilized writers and social activists. Calls for industry-wide changes have come only after protests, demonstrations, and the fight from grassroots social justice movements such as Dignidad Literaria (Literary Dignity) and the broader Black Lives Matter movement. The emergence of these social movements, and their members' efforts to showcase the ways in which publishing and cultural organizations exclude people of color, attests to how changes in publishing in academia occurred starting in the late 1960s only after extended periods of student protests and

3. A notable exception is Richard Jean So's *Redlining Culture.*
4. See Bowles, "*American Dirt* Is Proof."
5. See Cruz, "On the 'Simplicity.'" For an analysis on the influence of the Iowa Writers' Workshop on Cisneros's writing, see Cutler, *Ends of Assimilation* 118–34.

social activism. Likewise, the increasing number of students of color attending college continues to press universities for meaningful changes beyond statements on diversity and inclusion;[6] in their roles as creators and disseminators of knowledge, universities and their various constituencies influence what texts and fiction is read in their classrooms. Despite major shifts in the racial and ethnic backgrounds of incoming college students, changes and pledges for inclusion at colleges and university often lag behind. In English departments and literary studies, the emphasis on the Western and pre-1960s American literary traditions looms larger than we are comfortable acknowledging. Students of color at a college campus should not feel that the past experiences of their respective groups are an afterthought within a dominant historical or literary narrative or that texts by Black and Latinx writers that are worthy of study emerged only a few decades ago, given the vast history of Black and Latinx literary works published in the US dating back centuries. Likewise, within higher education, creative writing programs, since their rise in the 1960s, have remained for the most part, despite their diversity or inclusion efforts, predominantly white spaces when more often than not, the experiences of writers of color and their social justice grievances are diminished in favor of the emphasis on "craft."[7] The resistance to the histories and stories of people of color, along with the cutting and restructuring of ethnic studies programs and the devaluation of the work of faculty of color even at elite universities, attests that the fight for literary inclusion of writers and scholars of color in publishing and higher education remains an ongoing fight.[8]

While there are still challenges facing writers of color, there are reasons for optimism. As the previous struggles of the 1960s and 1970s at college campuses demonstrate, change often originates at key historical junctures and moments of social upheaval led by students and activists who are able to inspire others. An increasing number of writers and scholars of color continues to create and shape the ways in which a new generation of college students experiences the works of an increasingly multiethnic American literary tradition that reflects universities' student bodies. The inclusion of writers of color in publishing, literary studies, higher education, and cultural institutions is intrinsically connected to the struggles of people of color in American society, thus reflecting its challenges but also its possibilities.

---

6. A study by the American Council on Education found that in 2016 nearly half the undergraduate students were students of color (S. Brown).

7. See Chavez, *Anti-Racist Writing Workshop*; and Sáez, "Generation MFA."

8. As Kate Taylor describes in a 2020 *New York Times* article, Ivy League and other selective colleges continue to deny tenure to faculty of color whose scholarship specialized in the history of and experiences of people of color.

WORKS CITED

Acampora, Christa Davis. "On Unmaking and Remaking." Acampora and Cotten, pp. 1–17.

Acampora, Christa Davis, and Angela L. Cotten, editors. *Unmaking Race, Remaking Soul: Transformative Aesthetics and the Practice of Freedom.* State U of New York P, 2007.

Acosta-Belén, Edna, and Virginia Sánchez Korrol, editors. Introduction. *The Way It Was and Other Writings,* by Jesús Colón, Arte Público, 1993, pp. 13–30.

Acuña, Rodolfo F. *The Making of Chicana/o Studies: In the Trenches of Academia.* Rutgers UP, 2011.

———. *Occupied America: A History of Chicanos.* 2nd ed., Harper and Row, 1981.

Ainslie, Ricardo, and Daphny Domínguez. "Silent Wounds: Posttraumatic Stress Disorder and Latino World War II Veterans." Rivas-Rodríguez and Zamora, pp. 144–55.

Alcoff, Linda Martín. *The Future of Whiteness.* Polity, 2015.

———. "This Is Not Just about Junot Díaz." *New York Times,* 16 May 2018, https://www.nytimes.com/2018/05/16/opinion/junot-diaz-metoo.html. Accessed 1 Oct. 2019.

———. *Visible Identities: Race, Gender, and the Self.* Oxford UP, 2006.

Aldama, Frederick Luis. *Brown on Brown: Chicano/a Representations of Gender, Sexuality, and Ethnicity.* U of Texas P, 2005.

Alexander, Michelle. "The Injustice of This Moment Is Not an 'Aberration.'" *New York Times,* 17 Jan. 2020, https://www.nytimes.com/2020/01/17/opinion/sunday/michelle-alexander-new-jim-crow.html. Accessed 1 May 2020.

———. *The New Jim Crow: Mass Incarceration in the Age of Colorblindness.* New Press, 2012.

Alonzo, Juan J. *Badmen, Bandits, and Folk Heroes: The Ambivalence of Mexican American Identity in Literature and Film.* U of Arizona P, 2009.

Als, Hilton. "Edward P. Jones, The Art of Fiction." *Paris Review,* Winter 2013. https://www.theparisreview.org/interviews/6283/the-art-of-fiction-no-222-edward-p-jones. Accessed 8 Feb. 2018.

——. "Ghosts in the House: How Toni Morrison Fostered a Generation of Black Writers." *New Yorker,* 20 Oct. 2003, https://www.newyorker.com/magazine/2003/10/27/ghosts-in-the-house. Accessed 9 Apr. 2018.

Alvarez, Luis. "Transnational Latino Soldiering: Military Service and Ethnic Politics during World War II." Rivas-Rodriguez and Olgín, pp. 75–93.

Anaya, Rudolfo. "An Autobiography." González-T., pp. 359–88.

——. *Bless Me, Ultima.* Grand Central, 1994.

——. "An Interview with Rudolfo Anaya." Interview by Ishmael Reed. *Conversations,* edited by Dick and Sirias, pp. 1–10.

——. "The Magic of Words." *Rudolfo Anaya: The Essays,* edited by Robert Con Davis-Undiano, U of Oklahoma P, 2009, pp. 176–81.

——. "Rudolfo A. Anaya." Interview by Juan Bruce-Novoa. *Conversations,* edited by Dick and Sirias, pp. 11–28.

——. "The Silence of the Llano: Notes from the Author." *MELUS,* vol. 11, no. 4, 1984, pp. 47–57.

Andrews, William L. Introduction. *The Autobiography of an Ex-Colored Man,* by James Weldon Johnson, Penguin, 1990, pp. vii–xxvii.

——. Introduction. *Conjure Tales and Stories of the Colored Line,* by Charles W. Chesnutt, Penguin, 1992, pp. vii–xvii.

——. *The Literary Career of Charles W. Chesnutt.* Louisiana State UP, 1980.

Andrews, William L., Francis Smith Foster, and Trudier Harris, editors. *The Oxford Companion to African American Literature.* Oxford UP, 1997.

Androne, Helane Adams. "Revised Memories and Colliding Identities: Absence and Presence in Morrison's 'Recitatif' and Viramontes's 'Tears on My Pillow.'" *MELUS,* vol. 32, no. 2, 2007, pp. 133–50.

Anzaldúa, Gloria, editor. Introduction. *Making Face, Making Soul/Haciendo Caras: Creative and Critical Perspectives by Women of Color,* Aunt Lute Books, 1990, pp. xv–xviii.

Aranda, José F. *When We Arrive: A New Literary History of Mexican America.* U of Arizona P, 2003.

Augenbraum, Harold, and Margarite Fernández Olmos, editors. *The Latino Reader: An American Literary Tradition from 1542 to the Present.* Houghton Mifflin, 1997.

Babb, Valerie. *A History of the African American Novel.* Cambridge UP, 2017.

Baeza, Abelardo. *Man of Aztlán: A Biography of Rudolfo Anaya.* Eakin Press, 2001.

Baker, Houston A. *Blues, Ideology, and Afro-American Literature.* U of Chicago P, 1984.

——. "The Embattled Craftsman: An Essay on James Baldwin." Standley and Burt, pp. 62–77.

——. *Modernism and the Harlem Renaissance.* U of Chicago P, 1987.

Baldwin, James. "Autobiographical Notes." *Notes of A Native Son.* pp. 3–9.

——. "Everybody's Protest Novel." *Notes of a Native Son,* pp. 13–23

——. *The Fire Next Time.* Dial, 1963.

——. *Go Tell It on the Mountain.* Dial, 1953.

——. "Many Thousands Gone." *Notes of a Native Son,* pp. 25–45.

——. *No Name in the Street.* Dial, 1972.

——. *Notes of a Native Son.* Beacon, 1955.

———. *Tell Me How Long the Train's Been Gone*. Vintage, 1998.

Baraka, Amiri. *The Autobiography of LeRoi Jones/Amiri Baraka*. Freundlich, 1984.

———. "Black Is a Country." *Home: Social Essays*, pp. 82–86.

———. "Cold, Hurt, and Sorrow (Streets of Despair)." *Home: Social Essays*, pp. 94–96.

———. "Cuba Libre." *Home: Social Essays*, pp. 11–62.

———. "Cultural Revolution and the Literary Canon." *Callaloo*, vol. 14, no. 1, 1991, pp. 150–56.

———. *Home: Social Essays*. William Morrow, 1966.

———. Introduction. *The Motion of History and Other Plays*. William Morrow, 1978, pp. 11–16.

———. "The Legacy of Malcolm X, and the Coming of the Black Nation." *Home: Social Essays*, pp. 238–50.

———. "The Revolutionary Theatre." *Home: Social Essays*, pp. 210–15.

———. *The Slave. Dutchman and The Slave: Two Plays by LeRoi Jones*. William Morrow, 1964.

———. "Street Protest." *Home: Social Essays*, pp. 97–100.

———. "What Does Nonviolence Mean?" *Home: Social Essays*, pp. 133–54.

Baraka, Amiri, and Larry Neal, editors. *Black Fire: An Anthology of Afro-American Writing*. Black Classic, 1968.

Bentson, Kimberly. Introduction to *Dutchman*. *Political Stages: Plays that Shaped a Century*, edited by Emily Mann and David Roessel, Theatre and Cinema Books, 2002.

Berghahn, Marion. "Images of Africa in the Writings of James Baldwin." Bloom, *James Baldwin*, pp. 97–108.

Bigsby, C. W. E. "The Divided Mind of James Baldwin." Bloom, *James Baldwin*, pp. 113–29.

Blackwell, Maylei. *Chicana Power! Contested Histories of Feminism in the Chicano Movement*. U of Texas P, 2011.

Bloom, Harold, editor. *James Baldwin*. Chelsea, 1986.

———. *The Western Canon: The Books and School of the Ages*. Hardcourt Brace, 1994.

Boessenecker, John. *Bandido: The Life and Times of Tiburcio Vásquez*. U of Oklahoma P, 2010.

Bona, Mary Jo, and Irma Maini. *Multiethnic Literature and Canon Debates*. SUNY UP, 2006.

Booker, Bryan D. *African Americans in the United States Army in World War II*. MacFarland, 2008.

Bost, Suzanne. *Mulattas and Mestizas: Representing Mixed Identities in the Americas: 1850–2000*. U of Georgia P, 2005.

Bost, Suzanne, and Frances Aparicio, editors. Introduction. *The Routledge Companion to Latino/a Literature*. Routledge, 2012.

Bowles, David. "*American Dirt* Is Proof the Publishing Industry Is Broken." *New York Times*, 27 Jan. 2020, https://www.nytimes.com/2020/01/27/opinion/american-dirt-book.html. Accessed 2 Aug. 2020.

Brito, Manuel. "Widening the Paradigm of American Literature: Small Presses in the Publishing and Creation of New Hispanic Texts." Cottenet, pp. 79–94.

Brogan, Jacqueline Vaught. "Hemingway Talking to Walker Talking to Hemingway." *Hemingway Review*, vol. 30, no. 1, 2010, pp. 122–28.

Brown, Lloyd W. *Amiri Baraka*. Twayne, 1980.

Brown, Sarah. "Nearly Half of Undergraduates Are Students of Color. But Black Students Lag Behind." *Chronicle of Higher Education*, 14 Feb. 2019, https://www.chronicle.com/article/nearly-half-of-undergraduates-are-students-of-color-but-black-students-lag-behind/. Accessed 2 Aug. 2020.

Browner, Stephanie P., and Kenneth M. Price. "Charles Chesnutt and the Case for Hybrid Editing." *International Journal of Digital Humanities*, no. 1, 2019, pp. 165–78.

Broyles-González, Yolanda. *El Teatro Campesino: Theater in the Chicano Movement*. U of Texas P, 1994.

Bruce-Novoa, Juan. *RetroSpace: Collected Essays on Chicano Literature, Theory, and History*. Arte Público, 1990.

———. "Shipwrecked in the Seas of Signification: Cabeza the Vaca's *La Relación* and Chicano Literature." Herrera-Sobek, pp. 3–23.

Budd, Louis, J. "The American Background." *The Cambridge Companion to American Realism and Naturalism*, edited by Donald Pizer, Cambridge UP, 1995, pp. 21–46.

Bump, Philip. "The Most Likely Person to Read a Book? A College-Educated Black Woman." *Atlantic*. 16 Jan. 2014. https://www.theatlantic.com/culture/archive/2014/01/most-likely-person-read-book-college-educated-black-woman/357091/. Accessed 1 Sept. 2018.

Butler, Robert James. "Alice Walker's Vision of the South in *The Third Life of Grange Copeland*." *African American Review*, vol. 27, no. 2, 1993, pp. 195–204.

Byrd, Rudolph P., editor. Introduction. *The World Has Changed: Conversations with Alice Walker*, New Press, 2010, pp. 1–34.

Calderón, Héctor. *Narratives of Greater Mexico: Essays on Chicano Literary History, Genre, and Borders*. U of Texas P, 2004.

Calderón, Héctor, and José David Saldívar. Introduction. *Criticism in the Borderlands: Studies in Chicano Literature, Culture, and Ideology*. Duke UP, 1991, pp. 1–7.

Caminero-Santangelo, Marta. "'Jasón's Indian': Mexican Americans and the Denial of Indigenous Ethnicity in Anaya's *Bless Me, Ultima*." *Critique: Studies in Contemporary Fiction*, vol. 45, no. 2, 2004, pp. 115–28.

———. *On Latinidad: U.S. Latino Literature and the Construction of Ethnicity*. U of Florida P, 2007.

Campbell, James. *Talking at the Gates: A Life of James Baldwin*. Viking, 1991.

Cannon, Steve, Lennox Raphael, and James Thompson. "A Very Stern Discipline: An Interview with Ralph Ellison." Graham and Singh, pp. 109–35.

Cantú, Roberto. "Apocalypse as an Ideological Construct: The Storyteller's Art in *Bless Me, Ultima*." González-T., pp. 13–63.

Carby, Hazel V. *Reconstructing Womanhood: The Emergence of the Afro-American Woman Novelist*. Oxford UP, 1987.

Carretta, Vincent, editor. Introduction. *Phillis Wheatley, Complete Writings*. Penguin, 2001, pp. xiii–xxxviii.

Carretta, Vincent, and Philip Gould, editors. *Genius in Bondage: Literature of the Early Black Atlantic*. UP of Kentucky, 2001.

Cavitch, Max. "The Poetry of Phillis Wheatley in Slavery's Recollective Economies, 1773 to the Present." Cottenet, pp. 210–30.

Céspedes, Diógenes, Silvio Torres-Saillant, and Junot Díaz. "Fiction Is the Poor Man's Cinema: An Interview with Junot Díaz." *Callaloo*, vol. 23, no. 3, 2000, pp. 892–907.

Chavez, Felicia Rose. *The Anti-Racist Writing Workshop: How to Decolonize the Creative Classroom*. Haymarket, 2021.

Chester, Alfred, Vilma Howard, and Ralph Ellison. "Ralph Ellison, The Art of Fiction No. 8," *Paris Review*, vol. 8, 1955. https://www.theparisreview.org/interviews/5053/the-art-of-fiction-no-8-ralph-ellison. Accessed 20 March 2018.

Christian, Barbara. *Black Women Novelists: The Development of a Tradition, 1892–1976.* Greenwood, 1980.

Christie, John S. *Latino Fiction and the Modernist Imagination: Literature of the Borderlands.* Garland Publishing, 1998.

Cloutier, Jean-Christophe. *Shadow Archives: The Lifecycles of African American Literature.* Columbia UP, 2019.

Cohen, Lara Langer, and Jordan Alexander Stein, editors. *Early African American Print Culture.* U of Pennsylvania P, 2012.

Coleman, James W. *Understanding Edward P. Jones.* U of South Carolina P, 2016.

Colón, Jesús. *A Puerto Rican in New York and Other Sketches.* International, 1982.

———. *The Way It Was and Other Writings.* Edited by Edna Acosta-Belén and Virginia Sánchez Korrol, Arte Público, 1993.

Conner, Marc C., and Lucas E. Morel, editors. *The New Territory: Ralph Ellison and the Twenty-First Century.* U of Mississippi P, 2016.

Contreras, Alicia. "'I'll Publish Your Cowardice All Over California': María Amparo Ruiz de Burton's *The Squatter and the Don* in the Age of Howells." *American Literary Realism,* vol. 49, no. 3, 2017, pp. 210–25.

Cooper, David D., and Richard Rodriguez. "Interview with Richard Rodriguez." *Fourth Genre: Explorations in Nonfiction,* vol. 5, no. 2, 2003, pp. 104–32.

Cooper, Lydia R. "'Bone, Flesh, Feather, Fire': Symbol as Freedom in Helena María Viramontes's *Under the Feet of Jesus.*" *Critique,* vol. 51, no. 4, 2010, pp. 366–77.

Coronado, Raúl. "Historicizing Nineteenth-Century Latina/o Textuality." Lazo and Alemán, pp. 49–70.

———. *A World Not to Come: A History of Latino Writing and Print Culture.* Harvard UP, 2016.

Corpi, Lucha, editor. *Máscaras.* Third Woman, 1997.

Cotera, María Eugenia. *Native Speakers: Ella Deloria, Zora Neale Hurston, Jovita González, and the Poetics of Culture.* U of Texas P, 2008.

Cottenet, Cécile, editor. *Race, Ethnicity and Publishing in America.* Palgrave, 2014.

Cowart, David. *Trailing Clouds: Immigrant Fiction in Contemporary America.* Cornell UP, 2006.

Crawford, John F. "Rudolfo Anaya." Dick and Sirias, pp. 105–15.

Cruz, Felicia J. "On the 'Simplicity' of Sandra Cisneros's *House on Mango Street.*" *Modern Fiction Studies,* vol. 47, no. 4, 2001, pp. 910–46.

Curiel, Barbara Brinson. "'Had They Been Heading for the Barn All Along?': Viramontes's Chicana Feminist Revision of Steinbeck's Migrant Family." Gutiérrez y Muhs, pp. 27–47.

Cutler, John Alba. "At the Crossroads of Circulation and Translation: Rethinking US Latino/a Modernism." *Modernism/modernity,* vol. 3, cycle 3, 2018. https://doi.org/10.26597/mod.0069. Accessed 2 Aug. 2020.

———. *Ends of Assimilation: The Formation of Chicano Literature.* Oxford UP, 2015.

———. "Eusebio Chacón's America." *MELUS,* vol. 36, no. 1, 2011, pp. 109–34.

———. "Toward a Reading of Nineteenth-Century Latino/a Short Fiction." Lazo and Alemán, pp. 124–45.

Dalfiume, Richard M. *Desegregation of the U.S. Armed Forces: Fighting on Two Fronts 1939–1953.* U of Missouri P, 1969.

———. "The 'Forgotten Years' of the Negro Revolution." *Journal of American History,* vol. 55, no. 1, 1968, pp. 90–106.

Dalleo, Raphael, and Elena Machado Sáez. *The Latino/a Canon and the Emergence of Post-Sixties Literature.* Palgrave Macmillan, 2007.

Davies, Jude. "Naturalism and Class." Newlin, pp. 307–21.

Dávila, Arlene. *Latinos, Inc.: The Marketing and Making of a People.* U of California P, 2012.

———. *Latinx Art: Artists, Markets, and Politics.* Duke UP, 2020.

Davis, David A. "Southern Modernists and Modernity." *The Cambridge Companion to the Literature of the American South,* edited by Sharon Monteith, Cambridge UP, 2013. pp. 88–103.

Davis, Thadious. "Poetry as Preface to Fiction: Alice Walker's Recurrent Apprenticeship." *Mississippi Quarterly,* vol. 44, no. 2, 1991, pp. 133–42.

Deahl, Rachel. "Why Publishing Is So White." *Publishers Weekly.* 11 Mar. 2016. https://www.publishersweekly.com/pw/by-topic/industry-news/publisher-news/article/69653-why-publishing-is-so-white.html. Accessed 1 Nov. 2019.

de León, Concepción, and Elizabeth A. Harris. "#PublishingPaidMe and a Day of Action Reveal an Industry Reckoning." *New York Times,* 8 Jun. 2020, https://www.nytimes.com/2020/06/08/books/publishingpaidme-publishing-day-of-action.html. Accessed 2 Aug. 2020.

Díaz, Junot. *Drown.* Riverhead, 1996.

———. "MFA vs. POC." *New Yorker,* 30 Apr. 2014. https://www.newyorker.com/ books/page-turner/mfa-vs-poc. Accessed 1 Nov. 2019.

Dick, Bruce, and Silvio Sirias, editors. Introduction. *Conversations with Rudolfo Anaya.* U of Mississippi P, 1998, pp. ix–xiv.

Douglass, Frederick. *My Bondage and My Freedom.* Penguin, 2003.

Du Bois, W. E. B. *Dusk of Dawn: An Essay toward an Autobiography of a Race Concept.* Transaction, 1984.

Dudley, John. "African American Writers and Naturalism." Newlin, pp. 257–73.

Echevarría, Roberto González. Introduction. *José Martí: Selected Writings,* Penguin, 2002, pp. ix–xxxiv.

Edwards, Brent Hayes. *The Practice of Diaspora: Literature, Translation, and the Rise of Black Internationalism.* Harvard UP, 2003.

Eisenhower, John S. D. *So Far from God: The U.S. War with Mexico: 1846–1848.* Random House, 1989.

Elam, Harry J. *Taking It to the Streets: The Social Protest Theater of Luis Valdez and Amiri Baraka.* U of Michigan P, 1997.

Ellison, Ralph. "Alain Locke." *Collected Essays,* pp. 439–47.

———. *The Collected Essays of Ralph Ellison,* edited by John F. Callahan. Modern Library, 1995.

———. *Going to the Territory.* Random House, 1986.

———. "The Little Man at Chehaw Station." *Going to the Territory,* pp. 3–38.

———. "Remembering Richard Wright." *Going to the Territory,* pp. 198–216.

———. "Richard Wright's Blues." *Shadow and Act,* pp. 77–94.

———. *Shadow and Act.* Vintage, 1995.

———. "Twentieth-Century Fiction and the Black Mask of Humanity." *Shadow and Act,* pp. 24–44.

———. "What America Would Be Like without Blacks." *Going to the Territory,* pp. 104–12.

———. "The World and the Jug." *Shadow and Act,* pp. 107–43.

Encinias, Miguel, Alfred Rodríguez, and Joseph P. Sánchez. Introduction. *Historia de la Nueva México, 1610,* by Gaspar Pérez de Villagrá, U of New Mexico P, 1992, pp. xvii–xliii.

English, James F. *The Economy of Prestige: Prizes, Awards, and the Circulation of Cultural Value.* Harvard UP, 2005.

Ernest, John. *Chaotic Justice: Rethinking African American Literary History.* U of North Carolina P, 2009.

———. *Liberation Historiography: African American Writers and the Challenge of History, 1794–1861.* U of North Carolina P, 2004.

Espinosa, Lorelle L., Jonathan M. Turk, Morgan Taylor, and Hollie M. Chessman. "Race and Ethnicity in Higher Education: A Status Report." *American Council on Education.* https://www.equityinhighered.org/indicators/u-s-population-trends-and-educational-attainment/. Accessed 1 Nov. 2019.

Fagan, Benjamin. *The Black Newspaper and the Chosen Nation.* U of Georgia P, 2016.

Fanuzzi, Robert. "Frederick Douglass's 'Colored Newspaper': Identity Politics in Black and White." Vogel, pp. 55–70.

Fehrenbach, Heide. *Race after Hitler: Black Occupation Children in Postwar Germany and America.* Princeton UP, 2005.

Ferguson, Roderick A. *The Reorder of Things: The University and Its Pedagogies of Minority Difference.* U of Minnesota P, 2012.

Fernández Olmos, Margarite. *Rudolfo A. Anaya: A Critical Companion.* Greenwood, 1999.

Ferszt, Elizabeth. "Richard Rodriguez: Reluctant Romantic." *Early American Literature,* vol. 43, no. 2, 2008, pp. 443–52.

Field, Douglas. *All Those Strangers: The Art and Lives of James Baldwin.* Oxford UP, 2015.

Figueroa-Vásquez, Yomaira C. *Decolonizing Diasporas: Radical Mappings of Afro-Atlantic Literature.* Northwestern UP, 2020.

Fike, Matthew A. "Jean Toomer and Okot p'Bitek in Alice Walker's 'In Search of Our Mothers' Gardens.'" *MELUS,* vol. 25, no, 3, 2000, pp. 141–60.

Flores, Juan. Foreword. *A Puerto Rican in New York and Other Sketches,* by Jesús Colón, International, 1982, pp. ix–xvii.

———. *From Bomba to Hip-Hop: Puerto Rican Culture and Latino Identity.* Columbia UP, 2000.

———. "Life Off the Hyphen: Latino Literature and Nuyorican Traditions." *Mambo Montage: The Latinization of New York,* edited by Agustín Laó-Montes and Arlene Dávila, Columbia UP, 2001, pp. 185–206.

Fonseca-Chávez, Vanessa. *Colonial Legacies in Chicana/o Literature and Culture: Looking through the Kaleidoscope.* U of Arizona P, 2020.

Foreman, P. Gabrielle. *Activist Sentiments: Reading Black Women in the Nineteenth Century.* U of Illinois P, 2009.

Foster, Frances Smith. *Witnessing Slavery: The Development of the Ante-Bellum Slave Narratives.* Greenwood, 1979.

Franklin, John Hope, and Alfred A. Moss Jr. *From Slavery to Freedom: A History of African Americans.* 8th ed., Mcgraw-Hill, 2001.

Frydman, Jason. "Violence, Masculinity, and Upward Mobility in the Dominican Diaspora: Junot Díaz, the Media, and *Drown.*" *Bloom's Modern Critical Views: Hispanic-American Writers,* edited by Harold Bloom, Bloom's Literary Criticism, 2009, pp. 133–43.

Ganz, Marshall. *Why David Sometimes Wins: Leadership, Organization, and Strategy in the California Farm Worker Movement.* Oxford UP, 2009.

Garcia, Michael Nieto. *Autobiography in Black and Brown: Ethnic identity in Richard Wright and Richard Rodriguez.* U of New Mexico P, 2014.

García, Nasario. *Pláticas: Conversations with Hispano Writers of New Mexico.* Texas Tech UP, 2000.

Gardner, Eric. "African American Literary Reconstructions and the 'Propaganda of History.'" *American Literary History,* vol. 30, no. 3, 2018, pp. 429–49.

———. *Unexpected Places: Relocating Nineteenth-Century African American Literature.* U of Mississippi P, 2009.

Gates, David. "English Lessons." *New York Times,* 29 Sept. 1996. https://www.nytimes.com/1996/09/29/books/english-lessons.html. Accessed 8 Feb. 2018.

Gates, Henry Louis. *Figures in Black: Words, Signs, and the "Racial" Self.* Oxford UP, 1987.

———. *Loose Canons: Notes on the Culture Wars.* Oxford UP, 1993.

Gates, Henry Louis, and Nellie Y. McKay, editors. *The Norton Anthology of African American Literature.* Norton, 1997.

Geller, Allen. "An Interview with Ralph Ellison." Graham and Singh, pp. 70–86.

Genter, Robert. "Toward a Theory of Rhetoric: Ralph Ellison, Kenneth Burke and the Problem of Modernism." *Twentieth Century Literature,* vol. 48, no. 2, 2002, pp. 191–214.

Gil'Adí, Maia. "'I Think about You, X—': Re-Reading Junot Díaz after 'The Silence.'" *Latino Studies,* vol. 18, no. 1, 2020, pp. 507–30.

Giles, James R. "The Grotesque City, the City of Excess, and the City of Exile." Newlin, pp. 322–38.

Gillman, Susan. "Networking *Uncle Tom's Cabin*; or, Hyper Stowe in Early African American Print Culture." Cohen and Stein, pp. 231–49.

Gilroy, Paul. *The Black Atlantic: Modernity and Double Consciousness.* Harvard UP, 1993.

Goldberg, David Theo. *Racial Subjects: Writing on Race in America.* Routledge, 1997.

Goldsby, Jacqueline. Introduction. *The Autobiography of an Ex-Colored Man,* by James Weldon Johnson, Norton, 2015, pp. ix–lix.

Gonzales, Rodolfo. "We Demand: Statement of Chicanos of the Southwest in the Poor People's Campaign." *Aztlán: An Anthology of Mexican American Literature,* edited by Luis Valdez and Stan Steiner, Knopf, 1972, pp. 218–21.

González, Christopher. *Reading Junot Díaz.* U of Pittsburgh P, 2015.

González, John Morán. *Border Renaissance: The Texas Centennial and the Emergence of Mexican American Literature.* U of Texas P, 2009.

González, John Morán, and Laura Lomas, editors. *The Cambridge History of Latina/o American Literature.* Cambridge UP, 2018.

González, Juan. *Harvest of Empire: A History of Latinos in America.* Viking, 2000.

González, Matilde Martín. "Beyond Mainstream Presses: Publishing Women of Color as Cultural and Political Critique." Cottenet, pp. 143–67.

González-T., César A., editor. *Rudolfo A. Anaya: Focus on Criticism.* Lalo, 1990.

Goyal, Yogita. *Romance, Diaspora, and Black Atlantic Literature.* Cambridge UP, 2010.

Graham, Maryemma, editor. Introduction. *Conversations with Margaret Walker,* UP of Mississippi, 2002, pp. vii–xiv.

Graham, Maryemma, and Amritjit Singh, editors. *Conversations with Ralph Ellison.* UP of Mississippi, 1995.

Graham, Maryemma, and Edward P. Jones. "An Interview with Edward. P. Jones." *African American Review,* vol. 42, no. 3, 2008, pp. 421–38.

Graham, Maryemma, and Jerry W. Ward Jr., editors. *The Cambridge History of African American Literature*. Cambridge UP, 2011.

Gray, Thomas. *The Confessions of Nat Turner*. Lucas & Denver, 1831.

Griffin, Farah Jasmine. "Thirty Years of Black American Literature and Literary Studies." *Journal of Black Studies*, vol. 35, no. 2, 2004, pp. 165–74.

Grillo, Evelio. *Black Cuban, Black American: A Memoir*. Arte Público, 2000.

Griswold del Castillo, Richard. "The Paradox of War: Mexican American Patriotism, Racism, and Memory." Rivas-Rodríguez and Zamora, pp. 11–20.

———. "The War and Changing Identities: Personal Transformations." *World War II and Mexican American Civil Rights*, edited by Richard Griswold del Castillo, U of Texas P, 2008, pp. 49–73.

Gruesser, John Cullen. *Confluences: Postcolonialism, African American Literary Studies, and the Black Atlantic*. U of Georgia P, 2005.

Gruesz, Kirsten Silva. *Ambassadors of Culture: The Transamerican Origins of Latino Writing*. Princeton UP, 2002.

———. "The Once and Future Latino: Notes Toward a Literary History *Todavía Para Llegar*." Sandín and Perez, pp. 115–42.

———. "Transamerican New Orleans: Latino Literature of the Gulf, from the Spanish Colonial Period to Post-Katrina." González and Lomas, pp. 176–89.

———. "What Was Latino Literature?" *PMLA*, vol. 127, no. 2, 2012, pp. 335–41.

Gruesz, Kirsten Silva, and Rodrigo Lazo. "The Spanish Americas. Introduction." *Early American Literature*, vol. 53, no. 3, 2018, pp. 641–64.

Guajardo, Paul. *Chicano Controversy: Oscar Acosta and Richard Rodriguez*. Peter Lang, 2002.

Guillory, John. *Cultural Capital: The Problem of Literary Canon Formation*. U of Chicago P, 1993.

Gutiérrez y Muhs, Gabriella, editor. *Rebozos de Palabras: An Helena María Viramontes Critical Reader*. U of Arizona P, 2013.

Hall, Jacquelyn Down. "The Long Civil Rights Movement and the Political Uses of the Past." *Journal of American History*, vol. 91, no. 4, 2005. pp. 1233–63.

Hanna, Monica, Jennifer Harford Vargas, and José David Saldívar, editors. Introduction. *Junot Díaz and the Decolonial Imagination*, Duke UP, 2016, pp. 1–29.

Hargrove, Hondon B. *Buffalo Soldiers in Italy: Black Americans in World War II*. McFarland, 2003.

Harper, Phillip Brian. *Framing the Margins: The Social Logic of Postmodern Culture*. Oxford UP, 1994.

Hay, Samuel A. *African American Theatre: An Historical and Critical Analysis*. Cambridge UP, 2004.

Hernández, Guillermo E. *Chicano Satire: A Study in Literary Culture*. U of Texas P, 1991.

Herrera-Sobek, María. Introduction. *Reconstructing a Chicano/a Literary Heritage: Hispanic Colonial Literature of the Southwest*. U of Arizona P, 1993, pp. xix–xxxii.

Hill, Michael D. *The Ethics of Swagger: Prizewinning African American Novels, 1997–1993*. Ohio State UP, 2013.

———. "Timely Exile: James Alan McPherson, the Iowa Writers' Workshop, and Black Creativity." *After the Program Era: The Past, Present, and Future of Creative Writing in the University*, edited by Loren Glass, U of Iowa P, 2016, pp. 123–36.

Hine, Darlene Clark, and John McCluskey, editors. *The Black Chicago Renaissance*. U of Illinois P, 2012.

Hinojosa, Rolando. Introduction. *George Washington Gómez*, by Américo Paredes, Arte Público, 1990.

Holladay, Hilary. *Ann Petry*. Twayne P, 1996.

Holton, Adalaine. "'Little Things Are Big': Race and the Politics of Print Community in the Writings of Jesús Colón." *MELUS*, vol. 38 no. 2, 2013, pp. 5–23.

Howard, June. *Form and History in American Literary Naturalism*. U of North Carolina P, 1985.

Hubbs, Jolene. "William Faulkner's Rural Modernism." *Mississippi Quarterly*, vol. 61, no. 3, 2008, pp. 461–75.

Huerta, Jorge. *Chicano Drama: Performance, Society, and Myth*. Cambridge UP, 2000.

———. *Chicano Theater: Themes and Forms*. Bilingual Press, 1982.

———. Introduction to *The Shrunken Head of Pancho Villa. Necessary Theater: Six Plays about the Chicano Experience*, edited by Jorge Huerta, Arte Público, 1989, pp. 142–45.

———. "Looking for the Magic: Chicanos in the Mainstream." *Negotiating Performance: Gender, Sexuality, and Theatricality in Latin/o America*, edited by Diana Taylor and Juan Villegas, Duke UP, 1994, pp. 37–48.

———. "When Sleeping Giants Awaken: Chicano Theatre in the 1960s." *Theatre Survey*, vol. 43, no. 1, 2002, pp. 23–35.

Hurston, Zora Neale. "What White Publishers Won't Print." A. Mitchell, pp. 117–21.

Hutcheon, Linda. *A Poetics of Postmodernism: History, Theory and Fiction*. Routledge, 1988.

———. *A Theory of Parody: The Teachings of Twentieth-Century Art Forms*. Methuen, 1985.

Hutchinson, George. *The Harlem Renaissance in Black and White*. Harvard UP, 1995.

———. *In Search of Nella Larsen: A Biography of the Color Line*. Harvard UP, 2006.

Hutchinson, George, and John K. Young, editors. *Publishing Blackness: Textual Construction of Race Since 1850*. U of Michigan P, 2013.

Iglesias, Jorge. Introduction. *Outlaw: The Collected Works of Miguel Piñero*. Arte Público, 2010, pp. xv–xxvi.

Irizarry, Ylce. *Chicana/o and Latina/o Fiction: The New Memory of Latinidad*. U of Illinois P, 2016.

Jackson, Chris. "Widening the Gates: Why Publishing Needs Diversity." *What Editors Do: The Art, Craft, and Business of Book Editing*, edited by Peter Ginna, U of Chicago P, 2017, pp. 223–30.

Jackson, Lawrence P. *The Indignant Generation: A Narrative History of African American Writers and Critics 1934–1960*. Princeton UP, 2011.

———. *Ralph Ellison: Emergence of Genius*. John Wiley, 2002.

———. "Ralph Ellison's Invented Life: A Meeting with the Ancestors." *The Cambridge Companion to Ralph Ellison*, edited by Ross Posnock. Cambridge UP, 2005, pp. 11–34.

Jackson, Lawrence P., and Edward P. Jones. "An Interview with Edward P. Jones." *African American Review*, vol. 34, no. 1, 2000, pp. 95–103.

James, Henry. "Art of Fiction." *The House of Fiction: Essays on the Novel by Henry James*, edited by Leon Edel, Rupert Hart-Davis, 1957, pp. 23–45.

Jarrett, Gene Andrew. *Representing the Race: A New Political History of African American Literature*. New York UP, 2011.

Johnson, James Weldon. *Along This Way: The Autobiography of James Weldon Johnson*. Viking, 1954.

——, editor. Preface. *The Book of American Negro Poetry,* Harcourt Brace, 1922, pp. vii–xlviii.

——. "The Dilemma of the Negro Author." *The Essential Writings of James Weldon Johnson,* edited by Rudolph P. Byrd, Modern Library, 2008, pp. 201–8.

Jones, Edward P. "Edward P. Jones." Interview by Marita Golden. *The Word: Black Writers Talk about the Transformative Power of Reading and Writing,* edited by Golden. Broadway, 2011, pp. 47–60.

——. *Lost in the City.* Harper Collins, 1995.

Kaestle, Carl F., and Janice A. Radway, editors. *A History of the Book in America. Vol. 4, Print in Motion: The Expansion of Publishing and Reading in the United States, 1880–1940.* U of North Carolina P, 2009.

Kanellos, Nicolás. "Exiles, Immigrants, and Natives: Hispanic Print Culture in What Became the Mainland of the United States." Kaestle and Radway, pp. 312–38.

——, editor. *Herencia: The Anthology of Hispanic Literature of the United States.* Oxford UP, 2002.

——. *A History of Hispanic Theater in the United States: Origins to 1940.* U of Texas P, 1990.

——. "Sotero Figueroa: Writing Afro-Caribbeans into History in the Late Nineteenth Century." Lazo and Alemán, pp. 323–40.

Kanellos, Nicolás, and Jorge Huerta, editors. Introduction. *Nuevos Pasos: Chicano and Puerto Rican Drama.* Arte Público, 1989, pp. v–ix.

Kass, Jeff. "Writing Wrong: Helena María Viramontes Found Inspiration for Her Book and Her Activism While Living in Irvine." *Los Angeles Times,* 17 Sept. 1995. https://www.latimes.com/archives/la-xpm-1995-09-17-ls-46867-story.html Accessed 8 Sept. 2018.

Kennedy, J. Gerald, and Robert Beuka. "Imperilled Communities in Edward P. Jones's 'Lost in the City' and Dagoberto Gilb's 'The Magic of Blood.'" *Yearbook of English Studies,* vol. 31, no. 1, 2001, pp. 10–23.

Kevane, Bridget. *Latino Literature in America.* Greenwood, 2003.

King, Lovalerie, and Shirley Moody-Turner, editors. *Contemporary African American Literature: The Living Canon.* Indiana UP, 2012.

King, Martin Luther, Jr. *A Call to Conscience: The Landmark Speeches of Dr. Martin Luther King, Jr.* Warner, 2001.

Knauer, Christine. *Let Us Fight as Free Men: Black Soldiers and Civil Rights.* U of Pennsylvania P, 2014.

Krupat, Arnold. *The Voice in the Margin: Native American Literature and the Canon.* U of California P, 1989.

Latty, Yvonne, and Ron Tarver. *We Were There: Voices of African American Veterans, from World War II to the War in Iraq.* Amistad, 2004.

Lazo, Rodrigo. "Introduction: Historical Latinidades and Archival Encounters." Lazo and Alemán, pp. 1–19.

——. *Letters from Filadelfia: Early Latino Literature and the Trans-American Elite.* U of Virginia P, 2020.

——. "Trajectories of ExChange: Towards Histories of Latino/a Literature." González and Lomas, pp. 190–215.

Lazo, Rodrigo, and Jesse Alemán, editors. *The Latino Nineteenth Century.* New York UP, 2016.

Leal, Luis. "Poetic Discourse in Pérez de Villagrá's *Historia de la Nuevo México.*" Herrera-Sobek, pp. 95–117.

Leeming, David. *James Baldwin: A Biography.* Knopf, 1994.

Lehan, Richard. *Realism and Naturalism: The Novel in an Age of Transition.* U of Wisconsin P, 2005.

Levander, Caroline F., and Robert S. Levine, editors. *Hemispheric American Studies.* Rutgers UP, 2008.

Levine, Michael L. *African Americans and Civil Rights: From 1619 to the Present.* Oryx, 1996.

Levine, Robert S. *Martin Delany, Frederick Douglass, and the Politics of Representative Identity.* U of North Carolina P, 1997.

Levine, Robert S., John Stauffer, and John R. McKivigan, editors. Introduction. *The Heroic Slave: A Cultural and Critical Edition,* by Frederick Douglass, Yale UP, 2015, pp. xi–xxxvi.

Levy-Hussen, Aida. *How to Read African American Literature: Post-Civil Rights Fiction and the Task of Interpretation.* New York UP, 2016.

Lewis, David Levering. *When Harlem Was in Vogue.* Oxford UP, 1989.

Lima, Lázaro. *The Latino Body: Crisis Identities in American Literary and Cultural Memory.* New York UP, 2007.

Limón, José E. *Américo Paredes: Culture and Critique.* U of Texas P, 2012.

———. "Editor's Note on Richard Rodriguez." *Texas Studies in Literature and Language,* vol. 40, no. 4, 1998, pp. 389–95.

Lomas, Laura. "'El negro es tan capaz como el blanco': José Martí, 'Pachín' Marín, Lucy Parsons, and the Politics of Late-Nineteenth-Century *Latinidad.*" Lazo and Alemán, pp. 301–22.

———. *Translating Empire: José Martí, Migrant Latino Subject, and American Modernities.* Duke UP, 2008.

Lomelí, Francisco A. Introduction. *Chicano Sketches: Short Stories by Mario Suárez,* edited by Francisco A. Lomelí, Cecilia Cota-Robles Suárez, and Juan José Casillas-Núñez, U of Arizona P, 2004, pp. 1–5.

López, Antonio. *Unbecoming Blackness: The Diaspora Cultures of Afro-Cuban America.* New York UP, 2012.

López, Dennis. "Ghosts in the Barn: Dead Labor and Capital Accumulation in Helena María Viramontes's *Under the Feet of Jesus.*" *Twentieth-Century Literature,* vol. 65. no. 4, 2019, pp. 307–42.

———. "Good-Bye Revolution—Hello Cultural Mystique: Quinto Sol Publications and Chicano Literary Nationalism." *MELUS,* vol. 35, no. 3, 2010, pp. 183–210.

López, Marissa K. *Chicano Nations: The Hemispheric Origins of Mexican American Literature.* New York UP, 2011.

Luis, William. *Dance between Two Cultures: Latino Caribbean Literature Written in the United States.* Vanderbilt UP, 1997.

Lyne, William. "The Signifying Modernist: Ralph Ellison and the Limits of Double Consciousness." *PMLA,* vol. 107, no. 2, 1992, pp. 318–30.

Martín-Rodríguez, Manuel M. "An Epic Return(s): Gaspar de Villagrá and His *Historia de la nueva Mexico* in the Twenty-first Century." *Early American Literature,* vol. 53, no. 3, 2018, pp. 665–84.

———. *Life in Search of Readers: Reading (in) Chicano/a Literature.* U of New Mexico P, 2003.

Mason, Theodore O. "Alice Walker's *The Third Life of Grange Copeland*: The Dynamics of Enclosure." *Callaloo,* vol. 1, no. 39, 1989, pp. 297–309.

McGill, Meredith L. "Frances Ellen Watkins Harper and the Circuits of Abolitionist Poetry." Cohen and Stein, pp. 53–74.

McGurl, Mark. *The Novel Art: Elevations of American Fiction after Henry James.* Princeton UP, 2001.

———. *The Program Era: Fiction and the Rise of Creative Writing*. Harvard UP, 2011.

McHenry, Elizabeth. *Forgotten Readers: Recovering the Lost History of African American Literary Societies*. Duke UP, 2002.

McPherson, James Alan. "Indivisible Man." Graham and Singh, pp. 173–91.

Meléndez, A. Gabriel. "Growing Up: Book Culture in the Land of Scarcity and Want." *With a Book in Their Hands: Chicano/a Readers and Readership across the Centuries,* edited by Manuel M. Martín-Rodríguez, U of New Mexico P, 2014, pp. 131–41.

———. *So All Is Not Lost: The Poetics of Print in Nuevomexicano Communities, 1834–1958*. U of New Mexico P, 1997.

Meléndez, A. Gabriel, and Francisco A. Lomelí. Introduction. *The Writings of Eusebio Chacón,* U of New Mexico P, 2012, pp. 1–24.

Méndez, Danny. *Narratives of Migration and Displacement in Dominican Literature*. Routledge, 2012.

Milian, Claudia. *Latining America: Black-Brown Passages and the Coloring of Latino/a Studies*. U of Georgia P, 2013.

———. *LatinX*. U of Minnesota P, 2019.

Miller, D. Quentin. "Playing a Mean Guitar: The Legacy of Staggerlee in Baldwin and Morrison." *James Baldwin and Toni Morrison: Comparative Critical and Theoretical Essays,* edited by Lovalerie King and Lynn Orilla Scott, Palgrave Macmillan, 2006, pp. 121–48.

———. *The Routledge Introduction to African American Literature*. Routledge, 2016.

Miller, Henry D. *Theorizing Black Theater: Art Versus Protest in Critical Writings, 1898–1965*. McFarland, 2011.

Mills, Charles W. *The Racial Contract*. Cornell UP, 1997.

Minich, Julie Avril. "The Decolonizer's Guide to Disability." Hanna, Vargas, and Saldívar, pp. 49–67.

Mitchell, Angelyn, editor. *Within the Circle: An Anthology of African American Literary Criticism from the Harlem Renaissance to the Present*. Duke UP, 1994.

Mitchell, Koritha. Introduction. *Iola Leroy: or, Shadows Uplifted,* by Frances E. W. Harper, Broadview, 2018, pp. 13–50.

———. *Living with Lynching: African American Lynching Plays, Performance, and Citizenship, 1890–1930*. U of Illinois P, 2012.

Montes, Amelia María de la Luz. Introduction. *Who Would Have Thought It?,* by María Amparo Ruiz de Burton, Penguin, 2009, pp. xi–xxiii.

Morales, Ed. *Latinx: The New Force in American Politics and Culture*. Verso, 2019.

Moody, Joycelyn, and Howard Rambsy II. "Introduction: African American Print Culture." *MELUS,* vol. 40, no. 3, 2015, pp. 1–11.

Moore, Christopher Paul. *Fighting for America: Black Soldiers—The Unsung Heroes of World War II*. One World Ballantine, 2005.

Morín, José R. López. "The Life and Early Works of Américo Paredes." *Western Folklore,* vol. 64, no. 1, 2005, pp. 7–28.

Morrison, Toni. *Playing in the Dark: Whiteness and the Literary Imagination*. Vintage, 1993.

Moya, Paula M. L. *Learning from Experience: Minority Identities, Multicultural Struggles*. U of California P, 2002.

Murray, Albert. *The Omni-Americans: Black Experience and American Culture*. Da Capo, 1990.

Nadel, Alan. *Invisible Criticism: Ralph Ellison and the American Canon*. Iowa UP, 1988.

"National Book Awards 2019." *National Book Foundation.* https://www.nationalbook.org/awards-prizes/ national-book-awards-2019/. Accessed 1 Nov. 2019.

Neal, Larry. *Visions of a Liberated Future: Black Arts Movement Writings.* Thunder's Mouth, 1989.

Newlin, Keith. "Introduction: The Naturalistic Imagination and the Aesthetics of Excess." *The Oxford Handbook of American Literary Naturalism,* edited by Newlin, Oxford UP, 2011, pp. 3–17.

Nguyen, Viet Thanh. *Race and Resistance: Literature and Politics in Asian America.* Oxford UP, 2002.

North, Michael. *The Dialects of Modernism: Race, Language, Twentieth-Century Literature.* Oxford UP, 1994.

Nowlin, Michael. *Literary Ambition and the African American Novel.* Cambridge UP, 2019.

O'Meally, Robert, editor. *Living with Music: Ralph Ellison's Jazz Writings.* Modern Library, 2002.

Orchard, William, and Yolanda Padilla. Introduction. *The Plays of Josefina Niggli,* U of Wisconsin P, 2007, pp. 3–33.

Ortiz, Paul. *An African American and Latinx History of the United States.* Beacon, 2018.

Padilla, Genaro. *The Daring Flight of My Pen: Cultural Politics and Gaspar Pérez de Villagrá's Historia de la Nueva Mexico, 1610.* U of New Mexico P, 2010.

———. "Discontinuous Continuities: Remapping the Terrain of Spanish Colonial Narrative." Herrera-Sobek, pp. 24–36.

Paravisini-Gebert, Lizabeth. "Junot Díaz's *Drown*: Revisiting 'Those Mean Streets.'" *U.S. Latino Literature: A Critical Guide for Students and Teachers,* edited by Harold Augenbraum and Margarite Fernández Olmos, Greenwood, 2000, pp. 165–73.

Paredes, Américo. *The Hammon and the Beans and Other Stories.* Arte Público, 1994.

Perez, Richard. "Racial Spills and Disfigured Faces in Piri Thomas's *Down These Mean Streets* and Junot Díaz's 'Ysrael.'" Sandín and Perez, pp. 93–112.

Pérez-Torres, Rafael. *Mestizaje: Critical Uses of Race in Chicano Culture.* U of Minnesota P, 2006.

Phillips, L. Kimberley. *War! What Is It Good For? Black Freedom Struggles and the U.S. Military from World War II to Iraq.* U of North Carolina P, 2012.

Porter, Horace A. *Jazz Country: Ralph Ellison in America.* U of Iowa P, 2001.

———. "The South in *Go Tell it on the Mountain*: Baldwin's Personal Confrontation." *New Essays on Go Tell It on the Mountain,* edited by Trudier Harris. Cambridge UP, 1996. pp. 59–75.

Prentiss, Craig R. *Staging Faith: Religion and African American Theater from the Harlem Renaissance to World War II.* New York UP, 2013.

Puzo, Mario. "His Cardboard Lovers." Standley and Burt, pp. 155–58.

Rabinowitz, Paula. "Pulping Ann Petry: The Case of *Country Place.*" *Revising the Blueprint: Ann Petry and the Literary Left,* edited by Alex Lubin, UP of Mississippi, 2007, pp. 49–71.

Rampersad, Arnold. *Ralph Ellison: A Biography.* Vintage, 2008.

Reilly, Charlie, editor. *Conversations with Amiri Baraka.* UP of Mississippi, 1994.

Remnick, David. "Visible Man." Graham and Singh, pp. 392–401.

Rezek, Joseph. "The Print Atlantic: Phillis Wheatley, Ignatius Sancho, and the Cultural Significance of the Book." Cohen and Stein, pp. 19–39.

Rivas-Rodriguez, Maggie. "Framing Racism: Newspaper Coverage of the Three Rivers Incident," edited by Maggie Rivas-Rodriguez. *Mexican Americans and World War II.* U of Texas P, 2005, pp. 201–20.

Rivas-Rodriguez, Maggie, and B. V. Olgín, editors. *Latina/os and World War II: Mobility, Agency, and Ideology.* U of Texas P, 2014.

Rivas-Rodriguez, Maggie, and Emilio Zamora, editors. *Beyond the Latino World War II Hero: The Social and Political Legacy of a Generation.* U of Texas P, 2009.

Rivera, Tomás. "*Hunger of Memory* as Humanistic Antithesis." *MELUS,* vol. 11, no. 4, 1984, pp. 5–13.

Rodriguez, Ralph E. *Latinx Literature Unbound: Undoing Ethnic Expectation.* Fordham UP, 2018.

Rodriguez, Richard. "An American Writer." Sollors, pp. 3–13.

———. "Asians." *Days of Obligation,* pp. 158–74.

———. *Brown: The Last Discovery of America.* Penguin, 2003.

———. *Days of Obligation: An Argument with My Mexican Father.* Penguin, 1992.

———. "An Education in Language." *The State of the Language,* edited by Leonard Michaels and Christopher Ricks, U of California P, 1980, pp. 129–39.

———. "Going Home Again: The New American Scholarship Boy." *American Scholar,* vol. 44, no. 1, 1974, pp. 15–28.

———. *Hunger of Memory: The Education of Richard Rodriguez.* Bantam, 1982.

———. "Mexico's Children." *Days of Obligation,* pp. 48–79.

———. "Nothing Lasts a Hundred Years." *Days of Obligation,* pp. 201–30.

Rojas, Fabio. *From Black Power to Black Studies: How a Radical Social Movement Became an Academic Discipline.* Johns Hopkins UP, 2007.

Romero, Channette. *Activism and the American Novel: Religion and Resistance in Fiction by Women of Color.* U of Virginia P, 2012.

Rosales, Steven. *Soldados Razos at War: Chicano Politics, Identity, and Masculinity in the U.S. Military from World War II to Vietnam.* U of Arizona P, 2017.

Rossini, Jon D. *Contemporary Latina/o Theater: Wrighting Ethnicity.* Southern Illinois UP, 2008.

Rowell, Charles H. "Poetry, History, and Humanism: An Interview with Margaret Walker." Graham, pp. 19–31.

Royce, Edward. *The Origins of Southern Sharecropping.* Temple UP, 1993.

Sáez, Elena Machado. "Generation MFA: Neoliberalism and the Shifting Cultural Capital of US Latinx Writers." *Latino Studies,* vol. 16, no. 1, 2018, pp. 361–83.

Saldaña-Portillo, María Josefina. "Latino/a Literature: The Borders Are Burning." González and Lomas, pp. 737–47.

Saldívar, José David. *The Dialectics of Our American: Genealogy, Cultural Critique, and Literary History.* Duke UP, 1991.

Saldívar, Ramón. *Chicano Narrative: The Dialectics of Difference.* U of Wisconsin P, 1990.

———. "Historical Fantasy, Speculative Realism, and Postrace Aesthetics in Contemporary American Fiction." *American Literary History,* vol. 23, no. 3, 2011, pp. 574–99.

Sánchez, Marta E. "*Shakin' Up" Race and Gender: Intercultural Connections in Puerto Rican, African American, and Chicano Narratives and Culture (1965–1995).* U of Texas P, 2005.

Sánchez, Rosaura, and Beatrice Pita. Introduction. *The Squatter and the Don,* by María Amparo Ruiz de Burton, Arte Público, 1997, pp. 7–49.

Sandín, Lyn Di Iorio. *Killing Spanish: Literary Essays on Ambivalent U.S. Latino/a Identity.* Palgrave, 2004.

Sandín, Lyn Di Iorio, and Richard Perez, editors. *Contemporary U.S. Latino/a Literary Criticism.* Palgrave, 2007.

Scott, A. O. "In Search of the Best." *New York Times,* 21 May 2006. https://www.nytimes.com/2006/05/21/books/review/scott-essay.html. Accessed 1 Nov. 2019.

Scott, Lynn Orilla. *James Baldwin's Later Fiction: Witness to the Journey.* Michigan State UP, 2002.

Sedore, Timothy S., and Richard Rodriguez. "'Born at the Destination': An Interview with Richard Rodriguez." *New England Review,* vol. 22, no. 3, 2001, pp. 26–37.

Shatzkin, Mike, and Robert Paris Riger. *The Book Business: What Everyone Needs to Know.* Oxford UP, 2019.

Shea, Anne. "'Don't Let Them Make You Feel You Did a Crime': Immigration Law, Labor Rights, and Farmworker Testimony." *MELUS,* vol. 28, no. 1, 2003, pp. 123–44.

Sheffer, Debra J. *The Buffalo Soldiers: Their Epic Story and Major Campaigns.* Praeger, 2015.

Shumway, David R. *Creating American Civilization: A Genealogy of American Literature as an Academic Discipline.* U of Minnesota P, 1994.

Smethurst, James. *The Black Arts Movement: Literary Nationalism in the 1960s and 1970s.* U of North Carolina P, 2005.

So, Richard Jean. *Redlining Culture: A Data History of Racial Inequality in Postwar Fiction.* Columbia UP, 2020.

So, Richard Jean, and Gus Wezerek. "Just How White Is the Book Industry?" *New York Times,* 11 Dec. 2020. https://www.nytimes.com/interactive/2020/12/11/opinion/culture/diversity-publishing-industry.html. Accessed 4 Feb. 2021.

Sollors, Werner. *Amiri Baraka/LeRoi Jones: The Quest for a "Populist Modernism."* Columbia UP, 1978.

———, editor. Introduction. *The Invention of Ethnicity.* Oxford UP, 1989, pp. ix–xx.

———. "Jean Toomer's *Cane*: Modernism and Race in Interwar America." *Jean Toomer and the Harlem Renaissance,* edited by Geneviève Fabre and Michel Feith, Rutgers UP, 2001, pp. 18–37.

Spillers, Hortense J. "Who Cuts the Border? Some Readings on America." *Black, White, and In Color: Essays on American Literature and Culture,* by Spillers, U of Chicago P, 2003, pp. 319–35.

Spires, Derrick R. "Genealogies of Black Modernities." *American Literary History,* vol. 32, no. 4, 2020, pp. 611–22.

———. *The Practice of Citizenship: Black Politics and Print Culture in the Early United States.* U of Pennsylvania P, 2019.

Standley, Fred L. "James Baldwin: The Artist as Incorrigible Disturber of the Peace." Standley and Burt, pp. 43–54.

Standley, Fred L. and Nancy V. Burt, editors. *Critical Essays on James Baldwin.* G. K. Hall, 1988.

Staten, Henry. "Ethnic Authenticity, Class, and Autobiography: The Case of *Hunger of Memory.*" *PMLA,* vol. 113, no. 1, 1998, pp. 103–16.

Stavans, Ilan. Foreword. *Mexican Village and Other Works,* by Josefina Niggly, Northwestern UP, 2008.

———, editor. *The Norton Anthology of Latino Literature.* Norton, 2011.

Stepto, Robert B. *From Behind the Veil: A Study of Afro-American Narrative.* U of Illinois P, 1979.

Stewart, Barbara. "Outsider with a Voice." *New York Times,* 8 Dec. 1996. https://www.nytimes.com/1996/12/08/nyregion/outsider-with-a-voice.html. Accessed 8 Feb. 2018.

Stringer, Dorothy. "Passing and the State in Junot Díaz's 'Drown.'" *MELUS,* vol. 38, no. 2, 2013, pp. 111–26.

Sundquist, Eric J. "Dry Bones." *The Cambridge Companion to Ralph Ellison,* edited by Ross Posnock, Cambridge UP, 2005, pp. 217–30.

Taylor, Kate. "Denying a Professor Tenure, Harvard Sparks a Debate Over Ethnic Studies. *New York Times,* 2 Jan. 2020, https://www.nytimes.com/2020/01/02/us/harvard-latinos-diversity-debate.html. Accessed 2 Aug. 2020.

Taylor, Paul C. *Race: A Philosophical Introduction.* 2nd ed., Polity, 2013.

Thompson, John. "Baldwin: The Prophet as Artist." *Commentary,* 1 Jun. 1968. www.commentarymagazine.com/articles/baldwin-the-prophet-as-artist/. Accessed 8 Aug. 2018.

Thompson, John B. *Merchants of Culture: The Publishing Business in the Twenty-First Century.* Polity, 2010.

Tonn, Horst. "*Bless Me, Ultima*: Fictional Response to Times of Transition." González-T., pp. 1–12.

Torday, Daniel. "Young Boys and Old Lions: Fatalism in the Stories of Edward P. Jones." *Literary Imagination,* vol. 11, no. 3, 2009, pp. 349–65.

Torres, Hector A., and Richard Rodriguez. "'I Don't Think I Exist': Interview with Richard Rodriguez." *MELUS,* vol. 28, no. 2, 2003, pp. 164–202.

Torres-Saillant, Silvio. "Artistry, Ancestry, and Americanness in the Works of Junot Díaz." Hanna, Vargas, and Saldívar, pp. 115–46.

Valdez, Luis. *Bandido! Zoot Suit and Other Plays.* Arte Público, 1992.

———. "La Plebe." Introduction. *Aztlán: An Anthology of Mexican American Literature,* edited by Luis Valdez and Stan Steiner. Knopf, 1972, pp. xi–xxxvi.

———. *Luis Valdez—Early Works: Actos, Bernabé and Pensamiento Serpentino.* Arte Público, 1990.

———. "Notes on Chicano Theatre." *Luis Valdez—Early Works,* pp. 6–10.

———. "Pensamiento Serpentino." *Luis Valdez—Early Works,* pp. 168–99.

———. *Shrunken Head of Pancho Villa. Necessary Theater: Six Plays about the Chicano Experience,* edited by Jorge Huerta, Arte Público, 1989, pp. 146–207.

Vázquez, David James. "Their Bones Kept Them Moving: Latinx Studies, Helena María Viramontes's *Under the Feet of Jesus,* and the Crosscurrents of Ecocriticism." *Contemporary Literature,* vol. 58, no. 3, 2017, pp. 361–91.

Vega, Bernardo. *Memoirs of Bernardo Vega.* Translated by Juan Flores. Monthly Review, 1984.

Vélez-Ibáñez, Carlos G., Phillip B. Gonzales, Luis Plascencia, and Jesús Rosales. "Interrogating the Ethnogenesis of the Spanish and Mexican 'Other': The Literary Works of Aurelio M. Espinosa." *Aztlán,* vol. 44, no. 2, 2019, pp. 41–76.

Villaseñor Black, Charlene. "Founding Artists and the History of *Aztlán: A Journal of Chicano Studies*." *Diálogo,* vol. 20, no. 2, 2017, pp. 87–96.

Viramontes, Helena María. "Elevated Thinking, Metaphor Making, Aspired Imagining." Interview by Gabriella Gutiérrez y Muhs. Gutiérrez y Muhs, pp. 237–50.

———. "Faith in the Imagination." Interview by José Antonio Rodríguez. Gutiérrez y Muhs, pp. 251–63.

———. *Under the Feet of Jesus.* Plume, 1996.

Vogel, Todd, editor. *The Black Press: New Literary and Historical Essays.* Rutgers UP, 2002.

Walker, Alice. Afterword. *The Third Life of Grange Copeland.* Harcourt, 2003, pp. 313–18.

———. *In Search of Our Mothers' Gardens.* Harcourt, 2004.

——. "Interview with John O'Brien." Interview by John O'Brien. Byrd, pp. 35–57.

——. *The Third Life of Grange Copeland*. Harcourt, 2003.

Warren, Kenneth W. *So Black and Blue: Ralph Ellison and the Occasion of Criticism*. U of Chicago P, 2003.

——. *What Was African American Literature?* Harvard UP, 2011.

Watts, Jerry Gafio. *Amiri Baraka: The Politics and Art of a Black Intellectual*. New York UP, 2001.

——. *Heroism and the Black Intellectual: Ralph Ellison, Politics, and Afro-American Intellectual Life*. U of North Carolina P, 1994.

Weatherby, William J. *James Baldwin: Artist on Fire*. Donald I. Fine, 1989.

West, Cornel. *Race Matters*. Vintage, 2001.

Wilson, Ivy G. "The Brief Wondrous Life of the *Anglo-African Magazine*: Or, Antebellum African American Editorial Practice and Its Afterlives." Hutchinson and Young, pp. 18–38.

Wilson, William Julius. *When Work Disappears: The World of the New Urban Poor*. Knopf, 1996.

Whitaker, Mark. *Smoketown: The Untold Story of the Other Great Black Renaissance*. Simon and Schuster, 2019.

Womack, Autumn. "Reprinting the Past/Re-Ordering Black Social Life." *American Literary History*, vol. 32, no. 4, 2020, pp. 755–80.

Woodard, Komozi. *A Nation within a Nation: Amiri Baraka (LeRoi Jones) & Black Power Politics*. U of North Carolina P, 1999.

Worthen, W. B. "Staging América: The Subject of History in Chicano/a Theatre." *Theatre Journal*, vol. 49, no. 2, 1997, pp. 101–20.

Wright, Richard. *Black Boy*. Harper Collins, 1993.

——. "Blueprint for Negro Artists." A. Mitchell, pp. 97–106.

——. *Twelve Million Black Voices: A Folk History of the Negro in the United States*. Viking, 1941.

Wynn, Neil A. *The African American Experience during World War II*. Rowman and Littlefield, 2010.

Yarborough, Richard. Introduction. *Uncle Tom's Children,* by Richard Wright, Harper, 2004, pp. ix–xxix.

Yarbro-Bejarano, Yvonne. "Phantoms and Patch Quilt People: Narrative Art and Migrant Collectivity in Helena María Viramontes's *Under the Feet of Jesus*." Gutiérrez y Muhs, pp. 67–96.

Young, John K. *Black Writers, White Publishers: Marketplace Politics in Twentieth-Century African American Literature*. U of Mississippi P, 2006.

——. "'Quite as Human as It Is Negro': Subpersons and Textual Property in *Native Son* and *Black Boy*." Hutchinson and Young, pp. 67–92.

Zickuhr, Kathryn, and Lee Rainie. "E-Reading Rises as Device Ownership Jumps." *Pew Research Center*. 16 Jan. 2014. https://www.pewinternet.org/2014/01/16/e-reading-rises-as-device-ownership-jumps/. Accessed 1 Nov. 2019.

INDEX

Abbott, Robert S., 42

Abernathy, Ralph, 153, 154

Acampora, Christa Davis, 129n12

Acosta-Belén, Edna, 44n44, 47, 47n61

Acuña, Rodolfo, 57n91, 74, 87n21, 88n27, 132, 132n18

addiction, 151, 155, 162, 165

Adventures of Huckleberry Finn (Twain), 114n34, 116

aesthetics, 4, 6, 9, 13, 20–23, 36, 50

African American. *See* Black Arts Movement; Black Arts Repertory; Black civil rights movement; Black literary history; Black literary tradition; Black nationalism; Black print culture

Alarcón, Norma, 55

Alcoff, Linda Martín, 6, 10, 15–16, 17, 151

Alfred A. Knopf, 5n11, 44–45, 45n48, 45n50, 46, 56, 91

Als, Hilton, 57, 154n20, 157n28

American literary canon. *See* American literary tradition

American literary tradition: and aesthetics, 133, 142; and Black and Latinx authors,

9, 11, 21–23, 26, 80, 105, 126, 128, 168, 170; Black authors in, 4, 9, 22n55, 23, 23n56, 114, 117, 171; and Black print culture, 31, 35; and civil rights movements, 20, 22, 53, 141, 174; and Latinx authors, 23, 29, 122–23; and marginalization, 9, 20n47, 23; and MFA programs, 150; and New Spain chronicles, 34, 35n16; pre-1960s, 104, 174; and publishing industry, 7; and Spanish-language print culture, 31, 35

Anaya, Rudolfo: and aesthetics, 97–98, 97n47; art and social protest in, 24, 82, 85, 101; and Chicanx Movement, 82, 85, 96; and Latinx literature, 55; and Mexican American civil rights movement, 82, 85, 96; and *Nuevomexicano* communities, 90; publication history of, 55, 95–96; and World War II, 82, 90, 98–101. See also *Bless Me, Ultima*

Andrews, William, 12, 41, 42n38, 45n53, 46, 46n58, 148

Anglo-African Magazine, 35–36, 36nn19–20, 148

Anzaldúa, Gloria, 2, 108, 118, 129, 129n12

armed resistance, 62, 67, 67n27, 69, 72, 78. *See also* resistance

art. *See* aesthetics